Game of My Life
WASHINGTON REDSKINS

MEMORABLE STORIES OF REDSKINS FOOTBALL

Game of My Life
WASHINGTON REDSKINS

MEMORABLE STORIES OF
REDSKINS FOOTBALL

TOM MACKIE

SPORTS
PUBLISHING

Sports Publishing books may be purchased in bulk at special discounts for sales promotion, corporate gifts, fund-raising, or educational purposes. Special editions can also be created to specifications. For details, contact the Special Sales Department, Sports Publishing, 307 West 36th Street, 11th Floor, New York, NY 10018 or sportspubbooks@skyhorsepublishing.com.

Sports Publishing® is a registered trademark of Skyhorse Publishing, Inc.®, a Delaware corporation.

Visit our website at www.sportspubbooks.com.

10 9 8 7 6 5 4 3 2 1

Library of Congress Cataloging-in-Publication Data is available on file.

ISBN: 978-1-61321-330-8

Printed in the United States of America

For Ray Ciesinski, whose love for football, his country, and friends and family, continues to touch us.

EDITOR'S NOTE: While a new chapter has been added to this edition of *Game of My Life: Washington Redskins*, some statements and information in other chapters may be reflective of events that took place when the book was originally published in 2007.

CONTENTS

INTRODUCTION

It's been six years since this book was first published in 2007 and my attachment with the Washington Redskins has grown. My association with the Washington Redskins isn't your typical love affair. In fact, it's quite the opposite. I grew up cheering for the enemy: the Dallas Cowboys.

Being a Cowboys fan was probably inscribed on my birth certificate. My father served in the Navy, and both my uncles graduated from the Naval Academy. So in the fall of 1963, at eight months old, I was placed on my grandfather's lap every Saturday to watch Navy football. That season, the Midshipmen had a Heisman trophy candidate named Roger Staubach, who made so many jaw-dropping plays that president John F. Kennedy started attending games *and* practices. My mom says that whenever my grandfather got excited watching Roger the Dodger, he would jump up and down, causing me to wave my arms wildly in the air.

As I got a little older, and Staubach joined the Cowboys, everyone seemed to cheer for Dallas. But I shifted most of my allegiance to a team that no one on the east coast had even heard of: the Denver Broncos. What made a seven-year-old switch teams? I liked the horse on the helmet, and I discovered Denver had the league's most exciting star, Floyd Little. Still, the Cowboys remained a popular choice in the Mackie household. Since the Broncos were rarely on TV, we spent many Sundays watching Cowboys-Redskins games, along with the Giants and Cardinals, who seemed to be on TV more often than the local, usually blacked-out team, the lowly Eagles.

Due to the rivalry between the Pokes and the Skins, I knew Washington's players well. They had quarterback Billy Kilmer, one of the toughest guys I'd ever seen. His single-bar facemask was turned down so far it looked like he enjoyed having a perpetual bloody nose. They also had Larry Brown, a tireless runner who seemed to dish out as much punishment as he took.

Then there were defensive players like Diron Talbert and Pat Fischer. I didn't like Talbert because he always seemed to be sacking Staubach and dishing out verbal advice that would no doubt goad number 12. When I asked my dad what Talbert was saying, he replied with his usual eloquence: "He offered to piss in Staubach's cornflakes." Fischer also infuriated me. He was this little guy, but he seemed to beat the crap out of everyone around him. He'd shadow Bob Hayes into committing the dropsies, and knock the hell out of receivers like the Eagles' Harold Carmichael and the Cardinals' Mel Gray.

But the guy who annoyed me the most was Redskins coach George Allen. He was always licking his fingers and clapping his hands, walking up and down the sidelines nervously. I thought everyone was supposed to dress like Tom Landry, but Allen never wore a tie. The bottom line, though, was that Allen had transformed the Redskins into one of the most feared teams in the league. And I didn't like it.

A few years later, I started collecting autographs. My mom would take me to the Eagles training camp nearby at Widener College in Chester, Pennsylvania. There I got signatures from linebacker Bill Bergey, Carmichael, and a 30-year-old rookie named Vince Papale. In 2006, the movie *Invincible* surreally captured my memories of those summers. Seeing how much I loved going to pro training camps, my father decided to take me to my parents' alma mater, Dickinson College in Carlisle, Pennsylvania, to see the Redskins.

At first I didn't want to go. From pictures I'd seen, Dickinson was this small school in the middle of nowhere. Plus, the idea of watching the Redskins wasn't very appetizing. They were the enemy, after all. But the opportunity to spend time with my dad, now divorced, was something I always cherished. So I went.

Thanks to Ben James, a family friend who had a long association with Dickinson, I not only got to meet all the Redskins, I also toured the team's locker room. I saw names on lockers that I had only seen on TV: Kilmer, Talbert, Fischer, Roy Jefferson, and Ron McDole.

After that, I gained a new perspective and appreciation for the Redskins. They weren't this evil team, but a team of stars who contributed to the game I loved.

Fast forward to 2000. I'm living in Washington, D.C., and writing football articles for the Redskins organization. I'm strolling the halls of Redskin Park and routinely see Deion Sanders playing checkers, Bruce Smith riding the stair master, ageless Darrell Green looking like a tenth grader, and then-rookie LaVar Arrington surrounded by swarms of reporters. One day, coach Norv Turner came into our office after practice, his whistle dangling, and asked me how to use the fax machine. Suddenly, I was living in an ESPN commercial. I wrote articles for the Redskins for another four years: the Marty Schottenheimer era, ball coach Steve Spurrier's regime, and back to the future with Joe Gibbs.

In writing this book, I was able to reconnect with many of the Redskins stars I remembered so well as a kid growing up during the 1970s. I was also hit with another reality; even though a lot of these players were now in their 60s and 70s, many were still working full time. Up until a few years ago, I was naive in thinking that most former pro football players had become rich from the NFL and were living the good life somewhere on a Florida golf course.

Broncos Hall of Famer Floyd Little set me straight about that. Even though he'd been a highly successful owner of two car dealerships, Floyd told me about the NFL's embarrassing pension plan: what it provided players was below the poverty level. "It's the NFL's black eye that no one wants to talk about," he told me. "Many of my former teammates have not been as fortunate as I have. The NFL has turned its back on many of them."

As I put together this book, Redskins great Mike Bass continued to educate me about the lack of suitable health and pension plans. He talked at great length about players from the 1960s, '70s, and '80s, who were now in wheelchairs, and how the NFL had a bunch of lawyers telling them their condition was not a result of the game.

I looked into it and found that most players from those eras receive monthly pensions somewhere between $200 to $500 a month. This hardly covers the mounting medical expenses they're incurring.

One of the most heart-wrenching examples is Packers and Cowboys Hall of Famer Herb Adderly. He receives $126.82 a month. Because of the way he's been treated, Adderley refuses to wear his Super Bowl rings or his Hall of Fame ring. Still, *NFL Films* loves to show highlight reels of his tremendous impact to the game—including his interception return for a touchdown in Super Bowl II—to market the great tradition of the NFL.

As a result of their hardships and my experience in connecting with these players in writing this book, team colors and allegiances are now dissolved to me. The players who sacrificed their well-being for the future prosperity of the NFL that we all enjoy today are all heroes to me, regardless of team. The NFL may have forgotten them, but they are remembered here and in other forums where fans pay tribute. They were the guys I read about and followed as a kid. Because of their efforts, many of today's players will be able to retire wealthy, while these guys—the pioneers who made their riches possible—continue to work 9-to-5 jobs.

Enjoy reading the stories of these 21 Redskins legends. You'll see that their commitment, sacrifice, and love of the game are inspirations to anyone who is passionate about football, even if you once cheered for the Cowboys.

—TOM MACKIE

Chapter 1

SAM HUFF

Before Tom Landry became the iconic coach of the Dallas Cowboys, he was a player and defensive coordinator with the New York Giants. One day in 1956, Landry went to Giants head coach Jim Lee Howell and showed him a new defense he had devised where the middle guard actually stood up and positioned himself back a few yards behind the line of scrimmage.

Howell gazed at the young prodigy and smiled. Landry had just invented the 4-3 defense. And the person who became the stalwart of this new position—middle linebacker—was a rookie defensive tackle named Robert Lee (Sam) Huff.

"Coach Landry told me, 'You are now the quarterback of the defense,'" says Huff. "That made quite an impression on me. I really took that responsibility seriously and I always tried to set the tempo." For anyone who ever saw Huff play, "tempo" was just a euphemism for "devastating hit."

Born October 4, 1934, to Joseph and Catherine Huff, the future Hall of Famer learned honesty and discipline from his parents.

"I never stole anything, and my parents always taught me to have respect for my elders," says Huff. "I also learned about having a solid work ethic. My father was a coal miner. To this day, I've never worked harder than him."

Growing up in rural Farmington, West Virgina, Huff gravitated toward football because it seemed a natural fit for him. "I loved football and baseball," he says. "I couldn't really play basketball because I couldn't hit people. It was a game with too much finesse for me."

After being drafted out of West Virginia University in 1956 by the Giants in the third round, the former guard and defensive tackle suddenly became the NFL's most feared defensive player on one of the league's most recognized teams.

"A lot of people point to me when they talk about those great Giants teams in the 1950s," says Huff. "But I was just one component of the defense. We had a lot of great defensive players, like Andy Robustelli, Emlen Tunnell, Rosey Grier, Jimmy Patton, Jim Katcavage. Our offense had stars like Frank Gifford, Alex Webster, Charlie Conerly, Roosevelt Brown, and Kyle Rote. Plus, Vince Lombardi was our offensive coordinator!"

With Huff and his Giants playing in championships, and with the Yankees making so many World Series appearances, New York was ringing with sports heroes.

"The Yankees were in the World Series practically every year, so much that I even shared my locker at Yankee Stadium with Mickey Mantle," says Huff, about those 1950s teams. "We were young and well recognized everywhere we went. We won the NFL championship in 1956 and played for the championship in '58 and '59. It was a magical time and we felt like it would go on forever."

Sam Huff revolutionized the middle linebacker position. While with the New York Giants from 1956-63, Huff was the most feared man in the NFL. In 1964, Huff was traded to the Redskins, bringing his trademark toughness and winning attitude. *AP Images*

POLITICS AS USUAL

Teams inevitably change, and the Giants were no different. In 1959, Lombardi was tabbed as coach of the once-proud Green Bay Packers. The following year, Landry was named to lead the expansion Dallas Cowboys. By the end of the 1960 season, Howell retired as head coach.

"Even though we continued to play in championship games, facing Lombardi's Packers in 1961 and '62, and the Bears in '63, it became a different Giants team, especially the defense," says Huff, who doesn't hesitate to point to the man who, in his mind, ruined the team: "The guy who replaced Howell—new head coach Allie Sherman."

Instead of instructing Huff to play the middle with reckless abandon, Sherman forced the perennial Pro Bowler to play with more of a thinking-man's approach. "Allie Sherman didn't know anything about defenses. He was an offense guy and I think, out of jealousy for Tom Landry, he refused to run Landry's defense," says Huff.

Sherman changed the defense to one that reacts to what the offense was doing. Instead of roaming free to make tackles, Huff had gap responsibility. Being forced to stand his ground and not instinctively pursue the play reduced his role to that of a clogger.

"I became more like a defensive tackle," he says. "As a result, I had a blocker on me on every play. We had been so successful with Landry's 4-3. We didn't understand why we were changing. Guys like Andy Robustelli and Jim Patton didn't understand the new scheme, so I spent a lot of time trying to explain it. But it didn't make any sense to me."

The new, non-aggressive scheme made the Giants' defense average. But Huff was a team player, and because New York kept winning thanks to the offense's great production, he kept his mouth shut.

"We'd go the whole season outscoring teams," says Huff. "It wasn't until the championship games, when defenses really count, that Sherman's lackadaisical schemes were exposed."

In the '61 championship against the Packers, the Giants were blanked 37-0. In the '62 championship, they didn't fare much better, losing 6-7.

"By the time we faced the Bears in the '63 championship, I decided we had to make a statement or we were going to lose another championship," says Huff. "Sherman had no idea, but when we walked onto that soggy, freezing Wrigley Field, we decided to go back to playing Landry's 4-3 defense."

The Giants shut down the Bears offense most of the game and led 10-7 at halftime. Then Giants quarterback Y.A. Tittle had his knees shredded before the half by a vicious hit from linebacker Larry Morse. Huff told Tittle that he didn't need to play the second half for the Giants to win.

"But Y.A. was a proud quarterback who absolutely loved the game," Huff says. "He had never won an NFL championship and there was no way he wasn't going to play." Unfortunately, his knee clearly affected his play and Tittle threw five interceptions.

Chicago came back to win, 14-10, and Huff had had enough. "Before Sherman came along, I was making 15-20 tackles a game. Once he arrived, my tackles were about half that," says Huff. "He didn't even hire a defensive coordinator when Landry left. I became like a player-coach. I'm a team guy. I wouldn't have cared about my tackles if the defense was still performing at a high level, but we weren't. The offense was the best part of the team."

Huff decided to go to Sherman and talk about changing the defense back to Landry's 4-3. "Sherman's response to me was, 'You play what I tell you to play,'" says Huff. Shortly after their "discussion," Huff was traded to the Redskins for running back Dick James, defensive end Andy Stynchula, and an undisclosed draft pick. The Giants also unloaded defensive linemen Dick Modzelewski to the Cleveland Browns and Rosey Grier to the Los Angeles Rams.

"I was devastated," recalls Huff. "I had played for the Giants for eight seasons. My whole life was in New York. Then Sherman just tore up the team. I had to move my family to Washington. It was an extremely disruptive time."

Huff uprooted his family, pulling his kids out of school, and headed for his new team, the Redskins, who hadn't posted a winning record since 1955.

CHANGE OF SCENERY

Along with the trade for Huff in 1964, the Redskins decided to swap quarterbacks as well. They sent their starter, Norm Sneed, to Philadelphia for Eagles quarterback Sonny Jurgensen.

Like Huff, Jurgensen was a veteran player who'd had his share of success. He won an NFL championship in 1960 with the Eagles as a backup to quarterback Norm Van Brocklin. The following season, Jurgensen took over QB duties and led the NFL in passing yards and TDs. He continued to put up great numbers in 1962, but then suffered injuries in 1963 that limited his production.

"Sonny and I hit it off right away," says Huff. "We were both veterans who felt like we were treated badly by our former clubs. He quickly became the leader of the Redskins offense and I the defense."

With Huff and Jurgensen leading the Redskins, the team improved from 3-11 in 1963 to 6-8 in 1964. Meanwhile in New York, the Giants were just a shell of the 1963 championship team without Huff, registering a pathetic 2-10-2 record.

"I had made up my mind that I wasn't going to retire until I got back at Allie Sherman," says Huff.

GAME OF MY LIFE
BY SAM HUFF

Earlier in the 1966 season we had lost to the Giants in New York, 13-10. It always hurt losing to my former team, especially with Sherman standing across the field. The Giants won only one game that year, and it was against us.

By the time the Giants came to Washington, it was just after Thanksgiving and we had lost three straight games, two of which were on the road. I was glad to face my old team in front of the great Redskins fans.

Otto Graham, the great Browns quarterback legend, had taken over for coach Bill McPeak in '66 and we had one hell of an offense. Besides Jurgensen, there were Pro Bowl receivers Charley Taylor and Bobby Mitchell, and tight end Jerry Smith. We didn't have much of a running game back then, but our passing game was among the best in the league.

Typically before a game, I would watch the offense to see how they looked. But this time, I watched the Giants defense. I could tell right away that Sherman's defense was awful. I thought to myself, "This is my day." Sonny and I were captains and I looked over at him and said, "Sonny, we're going to kill them!" Just then, Otto Graham walked by holding a clipboard and he said, "What do you think about today?" I didn't blink. I said, "Otto, this is my day. This is revenge day. We will score over 60 points." He just stared at me, but Sonny blurted out, "You're crazy."

I told Sonny, "I know I'm nuts, but this is the worst defense I've ever seen. Don't show mercy today. This is what I've been waiting for."

I was counting on the offense because we didn't have the greatest defense. The Redskins offense had made some questionable decisions the past few years, like trading our Pro Bowl safety Paul Krause to the Vikings. I knew the Giants were going to score points on us, but I also knew our offense was going to torch them even worse.

As it turned out, our defense was on fire that day. We intercepted five passes, three of them by defensive back Brig Owens. He returned one 60 yards for a touchdown and later scooped up another fumble, racing 62 yards for another score. If the defense didn't score on our own, we turned it over to our offense, and Sonny and company lit up the scoreboard.

Sonny threw touchdown passes to running back A.D. Whitfield and two to Charley Taylor. Whitfield scored two other touchdowns, and even crazy Joe Don Looney scored a touchdown. We were up by some 20 points in the fourth quarter when Rickie Harris scored on a punt. Hell,

Bobby Mitchell even went back to playing running back and scored on a 45-yard run for our tenth touchdown of the game!

Bobby's touchdown made it 69-41. It seemed like every time I looked up, someone on our team was scoring. Not only was I loving every minute of it, I was savoring every hit. I must have looked like a madman out there. I didn't care. I think the Giants and some of my teammates were expecting me to let up, like when a fighter's down for the count. But I just wanted to get back at Sherman so badly. This became my defining Redskins moment. I was intent on smacking any Giants player who came my way, whether it was quarterback Gary Wood, or Joe Morrison, or Homer Jones—it didn't matter.

Finally, with the ball on the Giants 20 and with 20 seconds and counting left, I looked up at the scoreboard and saw the 69-41 score, then I looked at the fans cheering, and finally I saw the look of disgust on Sherman's face. Suddenly, I blurted out "Time-out, time-out!" Sonny looked over at me as if I were crazy. He knew what I wanted to do and called time out. Otto Graham was bewildered. He didn't know what was going on.

I told him, "Gogolak needs practice." This after Charlie had set an NFL record with nine straight extra points in the game. Before Otto could respond I had Charlie go out and try a 29-yarder. The funny thing was that Charlie's brother, Pete, was kicking for the Giants that day. So I'm sure Charlie felt strange.

The crowd went nuts as Charlie drilled those final three points for the 72-41 win. They were cheering, "Good-bye, Allie" and singing "Hail to the Redskins." Today, it's still the most points ever scored in a regular-season game.

All those feelings of anger and betrayal for the way I was treated by Sherman finally subsided a bit that day. For the first time, I felt justified and vindicated for what had happened. I'll never forget that look on Sherman's face either. He would step down as coach two years later.

STILL A REDSKIN

Huff retired from football in 1968, but his retirement was short-lived. Vince Lombardi, a year removed from being the general manager of the Packers, decided to return to coaching and replaced Otto Graham as the Redskins head coach. One of the first things Lombardi did as coach was ask Sam Huff to come out of retirement.

Huff didn't hesitate a second before saying yes. Huff returned to the gridiron as a player-coach. "I knew Lombardi during my days in New York when he was the offensive coordinator, so I was the only one who wasn't afraid of him," says Huff. "I remember his first comments to the Redskins team were, 'Gentleman, this is my belief: I believe football is won or lost in last two minutes of the half, and on conditioning. No one is going to out-condition this team.'"

Lombardi's emphasis on conditioning hit an all-time high—or low, depending on how you see it—on one of the hottest days at training camp. Huff remembers: "We were doing the old up-down drill: running in place and hitting the deck and getting back up to run in place. As a player-coach you would think I could bypass that old drill. But not when Lombardi was your coach. I remember being exhausted and looking over at Sonny, whose normally pale white face was Redskins burgundy. Then I heard Lombardi saying, 'Today is the day. Today is the day we're going to break the all-time record for up-downs.' Which, in case you didn't know, according to Lombardi, is 84."

The Redskins kept the up-downs going for several minutes, before Huff started worrying about Jurgensen. "Jurgensen's face was turning purple," says Huff. "Finally, I sidled up next to Lombardi and I said, 'You've got to stop this drill right now.' 'Why?' asked Lombardi. 'Because,' I paused, 'you're going to kill Sonny!'"

Lombardi looked over at Jurgensen's strawberry face and it alarmed him enough that he finally stopped the drill.

Raised in Hell's Kitchen in New York City, Lombardi was tough on everyone, even his wife. According to Huff, the coach would take catnaps on the Redskins bus. His wife, Marie, often rode with the team.

"One time the bus went over a bump and Lombardi woke up. Staring inches from his face was Marie. 'Where are we going to dinner tonight?' she demanded. 'Lady,' Lombardi replied, 'when you travel with the team you eat with the team.' I was sitting the next seat over and said, 'Coach, would you mind if I brought Mary—my wife—to be trained?' He said, 'Sam, I'm good, but I'm not that good.'"

It's easy to see that Lombardi liked to control situations. Huff says the legendary coach was even able to control religious services.

"At training camp Lombardi brought in a priest to stay in the room right next to his," says Huff. "The priest was a little guy from Carlisle, Father Sweata. One day I asked him, 'Coach, why do you have a priest next door?' He looked at me in all seriousness. 'Sam, I have to go to mass every morning. I want to make it convenient.'"

In just one year, Lombardi changed the Redskins' losing mentality and engrained in them confidence and a tireless work ethic. "Lombardi brought respectability back to the Redskins," says Huff about the coach who passed away the following year, in 1970, from cancer. "He helped us develop a tough mental attitude. You just loved playing for the guy, especially Sonny. He turned Sonny's life around."

LEGENDARY PRESENCE

Despite spending the first eight seasons of his career with the Giants, Huff has been a Redskins lifer ever since he hung up his cleats for good in 1969. He's a Hall of Famer and is one of the few legends who enjoyed outstanding careers on two teams.

He's stayed busy by working with Marriott Hotels, tending to his 23-acre horse farm in Middleburg, Virginia, and spending time in his radio programming facility and recording studio, the Middleburg Broadcasting Network, where he broadcasts his *Trackside* racing show. But most people know Huff as one of the voices of WJFK Redskins Radio, where, since 1973, he's called games alongside his buddy, Sonny Jurgensen.

"Sonny is my best friend," says Huff. "We came to the Redskins the same year and have been buddies ever since. He's like a brother to me."

Huff also spends a lot of time with his family, his children, his grandchildren, and his longtime companion, Carol Holt.

"I just love the game of football," he says. "I love everything about it. I did an NFL films episode with Ravens linebacker Ray Lewis and thoroughly enjoyed it. I'm glad to be a part of the Redskins organization. Leaving New York was a tough thing . . . New York had become my home. But the Redskins gave me the opportunity to start over . . . and exact a little revenge in the process."

Chapter 2

BILLY
KILMER

Billy Kilmer is the first to tell you that he didn't throw the prettiest pass.

"I don't have big hands, so I had to throw the ball with my thumb a lot," he says, relaxing at his home in Coral Springs, Florida. "Sometimes it would come out irregular or a bit wobbly, but it got there on time."

Redskins fans will also tell you that it didn't matter a lick what Kilmer's passes looked like; he was still a winner.

"People might not remember my passes as being rocket-armed because Sonny Jurgensen threw such a nice pass, but I had a strong arm," says Kilmer. "I was a baseball player and could throw the ball. I think my strength was that I had good timing and I worked on that a lot. I could throw to a hole or open area and have a receiver run into it. I also learned a lot from Jurgensen. He taught me a lot about how to throw the ball and maneuver it. Before going to the Redskins I always had a sore arm, but with the Redskins I learned to put my body into throws."

With Kilmer at the helm in George Allen's conservative offense, he was the perfect field general for someone who understood his role in a run-first, ball-control offense.

Born September 5, 1939, in Topeka, Kansas, Kilmer grew up in Azusa, California, and excelled in baseball, basketball, and football at

Citrus High School. He chose football and became an All-America quarterback at UCLA.

"I also played basketball for John Wooden at UCLA," says Kilmer. "I was All-California in high school and one of the top 30 players in the country. I also was good enough in baseball that the Pirates offered me a $50,000 contract." The San Francisco 49ers chose him in the first round of the 1961 draft (number 11 overall).

Kilmer considers himself lucky to have played for such a legendary coach as the fabled John Wooden. "I cracked my ankle during my junior year in football and I was going to come back and play for Wooden my senior year, but I had already been drafted by the 49ers in December and had a contract, so I was ineligible to play any more college sports."

"I count myself lucky, though, to have played for John Wooden. He taught me a lot about discipline and organization. The guy knew how to talk to kids. He said the right words, pushed the right buttons. It was a great experience. I didn't get to play a lot, but I practiced every day with the team."

GIVING IT HIS HEART AND SOUL IN SAN FRANCISCO

Kilmer's time with the 49ers was life-changing. 49ers coach Red Hickey had a lot of talent at quarterback; there was Y.A. Tittle, John Brodie, Bob Waters, as well as Kilmer. Lucky for Kilmer, Tittle was traded to the New York Giants before the start of the season, so Kilmer saw some playing time. It helped that Hickey had installed the shotgun that took advantage of Kilmer's athleticism.

"He alternated the three of us, John, Bobby, and me," says Kilmer. "I was a running quarterback, so I mostly ran."

After eight seasons with the 49ers and Saints, **Billy Kilmer** joined the Redskins in 1971, presumably to back up Sonny Jurgensen. That year, he led the Redskins to their first playoff appearance since 1945. In '72, he led them to the Super Bowl. The rest is history. *Diamond Images®*

Kilmer was such a great runner that he rushed for 509 yards and scored 10 TDs for a 5.3 average his rookie season. Still, Hickey didn't have that much success with the shotgun and scrapped it after six games. John Brodie became the full-time quarterback and Billy moved to running back as they started the 1962 season.

Now stationed behind Brodie, Kilmer rushed for 478 yards on 93 carries for a 5.1 average. Then with two games left in the '62 season, Kilmer's leg was shattered in a car accident.

"It nearly snapped my leg off and I was laid up in bed for a couple years," he says. The injury was so bad that he missed the entire 1963 season. "After that, I came back and played quarterback behind John Brodie and George Mira for a few seasons."

Kilmer's shifty running style was gone. And since he wasn't known for his pretty passes, Hickey didn't believe he had much of a chance to start, especially with Brodie playing so well.

"I had battled long and hard to get back," says Kilmer. "My leg had gotten infected and was almost amputated. Even after I was out of the hospital, they discovered I still had some bone chips in my leg, and so the [healing] process took even longer for me."

He came back for the 1964 season and played as a quarterback and a running back. His only play of note that gained any attention that season was a humorous one. Against the Vikings, Kilmer caught a short pass from John Brodie and, after maneuvering to get away from a defender, had the ball stripped from his hands. Minnesota defensive end Jim Marshall immediately scooped the ball up and ran it into the end zone—the wrong end zone. Marshall thought it was a touchdown, but it turned out to be a safety.

PRAYERS ANSWERED BY SAINTS

For many veteran players, being put on "the list"—that is, the expansion list—is a dubious honor. It means your team has left you unprotected, so the new club can claim you on waivers. When the New Orleans Saints became an expansion team in 1967, many great former players found themselves on the list, including two former Green Bay Packers, Jim Taylor and Paul Hornung. Taylor went to New Orleans for a year before calling is quits. Hornung retired.

"I remember when they called to tell me I had been taken in the expansion draft. I was playing golf at the time," recalls Kilmer. "I remember thinking, 'You know, this might be my big break. It'll give me a chance to play.' Tom Fears was the Saints coach and he had coached at UCLA. He knew me and gave me a chance. When I first went to New Orleans, I was the third quarterback, behind Gary Cuozzo and Gary Wood. I remember when they asked me to sign a contract, I didn't even look at what I was going to make. I just signed it and gave it back.

"All I said was, 'Just give me a chance to play. I don't care what I make.' And they did. I started the first three games of the season, then they went with Cuozzo for a time," he says. "We didn't have a lot of talent, but we played hard. I didn't like to lose, but it felt good to be playing."

Kilmer enjoyed some memorable games. In his first season with the Saints, he came off the bench to overtake the other expansion team, the Falcons, 27-24. The following year, Cuozzo was traded to the Vikings and Kilmer finally became a full-time starter. Despite missing two games, he threw for over 2,000 yards and 15 touchdowns. He also scored a pair of touchdowns on the ground.

"It was great to be out there playing," says Kilmer. "People don't realize this but during the Saints' first three years when I was at quarterback, we won more games than any other expansion club at the time." Indeed the Saints won 12 games from 1967-69, which is not bad when you consider that the 1960 expansion Cowboys didn't win a single game.

During his time at New Orleans, Kilmer also joined the record books with a spectacular 1969 game against the St. Louis Cardinals. The great Charley Johnson, one of the brightest and most underrated quarterbacks in NFL history, was quarterbacking St. Louis. On this day, Kilmer and Johnson shared a game for the ages. As if it were a touch football game in a nice breezy park, the two quarterbacks fired six touchdown passes apiece as the Saints won a wild 51-42 victory.

"I actually threw seven touchdowns and had one called back," Billy laughs. "Charley and I became real close friends later on and talked about that game. The funny thing is, we were 0-6 going into that game, and a friend of mine, George Owen, the personnel director, was fired before the game. I was told they were also going to fire Fears afterwards. That really upset me, because he had given me a chance. So I played my best for him."

Unfortunately for Billy, Fears was fired in the middle of the 1970 season and the team faltered after that.

The only good thing about the '70 season was beating the Detroit Lions on a last-second, 63-yard field goal by Tom Dempsey—an NFL record later shared by the Broncos' Jason Elam. With seconds left and the Saints driving to get into a possible field-goal try, Kilmer delivered a perfect 20-yard strike to receiver Al Dodd.

"Looking back, I didn't think Dempsey would make it, but I knew he was capable of kicking it that far," says Kilmer. "But you don't know. There's a lot of pressure on a kick like that. It's the end of the game, two seconds to go. But when he kicked that ball and I saw it take flight, I knew he was going to make it. The aftermath was quite a scene. The fans carried him on their shoulders for an hour. I didn't think they were ever going to let him down."

A WINNING MOVE

Redskins fans probably remember Kilmer coming to Washington and gracefully becoming the backup to Sonny Jurgensen. The truth is that Kilmer was upset he was going from being a starter to playing behind one of the greatest pure passers around.

"When I got traded to the Redskins, I knew I was going to be behind Jurgensen," says Kilmer. "It was upsetting because I was 31 years old. I wanted to play, and there were a few other teams I knew who wanted me. One was Denver; another was Green Bay. But I've always been a team guy, and I figured I'd play a year and then play out my option."

But the man who had endured so much pain and speculation about his ability to be a great quarterback became the recipient of a simple twist of fate. During an exhibition game against the Miami Dolphins, Jurgensen fractured the coracoid process of his left shoulder while making a tackle after an interception to safety Dick Anderson. Jurgensen missed most of the season, and the Redskins hopes for a strong 1971 season fell into the capable hands of number 17.

Kilmer led the Redskins to a 9-4-1 record and the team's first playoff appearance since 1945. "When Sonny got hurt, I got to play and everything fell into place," says Kilmer. "George and Sonny and the offensive coordinator, Ted Marchibroda, clashed a lot. Sonny had loved the way Lombardi had done things. I don't know what the deal was, but I know there was some animosity there. But when I got there, I just bought into their system, and as long as I was winning, they were going to keep me in there."

The first of many Redskins quarterback controversies arose during the 1972 season when Sonny, finally healthy, challenged Kilmer for the top spot. It appeared that Allen wanted to go with the hot hand. Kilmer started the '72 season with a victory against the Vikings on *Monday Night Football*. He followed that up with another win over St. Louis. Then the Redskins lost to the lowly Patriots, and Allen pulled the plug on Kilmer.

"I threw three touchdown passes that game," recalls Kilmer. "I almost had a fourth. They called Roy Jefferson out of bounds on a TD catch, but the replay indicated that he was in. Then Curt Knight missed a field goal at the end of the game we lost by one point, 23-24."

A loss was a loss in Allen's book, so he inserted the 38-year-old, 16-year veteran in Kilmer's place. Jurgensen won the next three games. For some, it was hard to argue about the switch; there was no denying Jurgensen's prowess as a passer. But the Redskins were no longer the pass-happy group they were in the 1960s when they had no defense. This was a George Allen team, and it had a stifling defense and a superb run game with Larry Brown and Charley Harraway.

In Week 6, at 5-1 and facing the much-improved 4-2 Giants, Kilmer got a second chance to show Allen that he was the man to lead them to the Super Bowl. Early in the game, Jurgensen snapped his Achilles tendon and limped off the field for the last time that season.

Kilmer came in and realized he didn't need to throw for 300 yards to beat the Giants. "I knew we could run on the Giants, so I kept calling running plays and Larry kept hitting the holes and making a ton of yards," says Kilmer. "I knew the defense wasn't going to let the Giants score a lot of points."

They didn't, and the Redskins won 23-16 as Brown raced for a career-best 191 yards. Said Giants defensive tackle Jack Gregory to reporters after the game: "Sonny is more dangerous, but the Redskins seem to play better with Kilmer."

The 6-foot, 204-pound Kilmer led the Redskins to five more victories and clinched the NFC East with two games to play. At that point, Allen rested most of the starters—except for Kilmer—and the Redskins lost the final two games, finishing 11-3.

"I don't blame George for doing that," says Kilmer, "you had to rest Larry for the playoffs."

The first team on the Redskins playoff docket in '72 was the Green Bay Packers. With Bart Starr retired, a young quarterback named Scott Hunter was the new leader of the Pack. Hunter became the hunted; the Redskins' tenacious defense featured a five-man front. With nowhere to run or pass, Hunter and the Packers fell easily to the Redskins, 16-3.

The only touchdown in the divisional playoff game came on a beautiful 32-yard scoring pass from Kilmer to Roy "Sweet Pea" Jefferson.

That left one game to go before the Washington Redskins would go to their first-ever Super Bowl. The 53,129 patient Redskins fans in attendance on that New Year's Eve night in D.C. got to see their arch-rival, the Dallas Cowboys, get humiliated.

GAME OF MY LIFE
BY BILLY KILMER

The championship against Dallas was probably the highlight of my career. After all, it got us to the Super Bowl.

Before the game, Cowboys coach Tom Landry casually said that I wasn't the athlete that his quarterback, Roger Staubach, was. I took it personally. Our team was already fired up and that comment got me really ready to play. Early that morning I was with Diron Talbert, Ron McDole, and Pat Fischer, and we were having coffee in the morning before the pregame meal. I think we were all reading the same paper and the same article. All of a sudden our heads popped up and we just looked at each other in disbelief. For someone like me who had been through some hardships and worked so hard to get my break, those comments by Landry stuck with me and gave me even more incentive to win. I tell you, I was ready to play right then.

A lot of people think no one hated the Cowboys as much as Diron Talbert hated them. Maybe that's true, but he didn't have to help me hate the Cowboys. I played the Cowboys a lot while with San Francisco, and at New Orleans we played them twice a year. I didn't hate the players much, but I didn't like the philosophy of Tex Schramm and the front-office people. They kind of ruled the league. They always seemed to get their way.

Before a game, George always wrote down his goals on a chalkboard as a way to remind us of what he wanted to accomplish. He had two goals against the Cowboys. He wanted our defense to pressure Staubach because he had missed the season with a separated shoulder, before coming off the bench the week before to throw those two touchdown passes. He believed that if we pressured him enough, he wouldn't be so effective. The second goal was that, offensively, he felt we could attack the Cowboys secondary, especially Charlie Waters' side. One reason was because on the other side was Pro Bowler Mel Renfro.

As the game went on, the defense got after Staubach. He didn't look so athletic running for his life. But I didn't worry much about that. I was focused on playing well, and I did. I threw two touchdown passes to Charley Taylor. After a scoreless first quarter, we added a field goal by Curt Knight and then we marched down near the goal line. The big play was a bomb I threw to Taylor over Waters. Then I threw a slant to him for a touchdown and a 10-0 lead.

They kicked a field goal and we led 10-3 at the half. We felt pretty good because we were controlling every aspect of the game. In the third quarter, the defense got after Staubach pretty well. He had nowhere to pass and was getting sacked.

By the fourth quarter, pure adrenaline took over our team. It was time to break open the game. Waters had broken his arm and they'd put in Mark Washington. I told Charley, "I know you can run by him," and I knew that in certain formations they would overplay Larry Brown. So I called a formation where I knew Charley would have single coverage. I thought I overthrew him but, boy, Charley put on some afterburners, and I think it was the best spiral I ever threw in my life.

After that, we just controlled the game. Knight kicked three more field goals and as the clock ran down, the fans crashed onto the field. We had won our division, beaten the Cowboys, and we were going to the Super Bowl. Knowing I had helped my team do that was the best feeling.

A DECADE OF SUCCESS

The world knows that the Redskins dream for a Super Bowl championship would fall to a Dolphin team of destiny. The Skins would fight valiantly but come up short, 14-7. Miami finished the NFL's only perfect season and would win the Super Bowl the next year as well.

For Kilmer and the rest of his teammates, the Redskins teams under George Allen would continue to make the playoffs for years to come. In 16 seasons, Kilmer the quarterback passed for 20,945 yards and 152 touchdowns.

Injuries to Kilmer in 1973 and 1974 would bring the ageless Jurgensen back onto the field for some welcomed heroics. But looking back, that magical 1972 season probably wouldn't have been possible without the talent and leadership of one William Orland Kilmer, Jr.

Kilmer retired in 1978, the year after George Allen left the Redskins.

"People talk about animosity between Sonny and me, but we supported whomever played. I've heard that we talked about wanting to play so much that we almost came to blows a few times, but that's a bunch of baloney. Sure, I wanted to play and he wanted to play. But the bottom line is we wanted to win. I had been in the league 10 years and never played for a winner. Sonny had been around with the Redskins all those years and had endured some miserable losing years. We knew we couldn't break up the team. Whoever was quarterback, we'd help each other. All we wanted to do was help the team win."

Today Kilmer considers Jurgensen and himself, "great pals." But his best friend on the Redskins remains Diron Talbert. "I'm still great friends with Diron, his brother Don, and his whole family. We like each other and like to go fishing and hunting. I just like to be around them. They're fun guys to be around. We just hit it off."

The personal side of Kilmer is equally refreshing. After retiring, Kilmer owned an automobile dealership for a while, and then became a marketing director for former Cowboys owner Clint Murchison, who owned several banks. He also hosted several golf tournaments over the years to raise money for charities concerned with cerebral palsy, which afflicts his daughter, Kathie.

"I've done what I can to help," says Kilmer. "The money raised from golf tournaments went toward the handicap section of Citrus Junior College in California, where she went for two years. She was Homecoming queen. They had an adaptive physical education deal, but they didn't have any equipment or stationary bikes. So we raised money to get them more equipment for adaptive physical education, for stroke victims and things like that. We did it for 19 years. We raised so much money and got so much equipment that the state came in and built a new building for them. I even go to it and help her work out."

When Kilmer thinks about his family, his daughter, Kathie, and his wife, Sandy, he counts himself extremely lucky. "My wife is incredible and my daughter is now 47. She has been in wheelchair her whole life and lives as normally as possible, and she's just the greatest person. When I played, I could throw three interceptions, but then I'd think about her and I wouldn't have any problems."

Like his daughter, Billy Kilmer continues to be an inspirational winner.

Chapter 3

DIRON TALBERT

If there was one player who helped to fuel the Redskins-Cowboys rivalry in the early 1970s, it was Diron Talbert.

There have been few players tougher or more outspoken than old number 72. Standing 6-foot-5 and weighing 255 pounds, Talbert backed it up with his play and his larger-than-life persona. He was a big man from a family of big men. His older brother, Don, who also measured 6-foot-5, played offensive tackle and linebacker for several teams, including the hated Cowboys. There was another Talbert son, Charlie, who was equally big. All three played at the University of Texas, and all three gave Abe Lincoln a run for their money in the candor department.

Pretentious is not a word ever associated with the Talberts.

"I was brought up to be honest," says Diron. "I never tried to be something I wasn't. If someone asked me a question, I'd answer it. No use in side-steppin' a subject."

That kind of raw honesty got Talbert into a feud with America's quarterback, the Dallas Cowboys' Cowboy, Roger Staubach. And it helped ignite a busted fuel line of contempt on an already wild, contentious, take-no-prisoners rivalry.

"We hated the Cowboys and they hated us," says Talbert. "It was a beautiful thing." He disliked everything about them, even the way the

25

offensive linemen would all stand up before kneeling down in their stances. "Stupid," he says.

That kind of honest orneriness made Talbert one of the most beloved Redskins of the George Allen era. Actually, he spent two eras with Allen: the first as a member of the Los Angeles Rams from 1967 to 1970; the second spanning seven years as one of the "Ramskins," 1971-77. He finished up in 1980 with Jack Pardee as coach. Talbert and his colleagues were so revered by Allen that one of the first things he did as the new Redskins coach was to trade for several of his old defensive players, such as Talbert, Pardee, Mo Pottios, Richie Petitbon, Maxie Baughan, and others.

Those "Ramskins," plus key trades bringing in receiver Roy Jefferson, quarterback Billy Kilmer, and defensive ends Ron McDole and Verlon Biggs, made Allen's Redskins one of the most talked about teams in the NFL.

"George wanted to simplify things by bringing in veterans that he didn't have to baby sit," says Talbert. "He believed in defense, a strong running game, and great special teams. So he brought in a lot of his own guys."

By giving away draft picks for proven veterans, Allen brought credence to his motto: The Future Is Now.

"We'd all been in the league and were hungry to win," says Talbert. "George had made us winners with the Rams; now we were going to win in Washington."

Winning and competing came naturally to Diron Vester Talbert. Born in Pascagoula, Mississippi on July 1, 1944, and raised in Texas City, Texas, about 40 miles south of Houston, the Talberts made the move to the big state of Texas a lasting one. The great flag of the second-biggest state became a symbol for the Talberts' Texas tough mentality.

When it came to fueling the Cowboys-Redskins rivalry, the undisputed ringleader was a tough, talented Texan named **Diron Talbert**. His running feud with "Captain America" Roger Staubach ignited a hatred toward Dallas that continues today. *Michael Zagaris/Getty Images*

After following in his brothers' footsteps to the University of Texas, Diron continued his football journey to the NFL with Don, who was drafted in 1962 by the Dallas Cowboys as an offensive tackle. Four years later, the Los Angeles Rams drafted Diron, then a junior, in the fifth round as a future pick in 1966.

"A lot of people think my hatred for the Cowboys and Roger Staubach started with the Redskins," says Talbert. "But it really began long before."

Talbert had played against Staubach and Navy for the national championship in the Cotton Bowl in 1963, the year "Roger the Dodger" had won the Heisman Trophy. After joining the Rams, Talbert discovered that was just the beginning of seeing number 12.

"George Allen was my coach with the Rams and we used to scrimmage the Cowboys all the time in training camp," says Talbert. "Even then, George always got us ready to play Dallas, whether it was regular season or a scrimmage."

The Cowboys held training camp in Thousand Oaks, California, a short drive north of Los Angeles, and the Rams would climb on a bus from their camp in Fullerton to scrimmage them during summer camp.

"They were a good team when I was on the Rams. Even then, George would get us psyched to play the Cowboys. He'd talk about all the great players they had and wondered how we would match up. He got us into a frenzy, and it was just a scrimmage."

As a defensive lineman with the Rams in the 1960s, Talbert got to rub massive shoulders with some of the game's legends. Though he was not one of the Fearsome Foursome, which included Rosie Grier, Deacon Jones, Merlin Olsen, and Lamar Lundy, he learned from the best.

When Bears legend Dick Butkus called the line the greatest in NFL history, the young Talbert got to be a part of the group. While Roger Brown replaced Grier in '67, Talbert and Coy Bacon began rotating with the foursome to keep the group fresh.

"I liked to call myself the fifth Beatle," says Talbert. "If one of them got hurt, I was first off the bench."

Talbert has many fond memories of his Rams days. "We sacked a lot of quarterbacks," he says. "I sacked Fran Tarkenton a few times when he was on the Giants. But probably my most memorable was during my first start. We were playing the Colts and I not only sacked Johnny Unitas, I got him three times!"

In Talbert's first year with the Rams, both the offense and defense were first in the NFL. The following year the defense was ranked third. In 1969 they came in fifth, and 1970 they were ranked third again. Though they never made it to the Super Bowl, it wasn't the defense's fault. The Rams never had the running game that Allen inherited when he became the Redskins coach in 1971.

SACKING CAPTAIN AMERICA

When Allen brought Talbert as part of the "Ramskins" deal, the Cowboys were still the team to beat in the NFC East. Talbert just picked up where he left off in hating the Cowboys.

"Even in the beginning with all those veterans from different teams you could sense something special," says Talbert. "We were all focused on playing like a team and winning."

Just as he'd predicted, the '71 Redskins didn't start out like a team that had a new coach and 20 new players. They won six of their first seven games and finished 9-4-1, earning a postseason berth for the first time since 1945. Those nine wins included a road victory over the Cowboys at brand-new Texas Stadium and at the Los Angeles Coliseum over Talbert and company's Rams.

"We lost in the playoffs, which was disappointing," says Talbert, "but we were excited about next season."

The 1971 season brought Washington's first victory over Dallas since 1967, the Redskins were primed for even more Dallas bashing in 1972. Both teams were 4-1 the first time they met at RFK Stadium on October 22 before 53,000 fans.

Dallas quarterback Staubach had suffered a dislocated shoulder, thanks to a preseason hit by Talbert's old team, the Rams. He was out not only for that game, but he was expected to miss most of the season. Craig Morton started for Dallas and Sonny Jurgensen for Washington. It didn't take long to figure out that both teams were the tops in the NFC. The Redskins won 24-20 with Larry Brown combining for 195 yards from scrimmage and Jurgensen making plays in the air.

"Allen said it felt like a Super Bowl," says Talbert. "He always stressed playing as a team. Back then there were only 40 guys on a team, so he loved saying '40 guys playing together can't lose!'"

The two teams met for a rematch at Texas Stadium on December 9, where the Redskins suffered their second loss of the season, losing 34-24 to the Cowboys. The Redskins would falter again the next week at home to the Bills, 24-17, and head into the playoffs facing the Packers with two-straight losses.

The Packers were no pushovers. The team had won its first division since Lombardi's legends won the '67 Super Bowl. Now, Bart Star was retired and a kid named Scott Hunter was taking snaps. Still, that didn't matter because Green Bay had two big, strong horses running the ball named John Brockington and MacArthur Lane. Allen knew that by stopping the running game, the team would have to win with the young quarterback's arm. Allen wasn't too concerned about Hunter passing the ball, so he focused on the ground game.

"George used a five-man front with Manny [Sistrunk] in the middle, and we stopped 'em cold," says Talbert. "I don't think those two big backs picked up a first down. We won on a bunch of field goals and a touchdown from Billy [Kilmer] to Roy [Jefferson]. Those Cowboys and Staubach were next."

GAME OF MY LIFE
BY DIRON TALBERT

There's no game that sticks out to me more than the 1972 NFC Championship Game. The Washington Redskins versus those hated Dallas Cowboys. What more could you want?

The Cowboys were the darlings of the media. They were America's Team. The Redskins had been nothing for so many years; you had to go back to 1945 for the last time we played for any kind of championship. We had had a great season, but that meant nothing if we couldn't beat the Cowboys.

People may not know this, but Craig Morton is a good friend of mine. We've known each other for a long time, and he's still a great friend. After Staubach dislocated his shoulder in the preseason against my old team, the Rams, Morton came off the bench to have a great season. He led them to 10 wins and a playoff berth. Then Staubach came in against the 49ers in the playoffs and helped them come from behind to win. All of a sudden Tom Landry names Staubach the starter for the championship game. Seriously, I felt bad for Craig, but deep down I was licking my chops.

I don't think there's ever been a team that was more prepared or ready to play than we were. Our plan on defense was pretty simple: we were going to chase Roger Staubach all over the doggone field. Well, we sacked Staubach a bunch of times in that championship game. He looked rusty and showed it. I don't even think he threw for 100 yards, and the Cowboys only managed one field goal. I remember roughing him up on a couple plays and having the time of my life. We crushed them 26-3 and we were going to the Super Bowl.

The thing I remember most about that game was trying to get to the locker room without getting killed. Before the game even ended, both teams were taken off the field. That gave us a good head start to the dugout. The Redskins fans were crazy. In seconds there were 30,000 fans on the field. Pat Fischer and I made a run for the dugout. All I remember was running, ramming into people to get by, and finally falling down inside the dugout exhausted. I was scared to get trampled and used Fischer almost as a shield. He was like a little rooster swinging his arms to get through.

After the game I was interviewed, I think, by Jerry Kramer on national television. He asked me about the game. I said, "I think they started the wrong quarterback." Well, of course, Staubach heard that, and it just added fuel to the rivalry. But if you look at his performance in the game, you know I was just being honest.

People think I played well in that game, but I really don't remember. That game was so emotionally loaded that I didn't know afterwards whether or not I'd done well. I look at it this way: we won, so I guess I must have played well.

GOING HOME TO TEXAS

Diron Talbert went on to play another eight seasons with the Redskins and retired in 1980 after a raucous 14-year career.

He continued to have a blast poking fun at Staubach over the next several years, and got some flak for dispensing more of his brutal honesty. Staubach's backup and Talbert's friend, Craig Morton, had been traded to the New York Giants a few weeks earlier. During the 1974 Thanksgiving game in Dallas, Talbert noticed that with Morton out of the picture, should anything happen to Staubach, a rookie named Clint Longley would have to play.

"If you can knock Staubach out, you've got that rookie [Longley] facing you," said Talbert at the time. "That's one of our goals. If we can do that, it's great."

There wasn't anything wrong with the thinking behind the statement, but only Talbert was frank enough to come out and say what every player and personnel coach around the league was thinking.

As everyone knows, the Redskins did level Staubach. Longley came off the bench and threw two fourth-quarter touchdowns to win, 24-23.

"I was just speaking the truth," says Talbert, about the famous quote. "Heck, they won that game, but they didn't make the playoffs, and we did."

Still, the Cowboys were the one team that always got him up the most.

"When you think about it, they always seemed to have more talent than us," he says. "They had a better running game, always had more Pro

Bowl players, but somehow we managed to win a lot of games against them. I think we split games with them each season or sometimes won them both. That just goes to show you how much we enjoyed playing them and beating them."

Since his playing days, Talbert has buried the hatchet with Staubach. "He's a nice enough fella," says Talbert. "I've played in some celebrity flag-football games with him and we've talked."

Talbert returned to Sugarland, Texas, just outside of Houston, and owns Talbert's Holiday Market and Deli with his brother, Don. In his spare time, he enjoys hunting and fishing. He's said about the latter, "There ain't but one time to go fishin' and that's whenever you can." His two children, Gregory and Amanda, both attended the University of Texas and he says so will his three "grandbabies."

Talbert is still tight with several Redskins from his playing days, including Billy Kilmer, Ron McDole, and Pat Fischer. Even though it's been more than 25 years since he retired, Talbert says he still gets letters from fans every week.

"People write to tell me that they appreciated me and love the Redskins. People asking for my autograph, it's flat-out crazy. People send me old football cards, some I've never seen before. Don't get me wrong; I don't dislike it. People send me stuff and I sign it. I just can't believe so many people remember us and appreciate what we did."

Redskins fans don't just remember Talbert; they'll never forget him.

Chapter 4

ROY JEFFERSON

Roy "Sweet Pea" Jefferson was different from most players when he joined the Redskins in 1971. Although he was part of George Allen's "The Future Is Now" movement, where Allen gave away draft picks for proven vets like him, Jefferson, unlike most of the "Over the Hill Gang," hadn't played for the Rams.

He came from the Baltimore Colts and was already a Pro Bowler. He even had a Super Bowl ring. So by the time he showed up at the Redskins camp in 1971, he had played with the likes of quarterback Johnny Unitas, and legends like John Mackey. Of course, he had also played with quarterbacks named Ed Brown, Ron Smith, and Kent Nix.

Because of this paradox, Jefferson was considered one of the best-kept secrets in the NFL. At 6-foot-2 and 195-pounds, he was a tall, fluid, gifted receiver who could dominate a game, yet he wasn't on the cover of any major sports magazines.

The media didn't really know him, but players from around the league sure did. In fact, teammate Mike Bass, who covered Jefferson when he was starring for the Pittsburgh Steelers, calls him one of the best receivers he ever faced. Because he played most of his career with the Steelers before coming to the Redskins, it may surprise people to hear that it was Jefferson, not Hall of Famer Charley Taylor, who posted back-to-back 1,000-yard receiving seasons. As great as Taylor was, he only had one 1,000-yard season.

So when Jefferson left the Steelers and joined the Colts in 1970 for their Super Bowl run, his prowess wasn't lost on then-Rams coach George Allen. Weeks after the Super Bowl, Jefferson got into a contract disagreement with Colts owner Carroll Rosenbloom and asked for his release. Allen was only too happy to snag him.

Jefferson spent his last six seasons with the Redskins and became a fan favorite, as much for his trademark sideburns as for his splendid play. Yet years later, when a "blue-ribbon" panel of supposed media experts was given the task of selecting the 70 Greatest Redskins, Jefferson wasn't named as one of them. Still, despite the incredible omission, the smile has never left Sweat Pea's face.

Roy Lee Jefferson, Jr. was born November 9, 1943, in Texarkana, Texas. When Roy was only two, his father died, and the family moved to Los Angeles shortly thereafter to be closer to other relatives. His mother was an honest and sometimes stern woman who fostered a lot of confidence in young Roy.

"My mom instilled in me at a very young age to always do what you're supposed to be doing," says Jefferson. "Then no one has a right to yell or scream at you."

There was little reason to object to anything Jefferson did on the athletic field. He excelled naturally in sports. He looked up to his cousin, Marv Fleming, a talented athlete who was a star at Compton High School who would earn four Super Bowl rings playing for the Green Bay Packers and Miami Dolphins. Jefferson was a year behind his cousin, and when Fleming accepted a scholarship at the University of Utah, young Roy followed him there.

Redskins great **Roy Jefferson** had a unique style on and off the field. That style, along with his trademark sideburns, made him a fan favorite. Defensive backs, however, knew him as an enormously talented receiver, one to be feared every time he lined up. *NFL/WireImage.com*

"I really wanted to go to UCLA," says Jefferson. "But you needed a 3.0 grade point average to go there, and my grades were a 2.7. Marv was at Utah and liked it, so I went too."

The nickname for Utah at the time was, ironically enough, the "Runnin' Redskins." Jefferson's coach, Ray Nagel, who led the Redskins from 1958-65, quickly recognized his numerous talents. In fact, when Jefferson graduated, Coach Nagel called him the "finest football player [he] ever coached."

"I got the opportunity to play a lot of positions and do lot of things at Utah," Jefferson says. "Because of that I was considered 'The Man.'"

He also got a chance to get an up-close look at a future teammate. "We were playing Arizona State and they had this pretty good tailback named Charley Taylor," says Jefferson. "He also played defensive back and tried to cover me."

Like Taylor, Jefferson was not only a star in his own right; he was one of the most exciting and versatile players in the country. In addition to playing running back and receiver, he also played linebacker and defensive back, and he returned kicks and handled most of the kicking duties.

Jefferson's talented exploits helped Utah earn a 9-2 record. In doing so, he was named All-American and voted the Western Athletic Conference (WAC) player of the year. Better yet, he led Utah to its first bowl game ever—the 1964 Liberty Bowl in Atlantic City. Even though he was known throughout the WAC, Jefferson's versatility and toughness gained him some national attention during the televised game.

Despite separating his shoulder, Jefferson managed to kick two field goals and an extra point, upsetting heavily favored West Virginia, 32-6.

"Utah had never been to a bowl game, so to go and upset West Virginia was pretty cool," says Jefferson. "It was upsetting to get hurt, but I still contributed." As his college career wound down and the NFL draft approached, Jefferson felt like he could go in the first couple rounds.

PITIFUL PITTSBURGH

It's difficult to think about the Pittsburgh Steelers without thinking about decades of success: the Super Bowl teams of the 1970s; years of winning in the '80s and '90s; the team's recent Super Bowl victory in 2005. But in 1965, the Steelers were perennial losers, and had been since the franchise began in 1933. Originally known as the Pittsburgh Pirates, the team had just five winning seasons in 32 years. So when Steelers head coach Mike Nixon used the team's first pick to get the sleek receiver from Utah, the young man knew he would be facing some tough years.

As a rookie, Jefferson had just 13 receptions, but those totaled 281 yards—a 22.1 average—and a touchdown. His lack of production was not surprising considering the quarterbacks working to get him the ball—Ed Brown, Bill Nelson, and Tommy Wade.

The following year, in 1966, the Steelers had another new coach: former Redskins coach Bill Austin. Jefferson quickly came into his own, snagging 32 receptions for 772 yards and four scores, not to mention a blistering 24.1 average. But more concerning was the number of new quarterbacks in the rotation—three.

By 1967, Jefferson's third season, the young speedster had to accommodate for another passer, rookie Kent Nix. Jefferson still grabbed 29 receptions and turned them into 459 yards and four scores.

"When I got to the Redskins, a lot of people started comparing my career with Charley Taylor's," says Jefferson. "He came in a year before and played with Sonny his whole career. I played with nine quarterbacks in Pittsburgh. Sometimes I was double and triple covered."

With Jefferson as the main target, opposing teams often put a linebacker on the line of scrimmage to bump him. Then he'd have to elude a cornerback and a safety before he could get open.

In 1968, with former Redskin Dick Shiner tossing most of the passes, Jefferson led the NFL in reception yards with 1,074 and 11 touchdowns. He also led the NFL in punt returns, fielding a league-high 28 for 274 yards and a touchdown. He was a unanimous Pro Bowler and should have been happy; Coach Austin had tried to switch Jefferson to defense during training camp, and his success on offense should have been vindicating. But Jefferson was furious with Austin about something much more appalling.

During a mid-season game at Atlanta, while the two teams were warming up, Jefferson heard Austin talking to Falcons coach Norm Van Brocklin about their teams.

"I heard Van Brocklin say, 'I can't get along with niggers,'" says Jefferson. "Then Austin replies, 'I can't get along with them either.'" Jefferson says other Falcons players he knew confirmed Van Brocklin's racial slurs.

The Steelers went 2-11-1 in 1968, and Austin was fired. The Steelers new coach was a 37-year-old assistant named Chuck Noll. Noll's first draft selection was defensive tackle Joe Greene. He also drafted quarterback Terry Hanratty. So Jefferson had to adapt to another new coach and another new quarterback. Somehow, some way, he put up another huge list of numbers. Even with the club going 1-13, Jefferson caught 67 balls for 1,079 yards and nine scores.

Again, he was named to the Pro Bowl. But again, he was tired of the losing. Noll was looking to put his own stamp on his team, and Jefferson wasn't so sure the young coach had all the answers.

"Coaches in those days wanted things their way," says Jefferson "Their approach was 'My way or the highway.' And Noll was no different. He didn't give you the opportunity to question anything. I just wasn't a player to be coached that way. People thought I was a free spirit, but I really wasn't so much. I'm an adult, a man. Allow me the flexibility to question what you're telling me. It's been proven coaches don't know it all."

Noll's response to the freethinking Jefferson was to trade him, along with a fourth-round draft pick, to Baltimore for receiver Willie

Richardson. A former Pro Bowler, Richardson never suited up for the Steelers and played a year in Miami before returning to the Colts in 1971.

UNITAS OVER HANRATTY

Once he joined the close-knit Baltimore Colts, Jefferson didn't need anyone to tell him that catching passes from Johnny Unitas was the way to go. The Colts were the NFL's best team in 1968 before being upset by the Joe Namath-led Jets in Super Bowl III. The next season, Baltimore went 8-5-1, and coach Don Shula left to go to Miami. Owner Carroll Rosenbloom elevated Don McCafferty, a Colts assistant, to head coach. McCafferty added Jefferson and another receiver, Eddie Hinton, to the offense, and the Colts were once again formidable. Jefferson was thrilled to finally play for a winner, not to mention a legend.

"Playing with Johnny Unitas was exciting," says Jefferson. "He was so cool under pressure. I remember one game, we got the ball with about a 1:30 to go and we needed to go 50 yards just to get into position for a field goal. Well, Unitas starts out the drive by throwing short passes: 10 yards to tight end John Mackey, 15 yards to me, and another few to a back. Then he threw incomplete a couple times. It was third-and-5 at our own 45. Unitas said, 'OK Roy, let's do an end-around to you.' As we broke the huddle, I thought, 'We can't do this. It's third down!' So I yelled over, 'Johnny, do you mean end-around pass?' because we had a play where receiver Sam Havrilak got the ball, faked it to me on the reverse and threw it. Unitas said, 'No, no, the run.' So I thought it made no sense to run this play with less than a minute to go. But who's going to argue with Unitas? So I ran the play and somehow I got around the end. I saw some daylight inside, but I was conscious of the clock and knew I had to get out of bounds. After that I caught another 15-yarder, Mackey snatched one, and we kicked a field goal to win the game."

Another game that not only showed the prowess of Unitas, but also the skill and focus of his new receiver, was against the Houston Oilers.

The night before the game, Jefferson spent time visiting his two aunts; one lived in Houston and the other he'd flown in from Texarkana, Texas.

"My Aunt Nell didn't know much about football, so she asked me what receivers do," recalls Jefferson. "My other aunt said, 'Why, they score touchdowns. Roy's the best at it.' So Aunt Nell asked me to score a touchdown for her against Houston." Jefferson instead scored two. "I scored one earlier in the game on a quick post, then another one to win the game. When I caught the ball at the goal line I held it up and threw it down hard. I said, 'This one's for you, Aunt Nell!'"

With Jefferson and Hinton catching passes from Unitas, the Colts went 11-2-1. In the playoffs, the Colts shut out the Bengals 17-0 thanks to 45-yard touchdown catch from Unitas to Jefferson on a key third-and-9 play. After knocking off the Oakland Raiders, 27-17, in the AFC Championship game, the Colts—and Roy Jefferson—were headed for the Super Bowl!

SUPER BOBBLE

Super Bowl V, the classic fumble-bumble bowl, was definitely not well played, but it was phenomenally exciting. The Baltimore Colts and the Dallas Cowboys combined for a mind-blowing 14 penalties and mind-numbing 10 turnovers.

Jefferson led the Colts with three catches for 52 yards and got the Colts close to scoring when he caught a 23-yard completion from Earl Morrall inside Dallas territory. Instead of trying to knock it in for a score, the Colts tried some trickery; Morrall pitched the ball back to receiver Sam Havrilak, who faked a reverse and threw to Hinton, who was close to the goal line before he coughed the ball up.

Jefferson remembers that play vividly: "I caught a pass from Earl by getting loose from the cornerback. A linebacker jumped on my back and I carried him another 5. I think if I had scored I would have been in contention for the MVP award. The next play, Eddie was hit and fumbled the ball into the end zone. One of their defensive backs went to jump on the ball, and I hit the guy just as he was grabbing it. The ball squirted out of the end zone for a touchback. I was so mad. I put a lot of effort into that hit."

But a quarter later, after rookie Jim O'Brien's 32-yarder flew through the uprights, Jefferson had earned a Super Bowl ring. In one year he went from being miserable on a 1-13 team to playing catch with Unitas and wearing a Super Bowl ring.

"It was quite a thrill to win a Super Bowl," says Jefferson. "It was a long time coming, but I was still young and had a lot of football left."

The only thing remaining for Jefferson to do was renegotiate his contract with owner Rosenbloom. When Jefferson arrived in Baltimore, he told Rosenbloom that he had no problem playing his first season with Baltimore under his existing contract, but if he had a good season, perhaps Rosenbloom would renegotiate it. Rosenbloom agreed. But, when Jefferson came back to negotiate a new deal, Rosenbloom claimed he never agreed to such a thing.

Jefferson was so upset he demanded to be traded. "I didn't want to play for a liar," he says. "A few years later, I saw Rosenbloom's son, Steve, at a playoff game in Minnesota and he apologized and said his father, who had since passed away from drowning accident, had agreed to renegotiate."

Lucky for Jefferson, 30 miles away in Washington, D.C., the Redskins' new coach, George Allen, was trading draft picks like they were the plague. He wanted experienced veterans over wide-eyed rookies. And the hard-playing, charismatic Jefferson was his kind of player.

A REDSKIN ONCE AGAIN

In July of 1971, the Redskins were already putting in sweat equity at their training camp in Carlisle, Pennsylvania, when Coach George Allen decided he wasn't too happy with his top pick, Texas receiver Cotton Speyrer. He wanted another proven receiver to go with his Pro Bowl split end, Charley Taylor. So he packed up Speyrer and sent him north to Baltimore, along with two mid-round picks, for Mr. Jefferson.

Once he got to Washington, Jefferson felt he had finally found a home. While he had some good times in Pittsburgh and enjoyed the town, he despised losing and felt he was treated as less than a man. Winning a Super Bowl ring in his lone season in Baltimore was memorable for a number of reasons, but in the end it came down to a lack of respect.

In Washington, Jefferson would find it all: happiness, respect, and—above all—wins.

"I loved George Allen right away," says Jefferson. "He liked veterans and treated us like men. There wasn't any need to yell at us or tell us what to do. We already knew what to do."

Fans gravitated toward Jefferson. Whether it was his trademark sideburns, his arresting smile, or his flashy clothes, he looked like a pro football star both on and off the field. He had earned the nickname "Sweat Pea" years earlier while in Pittsburgh.

"Joe Greene and another defensive tackle, Ben McGee, gave me that name," he recalls. "I was a pretty good dancer and wore some wild clothes. Somehow they heard this song from Tommy Roe called "Sweet Pea," and started calling me that: "Oh, Sweet Pea/Come on and dance with me/Come on, come on, come on and dance with me/Oh, Sweet Pea.""

On the field, Jefferson's moves were equally sweet. The Redskins quickly found they had something special. The 6-foot-2 Jefferson ran deep routes opposite the 6-foot-3 Taylor; the two former college rivals were now teammates, putting fear into defenses all over.

By making defenses wary of the deep ball, the Redskins running game grew more dangerous. "We became a ball-control offense with a great defense," says Jefferson. "But we were winning and that was the most important thing. All I wanted to do was make a big play when my number was called."

Jefferson proved to be the difference during a torrential downpour in a Week 3 contest against Dallas in 1971. After a 2-0 start, the Redskins played the Cowboys at Texas stadium with rain seemingly playing the spoiler.

The game was close and had gone back and forth. Finally, needing a big play, the Redskins turned to Jefferson. The running game was rolling well, so Kilmer called a play-action pass on third down at the 50-yard line. As Jefferson bolted down the field, Cowboys safety Cornell Greene bit on the fake. Jefferson smoothly gathered in the bullet and outraced everyone for the long touchdown.

Final score: Redskins 20, Dallas 16. The win catapulted the Redskins to 3-0 for the first time since 1943. Better yet, they finished 9-4-1 and made the playoffs for the first time since 1945.

Jefferson quickly realized that, unlike in Pittsburgh, he wasn't a one-man gang. He no longer had the bull's-eye on him. Of course, playing in a conservative but balanced offense meant he would never enjoy another 1,000-yard season. But that was fine with him; winning solved everything.

"That first season in Washington was great," says Jefferson. "We all came from different teams and different situations, good and bad. We quickly banded together and made the playoffs. Now we wanted to win the Super Bowl."

In fact, the '72 squad started much faster than the champions—going 11-1 to the Cowboys' 8-3 record. The Skins finished 11-3, the Pokes 10-4.

Washington not only won the NFC East, but they also earned home-field advantage throughout the playoffs. For the first time since 1942, the Redskins would host a playoff game. The opponent? The Green Bay Packers, who had won their division for the first time since 1967.

The Packers were considered one of the NFL's most dangerous teams. Green Bay had won six of its last seven games to win the NFC Central. They had a one-two punch at running back that teams couldn't stop. At tailback was second-year man John Brockington, a 6-foot-1, 225-pound player who had pounded out 1,027 yards and eight touchdowns. The fullback, MacArthur Lane, was tough, standing 6-foot-1 and weighing 220 pounds; he cracked through defenses for 821 yards and a 4.6 average—the probable equivalent to a 5.6 average today.

The two backs accumulated more yards than the Redskins duo of Brown and Harraway. In order for the Redskins to advance to a potential showdown with Dallas, they had to get past the Packers.

GAME OF MY LIFE
BY ROY JEFFERSON

I consider facing the Packers in that first round of the playoffs the game of my life because there was so much excitement. It was Christmas Eve, and it was the first playoff game at home in 30 years. We were confident we could win because we had beaten the Packers earlier in the season. But that had been before they'd started clicking.

We knew that the secret to beating Green Bay was stopping the running game. They had a phenomenal running game that just rolled over people thanks to those big backs, John Brockington and MacArthur Lane.

Well, George Allen loved a challenge. He really wanted to clog that middle, so he came up with a five-man line by putting defensive tackle Manny Sistrunk over Green Bay's center. That meant we had just two linebackers making the tackles. All I know is it worked—our defense suffocated their offense.

With our defense and powerful offense, we should have blown them away. Instead, we played very conservatively on offense. We kept them in the game with field goals instead of touchdowns. When you start playing like that and keep the opponent in the game, there's a good chance you might lose it.

Finally, Billy Kilmer got the right defense and called my number. It was something like "Double-sponge, Z post, X corner." That meant I would run a post and Charley would fake in and run to the flag. I got a good jump off the line, got between the linebacker and safety, and Billy led me perfectly. I never broke stride. I stretched my arms out and gathered in the ball and beat everyone to the end zone. The play gave us the lead and we never looked back.

When Billy threw me that pass, I knew we were going to win. That catch was the icing on the cake. I was happy to make a big play in a big game. But the defense set the tone. The defense was the key to that game. I was just so happy to help us win that first playoff game at home on Christmas Eve in front of those great Redskins fans.

SUPER BOWL AND THEN SOME

The next game, Washington's other receiver, Charley Taylor, grabbed the spotlight as the Redskins shot down the hated Cowboys 26-3 and advanced to the Super Bowl.

"It was great going back to the Super Bowl," says Jefferson. "Even though Miami hadn't lost a game all season, we were confident we could win. But it just wasn't our day."

Again, Jefferson stepped up in the big game—leading the team with five catches for 50 yards.

"There was something about playing in big games; it was always more exciting than anything," says Jefferson. "I always wanted to make a play to help the team."

Jefferson played four more seasons with Washington, and although the team didn't return to the Super Bowl, it wasn't for lack of effort from number 80. By the time he retired in 1976, he'd quietly put up monster numbers. His final stats read: 451 catches for 7,539 yards and 52 touchdowns. He also rushed for 188 yards and returned 58 punts for 436 yards and a touchdown. But what's more telling is

Jefferson's terrific playoff numbers: 30 catches for 435 yards and four touchdowns.

GREAT RECEPTIONS

Since his playing days, Jefferson has remained in the Washington, D.C. area. Gone are his trademark sideburns. But his passion and his numerous interests are as boundless as his NFL career was productive.

He's achieved success in all his post-football endeavors: selling building and kitchen supplies to contractors, hosting a children's television show called *It's Elementary*, working for the NFL Players Association, doing color commentary for CBS and ABC, getting his Series 7 and becoming a stockbroker, and finally owning a barbeque restaurant and a catering business.

Recently, Jefferson joined Wells Fargo in their insurance services division. However, his new passion is being a distributor and major endorser for an antioxidant-rich Southeast Asian Mango Juice called "Mangosteen."

"This juice is amazing," says Jefferson. "After retiring, every time I'd exercise I'd have to put ice on my joints. Whenever I played golf, I had to take Vicodin. Now, I've been drinking this juice for four months, and I don't have to ice my joints anymore or take pain relievers."

Still, his pride and joy is his family. Jefferson has been married for 43 years to his wife, Camille, better known as Candy. They have three children—two sons and a daughter—as well as two grandchildren.

Thinking back on his playing days, Jefferson values his time with the Redskins most. The camaraderie and winning attitude he experienced in Washington are just some of the reasons he still resides in the area. Even though he won a championship in Baltimore, it's now just a memory: he lost his ring in a bathroom at National Airport.

When people mention great receivers of the '60s and '70s, Jefferson's name doesn't usually come up. Though he was named to three Pro Bowls, led the NFL in receiving yards and punt returns, and stepped up in countless big games for the Burgundy and Gold, he was snubbed when the 70 Greatest Redskins list was announced. But the people who matter—the players and the fans—still know that there weren't many receivers as exceptional, exciting, or passionate as Roy "Sweet Pea" Jefferson.

Chapter 5

LARRY BROWN

Larry Brown played in an era when running backs took an unusual pounding. Specialty backs were not in vogue. If you weren't carrying the ball, you were blocking regardless of the down. Because offensive linemen couldn't extend or wrap their arms when they blocked, defenders could head slap, clothesline, and generally give ball carriers generous pops, usually without a flag. Backs rarely saw large, gaping holes found by today's running backs. Back then, you made your own holes.

In spite of being one of the smaller guys in the league at 5-11, 195 pounds, Larry Brown was such a back. A blocking back in college, Larry learned quickly from his first coach, the great Vince Lombardi, that he better run, catch, and block if he wanted to make his team.

"The one thing you quickly learned with Lombardi [was that] he was looking for that complete back, like he had in Green Bay with Jim Taylor and Paul Hornung," says Brown. "My whole thought process was to make sure I got his attention."

Brown did that by showing that he could hit. He could take contact and dish plenty out on his own. Learning to run and catch were something he had to develop, and quickly.

"My running style developed on its own," says Brown. "I was tough and not afraid to hit anyone. My quickness was developed from Vince

Lombardi telling me one day that every back must play by the same rules. Every back must hit the holes that the play was designed to make. He said if you do not stay with the hole, then you should never come up short, or you'd have to deal with him. I didn't want to deal with him, so I learned on hitting that hole fast."

To watch Brown run was to see the quintessential old-school back that isn't seen a lot in the modern game. He never ran out of bounds and he always lowered the boom. Despite his smaller stature, he ran as if he were 6-foot-2 and 230 pounds. He was also a terrific pass receiver, tallying more than 2,000 yards in receptions in just eight seasons.

"I played in an era where you had to be a complete back. You had to block, run the ball effectively, and catch the ball when asked. I didn't have the shiftiness of Floyd Little, a great back of my era who could set guys up and then break a long run. I just tried to gain positive yards. My focus was to find a hole and be effective. If I didn't stay with the hole that Lombardi or my other coach, George Allen, drew up I had to find another way to make positive yards. I didn't have a lot of time to make a decision. If that meant going head-to-head with a guy much bigger than me, so be it."

Born September 19, 1947, Brown learned his toughness while growing up in a slum section of Pittsburgh, Pennsylvania. One of three boys, he found sports to be a natural alternative to the streets. He excelled in baseball and football, but found the gridiron more to his liking.

"I think the contact, the hitting, wasn't something I shied away from," remembers Brown. "I was a tough kid in my neighborhood. I don't want to give the impression that I got in fights, but I wasn't afraid of physical challenges."

Growing up in the inner city of a tough steel town like Pittsburgh meant facing physical challenges every day. Pittsburgh was a large melting

Larry Brown is one of the most beloved Redskins of all time. Over eight seasons, 1969-76, the tough running back played in four Pro Bowls, led the NFL in rushing in 1970, and was named the NFL's MVP for helping to catapult the Redskins to their first Super Bowl in 1972.

Diamond Images/Getty Images

pot of people from various ethnic backgrounds. It was a blue-collar neighborhood where people worked in factories and steel mills.

"It wasn't easy to survive in that kind of environment," says Brown. "People worked hard and the kids were pretty tough."

Brown's parents wanted something better for their children and felt going to college was the way out. With money scarce, Brown looked at football as his best way to get a college scholarship.

Brown didn't get any love from the big schools in his area—Pitt, Penn State, West Virginia, or Ohio State. Finally he got the opportunity to play college football at Dodge City Community College in Kansas and accepted their offer. There he blocked more than he carried the ball. After two years, he transferred to Kansas State, and again Brown found himself blocking for another back, Cornelius Davis, who was the Big 8's leading rusher.

LOMBARDI CALLS

Most pro scouts didn't even have Brown on their radars because he never rushed for more than 400 yards a season.

The Redskins, however, were a different team. Despite having a less than dominating defense, Washington had one of the NFL's premier offenses. Future Hall of Famers Sonny Jurgensen, Charley Taylor, and Bobby Mitchell displayed perhaps the NFL's best aerial circus. They had a solid line led by Pro Bowl center Len Hauss. What they were lacking, however, was a proven running back.

During the 1969 draft, Lombardi came out of retirement from a front-office job with the Packers to coach the Redskins. He knew upgrading the running game was paramount to his Lombardi-style football, so he drafted Ed Cross from Arkansas Pine-Bluff in the third round. Not satisfied with one back, Lombardi spent his seventh-round pick on another, Jeff Anderson from Virginia. The next round, he remembered scouts talking about a kid from Kansas State who loved contact and displayed a never-say-quit toughness.

So with two backs already drafted, Lombardi took a flier on yet another running back: Larry Brown.

"During that period Lombardi had an open-door policy in terms of finding a good back," says Brown. "He wanted to look at a lot of backs because I don't think he was happy with the ones he'd inherited. Nor was he happy with the draft choices before he got there. I realized pretty quickly that I had a strong point in that I could block. I also knew that he was the person who called the shots, he was the person who made the decision about who stayed and who didn't. I felt the only way to get his attention was to show that I was a tough back who wasn't afraid to hit someone."

But as impressed with Lombardi as Brown was, the opposite wasn't true for the legendary coach. Brown was great in drills, knocking much bigger defenders backwards. But he didn't seem like he knew the plays and appeared to be a half-second short off the snap of the ball. Chances are an average coach would have just cut a late rounder like Brown. But it bothered Lombardi that the tough kid from Kansas State seemed slow to the punch.

Finally, one day after a long interrogation by Lombardi as to why Brown wasn't hitting the holes quickly enough, the quiet young man let the coach in on a secret: Brown was deaf in his right ear. Between plays, Brown huddled up on the opposite side of Jurgensen and couldn't always hear the play called. So instead of going on the snap count, Brown waited for others to move first before he took a step.

Lombardi used his powers of persuasion to change all that. Despite a rule not allowing players to be wired with sound, the legendary coach convinced then-commissioner Pete Rozelle to make an exception.

Brown's headgear became known as the "$400 Helmet." With a hearing aid firmly secured in his helmet, Brown not only showed prowess as a blocker, but he started turning heads as a runner.

"As a rookie, [I was] reluctant to say I couldn't hear the snap count," says Brown. "Instead, I turned my head and tried to time my movement with the snap of the ball. Well, obviously, someone filming it would be able to tell that I was out of sync. When I got the $400 helmet, I learned pretty quickly that the hearing aid was not going to survive all the punishment I was taking during a game. It helped tremendously in the beginning, but in the long run, there were problems."

After a few seasons, Brown stopped wearing the special helmet because it simply didn't work anymore. By then, he knew the offense front and back and relied on his experience to overcome his auditory deficiency.

RUNNING STRONG

As a rookie in 1969, Brown became the starting halfback and finished fourth in the NFL with 888 yards rushing. It was an amazing achievement for an unknown, eighth-round pick who'd primarily been a blocker in college.

"My rookie year, my first goal was to make the team. My second was to start," says Brown. "I was just fortunate my rookie year that I was able to accomplish those two goals. After that it was a game-by-game thing for me, trying to be successful to the extent that I satisfied Vince Lombardi."

Lombardi never wanted players to feel too confident about their status on the team; they were only as good as their last run. "There was something going on in my head about Lombardi, getting him off my back," says Brown. "It was an ongoing battle of head games between Lombardi and myself. He was going to make sure that I did not end up with a swollen head. Even when I began to show some signs of running the ball well, he would constantly make it difficult for anyone to be satisfied with what they were doing."

The legendary coach passed away before the 1970 season. Assistant Bill Austin took over, and Brown, in just his second season, led the entire NFL with 1,125 yards.

The following year, however, teams started keying in on Brown, but he still pounded out 948 yards despite missing a game due to injury. The good news for Brown, though, was that former Rams coach George Allen had replaced Austin and instituted a run-first offense. The perennial Pro

Bowler, Charley Taylor, was still out on the end. But Allen started relying more on backup quarterback Billy Kilmer—a former Saints quarterback who was known for his toughness more than his passes—than on the flamethrower Sonny Jurgensen. Still, during the '72 season, Jurgensen won back the quarterback spot and at 38, he played well early on.

"I was fortunate to play with two Hall of Fame coaches in Vince Lombardi and George Allen," says Brown. "We had a pretty talented team with Hall of Famers Sonny Jurgensen and Charley Taylor on offense and safety Ken Houston on defense."

Still, despite the passing talent of the Redskins, Allen preferred a grind-it-out ground game, and Brown was prepared to carry the load going into the 1972 season. The Redskins had gone from 6-8 in 1970 under Austin to 9-4-1 under Allen in 1971, making their first playoff appearance since 1945. Going into 1972, the team wanted more, and Brown was ready to shoulder the offense.

The 1972 season would become Brown's best year. After winning Super Bowl VI in '71, the Cowboys were a marked team. None zeroed in on them more than the Redskins. Even during the 1960s, when the Redskins had a string of losing seasons, they always played the Cowboys tough. The high-powered offense kept the team in the game against Dallas' Doomsday defense during those years. But now, the Redskins were a team of veterans, pieced together by Allen not just to beat Dallas, but to beat *up* Dallas.

"George hated Dallas, plain and simple," says Brown. "He would do something to get us to feel the same way about them. That started the first day of training camp. He made it perfectly clear that in order for us to win our conference, we had to beat Dallas. George reminded us that they were the only team that called itself America's Team, which was very arrogant."

Allen went to extremes to drive home his hatred for the Cowboys. He even brought in June Rhee, a world-renowned karate and tae kwon do expert. After one practice, Allen presented Rhee to the team, and the skilled expert easily split a pair of wood two-by-fours. Allen then took the two-by-fours and told the squad that the blocks of wood represented the Dallas Cowboys. Allen got in his best karate pose and slammed his hand on the two-by-fours. The boards split, but a few splinters pierced his skin and cut his eye.

With blood dropping from his face, Allen said, "Thus ends the lesson," and went down to the trainers' table to get patched up.

SUPER SEASON

The '72 Redskins set out to win their division, something they hadn't accomplished since Dallas' inception in 1960. The season started at Minnesota with a nail-biting win, 24-21, and Brown slugging out 105 yards and a touchdown. They followed that up with a solid 24-10 victory at home over the St. Louis Cardinals. The ground game took control as Brown turned in his second-best game as a pro with 148 yards.

The confidence was flowing in D.C. But playing in the NFL can be a humbling experience; the Redskins took a step back by dropping a road game against the lowly New England Patriots, 23-24, a team that would win only three games that season. Still, Brown crossed the century mark for the third-straight week with 113 yards.

At 2-1, the Redskins were presented with the perfect opportunity to measure themselves against their rivals—each of their next four games would be against NFC East opponents. Thanks to the running of Brown and the Redskins-sublime defense, Washington quickly returned to its winning ways and captured the attention of the national media in the process.

They blanked the Philadelphia Eagles 14-0 in Week 4. The next week they traveled to St. Louis for a rematch game. Both the games proved easy challenges, since the Cardinals and Eagles were poor teams, who would go 4-9-1 and 2-11-1, respectively, that season.

"We knew the only way to properly measure ourselves was against the better teams in our division, like the Cowboys and Giants," said Brown.

Brown and the Redskins got their wish. Both teams were 4-1 and atop the division when they met October 22 in front of 53,039 fans at RFK. Brown displayed toughness on the ground and in the air. He hammered out 95 yards on 26 carries, and nabbed seven passes for an even 100. The Redskins won 24-20, and Coach Allen declared the atmosphere similar to that of a Super Bowl. For the Redskins, the win put them alone at the top of their division for the first time since the Eisenhower administration in the 1950s.

There was one more important division game left now. They would travel to New York to face the much-improved Giants.

GAME OF MY LIFE
BY LARRY BROWN

As much as that victory over the Dallas Cowboys the week before meant to me, playing the Giants in New York presented a tremendous challenge. After a big win, it's easy to look past the next opponent. But we were determined not to do that, and I was even more determined because it was in New York, the big media capital of the world.

The Giants had a much-improved team from the year before. We were 5-1 and they were 4-2 when we met that overcast day at Yankee Stadium. They had a veteran quarterback in Norm Snead, a former Redskin who played for us in the early '60s, plus a good running back, Ron Johnson. George wanted to show the Giants and the rest of the NFL that the Redskins were tougher and more hard-nosed than other teams, especially those in the NFC East.

His focus was defense when he came to the Redskins, which was a big weakness of ours at the time. He believed in great defense and pounding the ball. He was the type of person who didn't believe in a lot of people touching the ball. So if he was comfortable with you, you could expect the ball a lot. He didn't like substituting. At that point in time, if you were going to be successful, if you were going to get a lot of notoriety for your work, then you had to touch the ball. The more I got the ball, the better I performed.

I got into a great rhythm in the Giants game. I honestly didn't go into the huddle hoping someone would give me the ball. That was selfish. I was more concerned with doing my job on every play whether I was carrying the ball or not. I made sure that I didn't make any mistakes and that I did everything I was supposed to do. When you look at a play and how it's drawn up, you know that everything that each member of the team does is for a purpose. And if someone doesn't do something correctly, it fouls up the play. It may negatively impact the outcome of the whole game.

It was an unusually hot game for October. But I knew I was going to have a good game when I gained 25 yards on the second play. The line was blocking great. Len Hauss was handling their tough guy in the middle, John Mendenhall, and the offense was popping on all cylinders. That is, until Sonny Jurgensen got hurt. In the second quarter, he ruptured his Achilles tendon and limped off the field. Little did we know he was done for the season. Luckily, we had Billy Kilmer who stepped in, and after a slow start did a tremendous job.

The thing that was so great about Billy was his enthusiasm. He hadn't played in a few weeks, but he came in and started clapping his hands, patting guys on the back, encouraging us. It took a few plays to get the tempo going, though. We tried a few passes but couldn't get a first down. So we returned to running the ball and that loosened things up. As the holes began opening again, Billy kept calling my number. He was always about winning and doing the best for the team.

I caught a short touchdown pass from Billy and that tied the game. Then Mike Bass hit Giants running back Ron Johnson and slowed him up enough for Chris Hanburger to take the ball. The Giants argued the play should have been stopped by forward progress, and the New York fans were going nuts.

Well, while they were arguing, Billy called a simple, quick off-tackle play. I think the Giants were still preoccupied by the call, because I took the handoff and it caught them off guard. I started toward the hole, saw it was clogged, and burst outside where there was lots of space. No one was there except a DB and I ripped past him for a 38-yard touchdown. We never looked back after that and won (23-16).

As I was walking into the locker room, some fan threw a beer on me. I just remember going off after that, telling reporters that the Redskins didn't get any respect and that we were now on top of the Big Apple. I remember this game, because the win, along with the previous one over the Cowboys, finally made the national media look at us. The Redskins were a team to be reckoned with. Thanks to my teammates and their hard work, I rushed for a career-high 191 yards in that game, and made the cover of *Sports Illustrated* that week.

We went on to win another five games and clinch the division by Week 12 with an 11-1 mark. We were on a roll . . . all the way to the Super Bowl.

A VALIANT EFFORT

Although the Redskins would lose Super Bowl VII, there was no denying the impact of the Redskins and the performance of Larry Brown during that incredible 1972 season. He rushed for an NFC-leading 1,216 yards and won the NFL's coveted MVP Award.

Rarely has a team ever ridden one player to victory as often as the Redskins did with Larry Brown. He hoisted Allen's conservative run-offense on his surprisingly strong 5-11, 195-pound frame and carried the load week after week.

"I guess it's the highest award of recognition you can achieve as a player," says Brown of the MVP Award. "Obviously, I was happy and excited to achieve that goal. But that recognition was all done in the spirit of the team. I didn't set out for it to happen. It just happened on the way to the Super Bowl. It's good to know that people felt very good about the way you carried on your work as part of the Washington Redskins organization."

Brown retired in 1976 when, according to him, his knees and age finally caught up with him. "The older you get," he says, "the injuries that used to go away in a day or two were still around the following

Sunday. That's a telling sign. Besides, it's hard to just hang around when you can't perform the way the public expects you to play. I knew it was time."

After working for EF Hutton, Xerox, Oracle, and doing other consulting work in the area, Brown hooked up with the Michael Company, Inc., a full-service commercial real estate firm in Prince George's County, where he's worked since 1996. When he's not working, he spends time with his wife, Janet, and their two daughters, Lauren and Tonya.

In eight seasons, Brown totaled 5,875 yards on the ground and another 2,485 in receptions. He played in four consecutive Pro Bowls from 1969-73 and scored 55 touchdowns. For younger fans the totals may not compare with today's running backs. But it was a different era, when halfbacks split carries with fullbacks, and the rules for defenses allowed them to easily prevail over offenses.

Still, pound for pound, there were few running backs that came tougher than Larry Brown.

Chapter 6

RICK WALKER

Rick Walker never thought of himself as anything but a Californian. Growing up in the warm, sun-splashed world of Los Angeles, Walker was able to enjoy sports all day, every day.

That love of sports and natural talent led to a football scholarship at nearby UCLA. By the time his senior year rolled around, the budding tight end was an All-American and an explosive pro prospect thanks to his blocking skills and his pass-catching abilities.

In April 1977, his California world of sunshine changed forever when the Cincinnati Bengals selected him in the fourth round of the NFL draft.

"To go from L.A. to Cincinnati was a social shock," says Walker, who admitted it took some adjusting to go from the laidback California lifestyle to the conservative Midwestern Ohio town.

Despite being surrounded by stars like quarterback Ken Anderson, receiver Isaac Curtis, and cornerback Ken Riley, Walker and the rest of the team never reached their potential. A broken arm and a disagreement about his rehabilitation gave Walker the foresight to pursue other opportunities. Instead of heading back to California, Walker was asked to venture farther east and become a Washington Redskin.

The decision to give the Burgundy and Gold a try changed Walker's life forever by playing in two Super Bowls and being an integral part of the franchise's first modern championship, Walker became eternally etched into the minds of Redskins fans. He's become so engrained in the fabric of Redskins football that today he eschews his previous California life for the cooler temperatures and heated sports talk of Washington, D.C.

The son of a Marine, Walker was born May 28, 1955, in North Carolina. His father got transferred to El Toro Marine Corps Air Station in Shasta, California, when Walker was just two years old. The family settled in Santa Ana near Los Angeles. There he fell in love with the year-round outdoor playground of southern California.

"I lived near one of those great little league ball parks," remembers Walker. "It was first class with sponsor boards everywhere. I played shortstop and pitched. I could really throw some gas."

It was a different era back then, Walker recalls. Kids didn't sit in front of a television or play video games. "It was an era where having a new glove was important. You'd put oil in it, place a ball in there and sleep with it. I'd keep a bat in my room and watch my swing in the mirror," he says. "There was always something to do outside. If you weren't playing football or baseball, there'd be stickball or bottle caps. You were constantly competing."

Attending Valley High School made Walker just one of the young prospects that college coaches flocked around. Walker wanted to play major league baseball but threw his arm out at a young age. Suddenly football became his sport of choice. He played quarterback early on but realized that because of his arm, he wouldn't make it on the college level, so he switched his focus to playing receiver.

Rick Walker came to the Redskins from Cincinnati in 1980, becoming a key blocker and receiver in Joe Gibbs' explosive offense. Today the former Californian is a Washington, D.C. fixture, busy with various radio and TV shows while working with numerous charitable causes.

Nate Fine/WireImage.com

Playing at a big-time high school where sports reigned gave Walker the temperament to play in big games. The team played on Friday nights under the lights.

"Our team progressed each year," says Walker. "We went 0-9 my freshman year, then 5-6, 6-5 and won a championship my senior year. We attracted between 7,000 and 10,000 fans a game. That doesn't happen here on the East Coast."

As he prepared to attend UCLA, Walker wanted to get a head start; he took eight credits of college courses. Later he was told that by taking eight credits instead of the required load of 12, he'd be in violation of some rule, so he ended up enrolling at Rancho Santiago Junior College for a semester.

THE BIG TIME: UCLA

When Walker's circuitous route finally landed him at UCLA, he discovered that he was just beginning his hard-fought road to success. His college coach was an intense, hardworking young man named Dick Vermeil.

Today football fans know Vermeil as much for his emotional post-game speeches as for his coaching success. Walker attests that Vermeil was no different back in the mid-1970s.

Vermeil put his young troops through ten 100-yard dashes every practice under time. "He was an excellent organizer and a terrific coach," says Walker. "But he worked the dog manure out of you. Thank God I was young. He worked you so hard in practice that he was like a lunatic. One day he was working us so bad that we hit a wall and we were like, 'Enough is enough. This guy is killing us.'"

After practice, Vermeil led his team over to a dorm room and shut the door. There, his emotions got the best of him. "He told us how proud he was of everyone. How hard we all worked. How we did everything he asked and no one missed any practice. He started crying and we didn't know how to react. Football is so bad in that any emotion you display, you're not a man. I mean, back then you were considered less than a man if you took a break to drink water. That's how unsophisticated the game was back then."

UCLA went on to beat USC in the cross-town rival showdown and topple Ohio State in the Rose Bowl. "To this day, the Vermeil's practices were the hardest things I ever had to do," says Walker.

Vermeil left UCLA to become the Philadelphia Eagles coach, and Terry Donohue became Walker's new coach. The young receiver was now converted to tight end because Donohue wanted the best 11 guys on the field and was weak at tight end.

College taught Walker a lot about the landscape of college football. "I tell kids all the time, don't believe what you read about other players," says Walker. "I went to UCLA and I found they had some big-name high school receiver stars who couldn't catch. But if you'd just read about them you'd thought they were the greatest things since sliced bread."

On top of being influenced by Vermeil and Donohue, Walker found his greatest inspiration from his tight end position coach, Frank Ganz. A respected assistant coach in the college and pro ranks, Ganz eventually coached the Kansas City Chiefs for two seasons, 1987-88.

"Frank Ganz was a great coach," says Walker. "He was the best coach I've ever been around in terms of teaching you, working with you, and making sure you understood what he was asking of you."

Part of Ganz's expertise was in teaching fundamentals. According to Giants coach Tom Coughlin, Ganz was the one responsible for helping him develop the proper ball-carrying technique to prevent fumbles. It was Ganz's technique that Coughlin brought to New York to help the then-chronic fumbler, Tiki Barber, change his reputation.

"It wasn't just football with Frank. He was great with life skills, academics, socialization. He was unbelievable," says Walker. "I got used to winning at UCLA. So when the draft came around I was just hoping to go to a team committed to winning."

QUEEN CITY CALLS

When the UCLA senior tight end heard the phone ring on draft day in 1977, he knew a team had just selected him. He was hoping it would be his favorite team, the Raiders. Instead it was the team the Raiders had beaten in the playoffs the year before, the Bengals.

Along with facing the rigors of being a rookie in the NFL, Walker underwent a cultural shock as well.

"When you're in L.A. and you're a Laker or a Dodger, you can't compare that to anywhere else," he says. "Things are open till 4:30 a.m. Then to go to Cincinnati, where baseball rules and everything closes at 11:30, that's something."

Cincinnati was different on the field as well. Legendary coach Paul Brown had retired after the '75 season and was replaced by Bill "Tiger" Johnson. Brown's son, Mike Brown, was the general manager. The Browns didn't run the team like the well-off family that they were. "They had a lot of money but they were running the organization like they were on a shoestring budget," says Walker. "That's when Mike Brown became infamous."

Ironically, it was Brown's cheap ways that helped Walker mature as a young man. After being drafted to the Bengals, Walker started spending money like a rich athlete. But the more he watched Brown and spoke to him about fiscal responsibility, the smarter he got with his newfound "riches."

"Mike Brown was famous for being cheap," says Walker, "but today I respect the heck out of him because he taught me economics. Best lesson ever. I was under the assumption that when you got to the NFL, you'd made it. Well, in college, you're basically broke the whole time. So any money you get in the NFL, even back then, was big money. But in the scheme of things, they were one of the worst paying teams in the NFL . . . but they ran the business to make a profit.

"We practiced at a place called Spinny Field, where they recycled and made trash receptacles," says Walker. "There was soot on your car from it every day. We're talking an eighth of an inch of soot. That tells you that if it's on your car, it's in your lungs."

Time-wise the Bengals went from being a playoff team the previous year in '76 to 8-6 in '77, followed by back-to-back 4-12 seasons in '78 and '79. After leading the Bengals to a 10-4 record in '76, Johnson's teams tanked and he was fired after a 0-5 start to the '78 season. Homer Rice replaced him, but didn't fair much better: he won just four games. He got his walking papers after the '79 season and was replaced by former Packer great Forrest Gregg.

"It was a tough time," he remembers. "I went through three coaches in four years. I broke my arm as a rookie and tried to come back too fast. Then I broke it again against Denver. I was just trying to prove my worth."

Walker says the final straw for him was when Gregg took over and had a disagreement with him after hurting his shoulder during a preseason game. "He wanted me to take a cortisone shot injection and go back into the game—and this was preseason," he says. "I couldn't believe it. He finally turned things around [after I left], but his approach was totally Neanderthal."

Walker began to realize that his dream of playing for an NFL championship team wasn't going to materialize in Cincinnati. He got a call from Redskins GM Bobby Beathard that changed everything.

GO EAST, YOUNG MAN

For a West Coast kid like Walker, going east was the opposite direction he wanted to travel. But he was happy to get away from Cincinnati.

The 1980 Redskins had some talent, but they were in transition. Running back John Riggins decided to take a year off, so Wilbur Jackson took over the ground duties. There were some positive sides, like the drafting of Art Monk, the signing of CFL star Mike Nelms, and the free agent pickup of center Jeff Bostic. But the team fell way short of a winning season and went 6-10, leaving the Eagles and Cowboys to fight it out in the NFC Championship game.

"The next year Joe Gibbs arrived and everything changed," says Walker. "All of a sudden everyone was competing for a job. It didn't matter if you were a veteran, a young vet like me, or a super rookie."

As most Redskins fans remember, the 1981 Draft had its share of super rookies. It was a phenomenal group that stocked the Redskins for years to come. The well-documented draft included Mark May, Russ Grimm, Dexter Manley, Darryl Grant, receiver Charlie Brown, and tight end Clint Didier. With so much talent on the offensive line, the team went to a power offense with two tight ends and one running back, John Riggins or Joe Washington, depending on the situation.

Because the young group of players was still learning the rigors of the NFL, success didn't happen overnight. The '81 Redskins started slow before winning eight of their final 11 games to wind up 8-8.

"If you wanted to watch smash-mouth football, the NFC East was the place to be then," says Walker. "Everybody knew each other," recalls Walker. "It was always a good matchup when you played NFC East foes like the Giants. They had Harry Carson, Beasley Reece, Phil Simms, and more. We knew those guys. It was a great time playing against Bill Parcells. They were all close games. It usually came down to a field goal."

Two games that stuck out to Walker during the '81 season were going to New York to beat the Giants, 30-27, and then flying home to L.A. to rock the Rams, 30-7.

"Beating the Rams was great, but it wasn't a playoff game. You always want to play your best when the game means the most," says Walker.

In 1982, Walker and his Redskins got lots of chances to step up in big games. The players' strike shortened the season to nine games and meant the top eight teams would make the playoffs regardless of division.

Still, the division games were the best. "We beat the Eagles by three points in the first week at Philly, then beat them again at home in another close one," says Walker. "We lost at home to Dallas, then went on the road and just squeaked by St. Louis. Then late in the season we won a close one at home against—whom else—the Giants."

Finishing the shortened season at 8-1, the Redskins had home-field advantage throughout the playoffs.

"We beat the Lions 31-7, and then faced the Vikings," says Walker. "I remember the d-line coach said they were going to butcher the Hogs. Well, we ran the ball a lot in that game. Riggins had asked for the ball at the start of the playoffs and he sure got it—37 times for 185 yards. RFK was shaking and chanting, 'We want Dallas.' It was one of those feelings when you go in and are expected to win and someone doubts you. But you still go out and crush them."

The '82 NFC Championship game was a huge deal for the Redskins and their fans. It marked the 10-year anniversary of when the '72 Redskins faced the Cowboys for the right to go to Super Bowl VII. Now, 10 years later, the scenario was the same. The names were different, the fans perhaps a generation older, but the passion and hatred for America's Team was palpable.

The Redskins battled the Cowboys throughout the game before pulling away and winning 31-17.

"Winning those playoff games at RFK, well, I get goose bumps just thinking about it," says Walker. After the game, the thing that was on Walker's mind of course was again going home to Los Angeles. But this time it was for a game that counted: the Super Bowl. Against a team—the Dolphins—the Redskins had played 10 years earlier in the same city, in a game they had lost.

GAME OF MY LIFE
BY RICK WALKER

Anybody that dreams of playing in a Super Bowl usually dreams about playing the game near their home, where they grew up and, for me, where I played my college ball—at the Rose Bowl in Pasadena.

It was almost overwhelming. Thank goodness we didn't have two weeks to think about it, because of the strike. It was a compressed week.

We beat Dallas on a Sunday, and the next Sunday was the Super Bowl. I'm glad the game was the following week because, being at home, it would have been filled with too many distractions. Tickets were overwhelming; I had something like 62 tickets that I had to get for family, friends, and classmates. It was almost a burden, but it all worked out.

Being at the Rose Bowl brought back so many memories. Not only did I play my college ball there, but in the '76 Rose Bowl, we beat Ohio State there. Now, to be here for the Super Bowl and to beat the Dolphins to become world champions—it's difficult to make the scenario any better than that.

Of course, when people think of Super Bowl XVII, they think of the famous run by John Riggins in the fourth quarter. We were down 17-13 and it was a fourth-and-1 play called 70 Chip. I was lined up on the left side next to tackle Joe Jacoby. In a play like that you just want to stay engaged with the guy in front of you; you try to get as much momentum as possible. I remember Otis Wonsley was the fullback and Clint Didier was the motion guy, so their job was to clean up anybody who broke through.

We blocked our guys, and Dolphins safety Don McNeal slipped a little bit due to the fake motion by Didier, and that little bit of a slip, plus Clint getting a piece of him, was enough that when JR came through at 250 pounds going full boar, that's a mismatch, and that's what you really try to do with that play.

Next thing I know everyone is going nuts seeing big number 44 taking it to the end zone. That was just an incredible high moment. A lot has been said about that play. But a lot of times, in short yardage, you'll get a play like that because everyone is so clustered in to prevent the short yardage. Inevitably, if you're able to break through, you'll score a touchdown, and that's what happened.

After the game, the feeling was overwhelming, almost numbing. I was there with my teammates and owner Jack Kent Cooke and Coach Joe. It was just an incredible time. We started that week beating the Cowboys at home in an epic game, and then a week later we'd won a world championship in my hometown. We had so many fans there, too. It was like a home game away from home.

I also remember my mom and my aunt having the majority of the team over. We had ribs and some great food. It was a magical time with the Hogs, the Fun Bunch, Pearl Harbor Crew, all those zany groups we had going. It was just picture-perfect. There's really no way to explain how everything just fell in place.

BIG GAMES, BLOWOUTS, AND LIFE AFTER FOOTBALL

The following year, Walker and his teammates again rolled through the regular season going 14-2. The offense was unstoppable.

"JR had 24 touchdowns and we scored over 500 points on offense," says Walker. "We started fast and then won the final nine to get into the playoffs."

Walker enjoyed one of his most satisfying moments. It was a home playoff game against the other L.A. team, the Los Angeles Rams, and it was just one of those rare times in sports where everything works to perfection.

"You always want to beat the team where you're from," says Walker. "So I was happy to be playing the Rams. It became one of our finest moments as a team. Every part of our team worked. We probably peaked too soon as a team, but it was the perfect game because it was total domination. That's tough in any game, but in the playoffs, that's extremely difficult. We crushed the Rams 51-7. That's 51-7 in a playoff game. And we did it at home in front of our great fans.

"I remember feeling so happy and confident after that game. Everything worked. I wasn't a Rams fan growing up, I liked the Raiders, Silver and Black. But it was always cool to beat the Rams, and this was an ass kicking. It was an embarrassment."

The Redskins beat the 49ers in the NFC Championship game and, again, were headed for the Super Bowl. It would be in Tampa against

Walker's favorite childhood team, the Los Angeles Raiders. But this time, the Raiders rocked the Redskins, 38-9.

"I just think we peaked too soon," says Walker. "We scored 51 points in the first round, 21 points against the 49ers in the first half of the championship game to win 24-3. And we never really scored after that in the Super Bowl."

Walker played two more seasons before retiring in 1985. During his nine seasons, he was an integral part of the famous Hogs and had come up with the name for the Fun Bunch. He also caught 70 passes for 673 yards and nine touchdowns, and he'd run 10 times for another 36 yards. Though his job was mostly opening holes for Riggins and Washington, he was often a reliable third-down mark. His 6-foot-4, 235-pound frame was a big target for Theismann.

For all of Walker's love for the West Coast, he decided to set down routes in his East Coast hometown, Washington, D.C. He's been married 21 years to his wife, Carol, a realtor, and they have three children, ages 13-18. "They're all proactive, love sports, all good kids," says Walker.

Though he retired more than 20 years ago, Walker is one of the most visible former Redskins in this Redskins-crazy town. He hosts a radio show on *SportsTalk 980* with Georgetown basketball legend John Thompson, and he spent 15 years broadcasting NFL games on CBS-Westwood One and ACC college football games on Jefferson Pilot Sports. He's also the host of *ProView*—a popular Sunday night sports show on Comcast SportsNet, where he interviews legends of the game, as he says, "So fans will understand more about sports and [have] an insider's look at the game."

Walker is also a sought-after motivational speaker. Recently *Selling Power Magazine* rated Walker as one of the region's top motivational speakers. He's also donated much of his time to charity work. Among his many charities are the Muscular Dystrophy Association, the Cystic Fibrosis Foundation, and the YMCA. He also hosts the annual Doc Walker Alzheimer's Golf Tournament, now in its tenth year.

But when he's not spending time with his family, "Doc" really enjoys his show *ProView.* Walker has a lot of his former teammates on the show to talk about some of their famous games. "I interview former Redskins about their moments and talk about games of significance. I always laugh when people talk about how many points we scored. Its not about scoring points, it's about winning."

Walker and his teammates did a lot of both.

Chapter 7

KEN HARVEY

There are few plays in football more scintillating than the quarterback sack. Watching the quarterback stand behind a fortress of linemen with defenders bearing down, sweeping in like tornadoes to collapse the pocket, is to witness perhaps the most havoc-wrecking play in sports. Redskins player Ken Harvey was one of the league's best at creating that kind of game-changing destruction.

"I had a lot of problems handling pressure growing up, so football became my outlet," Harvey says. "I wasn't a very good student early on. I was shy and a bit of an introvert. Football was the only place where I could go all out and not have to worry about anything."

When he retired in 1998 after 11 NFL seasons, six with the Phoenix Cardinals and the final five with the Redskins, it was clear that Harvey had successfully funneled that pressure into his opponents. He notched an incredible 89 career sacks from his linebacker position—including an NFC-leading 13.5 sacks in 1994. During his five years with Washington, Harvey was named to four straight Pro Bowls from 1994-97, and in 2002 he was voted one of the 70 Greatest Redskins.

Born in Austin, Texas, on May 6, 1965, Kenneth Ray Harvey was one of seven children born to his parents, Albert and Carolyn. "I grew up in a loving, hard-working family," says Harvey. "Everyone pulled their own weight. But the idea of going to college or seeing beyond the area wasn't discussed. It was, 'Get a good job with the city and gain security by having good benefits.' I wasn't sure what I wanted, but I knew there was a bigger world out there than my hometown."

Harvey knew that sports were a way out. Unfortunately, he had some inner demons that kept him from his goal. He had some good games at Lanier High School in Austin, but he was shy and had difficulty dealing with the attention. "I kept to myself, so when people started recognizing me for my play on the field, it shocked me. I didn't like having that kind of attention. I wasn't ready for it. So I sabotaged it by breaking rules, missing school."

The problem became so severe that he dropped out of high school. Six months passed and so did his senior season. It was too late to go back. Harvey started looking in the newspaper for jobs and discovered that there were few jobs available for high-school dropouts.

"No college would touch me," Harvey says, "so I went back to school to finish up with a high school diploma, but that didn't seem to matter either. I started praying. I said, 'God, why am I here? Please tell me my purpose.'"

Harvey would soon discover his purpose while working out at his local gym. One day he lifted with a guy who told him about a junior college in California that might give him a chance. Harvey practically dropped the barbell he was holding and scraped enough money together to head to Laney JC, a city college in Oakland, California.

"Laney College proved to be a great lesson for me," says Harvey. "It was located in a tough section in downtown Oakland, a sort of haven for second chances. It presented me a whole different experience than the country life of growing up in Texas."

Like Harvey, his new teammates were trying to overcome earlier failures. Some had drug problems, others had been in jail, and many

Although he played just five seasons for the Redskins, linebacker and sack specialist **Ken Harvey** quickly made a big impact. After joining the team in 1994, Harvey was voted to four straight Pro Bowls, and he was eventually selected as one of the 70 Greatest Redskins. *Doug Pensinger/Getty Images*

worked multiple jobs. "The coach, Stan Peters, really emphasized responsibility and discipline. It was his way or the highway," says Harvey. "He really cared about his players. He wanted everyone to graduate and go on to a four-year college. He even made everyone take a speech class so we could represent the school well whenever we spoke to the media."

Harvey flourished in this tough-love environment. As in high school, Harvey quickly became one of the best players on the team. With the help of his counselor and his position coach, he maintained decent grades and met an English girl, Janice, who would become his wife.

After two stellar seasons, Harvey got a few scholarship offers and accepted one at the University of California at Berkeley.

"I chose Cal because it was close to Oakland and they had a pretty good defense," says Harvey. "Hardy Nickerson was there and he ended up being drafted by the Pittsburgh Steelers in 1987, after my junior season," he says. "I learned a lot about dedication and hard work from Hardy and another guy, Don Nobles, who became a life-long friend."

As he had done on every level, Harvey dominated at Cal. It seemed like every Pac 10 quarterback had met him personally. The Phoenix Cardinals, who had just moved from St. Louis, wasted no time drafting Harvey No. 1 in the 1988 draft.

STRANDED IN THE DESERT

"As a first-round draft pick, I guess a lot of people would think they had made it by then," says Harvey. "But I had come too far to let this opportunity slip by. I wanted to take it as far as I could."

Unfortunately for Harvey and the rest of his Cardinals teammates, the change of scenery from St. Louis to Phoenix didn't change their bleak outlook. Gene Stallings, who would later win a national championship at Alabama, was in his fourth season as the Cardinals coach. After sporting a 7-9 record during Harvey's first season in 1988, Stallings was fired with five games left in the '89 season and replaced by assistant coach Hank Kuhlmann. He faired even worse, losing all five games. The team stumbled to a 5-11 record.

"Coach Stallings was a good coach," says Harvey. "He really took care of the veterans, who made sure everyone worked hard and knew their playbook."

In 1990, Redskins legendary coach Joe Bugel became the Cardinals coach. Like a lot of great assistants, Bugel proved to be a better assistant than head coach. In four years at the helm, Bugel's record was 20-44.

What the Cardinals lacked most, however, was consistency at quarterback. Incredibly, a new quarterback led the team in each of Harvey's six seasons in Phoenix: Neil Lomax in '88; Gary Hogeboom in '89; Timm Rosenbach in '90; Stan Gelbaugh in '91; Chris Chandler in '92; and Steve Beurlein in '93.

"Stability at quarterback was just one of the challenges we endured in Phoenix," says Harvey. "I think the ownership and the way we came to Phoenix put a strain on our fan base and our team."

Some teams had hands-on owners, but Cardinals owner Bill Bidwell wasn't one of them. "I think Mr. Bidwell enjoys the game," says Harvey of the man who inherited the team from his father, Charlie Bidwell, a member of the Pro Football Hall of Fame. "But I don't know if he's a real student of the game. He seemed detached. One time I was in the elevator with him, just him and me, and he didn't say a word. Frankly, I don't think he knew who I was."

Bidwell, long known as one of the more frugal owners in the league, did something else that didn't sit well in the Phoenix community. After moving the Cardinals to the desert to increase revenue and fan base, Bidwell charged the highest ticket prices in the NFL.

"I think the high ticket prices really hurt our fan base and soured the Cardinals in the community," notes Harvey. "Sometimes we would only get 25,000 fans to our home games—and most of those cheered for the visiting team."

A NEW START

One of the teams that attracted a lot of fans at Cardinals games was the Redskins. "That really impressed me," says Harvey. "I wasn't an east-coast guy, so I didn't know a lot about Washington, but Redskins fans were all over Arizona. I learned pretty quickly about Redskins Nation."

Harvey had a lot of admiration for the Burgundy and Gold. What he didn't realize was that the Redskins felt the same way about him.

"I had a chance to go to another team in 1994 because of the new Plan B free agency," says Harvey. "But because the Cardinals were hardly ever on national television, I didn't think I would get much notice. The Cardinals had some great players who, like me, didn't get much publicity."

Players like Harvey, safety Tim McDonald, and tight end Jay Novacek, were highly regarded in the NFL, only they didn't realize it. While McDonald and Novacek would go on to Super Bowl teams with the 49ers and Cowboys, respectively, Harvey was thrilled to go to a good organization. The Redskins were equally ecstatic to sign their new sack specialist; Harvey notched 47.5 sacks in just six seasons with Phoenix.

"Going from the Cardinals to the Redskins was just incredible," says Harvey. "RFK Stadium wasn't as big as Sun Devils Stadium but, boy, Redskins fans packed every seat and aisle in old RFK. The noise was like listening to jets take off."

In his first season with Washington, Harvey led the NFC with 13.5 sacks and garnered his first Pro Bowl selection.

"I was truly humbled," says Harvey. He remembers that the three NFC quarterbacks that day—Troy Aikman, Steve Young, and Warren Moon—all became Hall of Famers. "There also was Barry Sanders, Emmitt Smith, Jerry Rice, Reggie White, and Deion Sanders." But what Harvey remembers most fondly was that his former Cardinals teammates, McDonald and Novacek, were representing their new teams in the Pro Bowl, just like him.

"We just looked at each other and laughed," recalls Harvey. "We didn't get a lot of respect in Phoenix. But now that we were in great organizations, all the pieces fell together for us. It took me going to the Redskins to finally get recognition."

GAME OF MY LIFE
BY KEN HARVEY

My second Pro Bowl game following the 1995 season was the game of my life. Don't get me wrong, that first Pro Bowl with the Redskins was special. The 1994 season was a great one personally for me, but not for our team. We won only three games that season, coach Norv Turner's first year as a head coach. Because of the poor record, I was the only player representing the Redskins at the Pro Bowl that year.

Being named to my second Pro Bowl in '95 was even more special to me because it proved the first one wasn't a fluke. It gave me the validation that I deserved to be there. When I first arrived in Washington, no one knew who I was. I remember driving from the airport with defensive coordinator Ron Lynn, and someone on the radio said, "The Redskins just signed Ken Harr-a-vey from the Cardinals. Never heard of him!" Coach Lynn couldn't turn the radio off fast enough. So to make a statement that first year by leading the NFC in sacks and being the only Redskin in the Pro Bowl, I felt at least the fans and maybe even that radio guy knew who I was now.

But the second time around, I wasn't alone. Brian Mitchell was also named to the team, so I had a teammate to experience the thrill with me. I also brought a lot of my family. I didn't know if I'd be back again, so I felt if I went to the Pro Bowl then some of my family should go. I just wanted them to know that I appreciated them. Tim McDonald and Jay Novacek were there again, so I really felt at home.

As I sat around the locker room this time before the game, I really soaked everything in. I saw Jerry Rice, Emmitt Smith, and a first-time Pro Bowl quarterback named Brett Favre. I started smiling inside and out. I thought, "I feel like a kid in the candy store. If I wasn't a player, I'd be scrambling to get their autographs!" But then I looked around and noticed something that both bothered and motivated me: there were 10 players from the 49ers representing the NFC and, worse, 10 from our rival Dallas Cowboys—including my buddy, Jay.

It really irked me that more Redskins weren't recognized. I ran out on that field with something to prove. As I hit the field, I noticed Joe Gibbs was there being honored as one of the newest Hall of Famers. Right then I knew it wasn't just about representing my family and friends, it was more important to make a statement about the Redskins and the great Washington fans.

Because they don't allow blitzing in the Pro Bowl, I knew that I would be asked to do something beyond my specialty; that is, pass coverage. Since I was always rushing the passer, I'd never intercepted the ball up to that point. I even became paranoid about whether or not I could even catch the ball. I was known for my hits, not my hands.

The game started out dramatically with AFC quarterback Jeff Blake completing a 93-yard touchdown strike to Yancy Thigpen. Just like that we were down 7-0. We answered with a field goal, then a touchdown pass of our own: Brett Favre to Jerry Rice.

Only down 10-7, the AFC for some reason started passing on every down. Suddenly I was backpedaling more than a politician. I remember trying to cover on two straight pass plays, including tailing the slippery Glyn Milburn of the Broncos on a quick out. Quarterback Jim Harbaugh overthrew Milburn, and I came back to the huddle winded. On third-and-4 on our 36-yard line, Harbaugh dropped back and threw a high pass right down the middle to Buffalo's Steve Tasker.

I sprinted back in coverage and saw the ball beginning to sail. I'm sure Jim never saw me, but I instinctively closed on the ball as if I had done it countless times before. I stepped in front of Tasker and snagged the ball high above my shoulders. The ball stuck in my hands and I remember freezing for a second, shocked that I had caught it. Then I just took off for the goal line. Because this was my first interception, I was afraid I would drop the ball or stumble to the ground. I felt Tasker right behind me. The end zone seemed a mile away. I pictured I was Leon Lett in that Super Bowl and Don Beebe of the Bills chasing him down. I didn't want that to be me. I just prayed to God that Tasker wouldn't catch me. I ran straight for the corner of the end zone, still 36 yards away. Tasker dove to strip the ball. But he missed! Harbaugh had an angle on me as well, but somehow I outraced him for the corner.

One of the things I remember most about that moment was that my former teammate, Tim McDonald, was one of the first to congratulate me. I was so happy I just tossed the ball away and I never got it back.

Steeler great Lynn Swann was working as a sideline reporter that day for ABC and he interviewed me right after the touchdown. It was surreal talking to a Hall of Famer known for having one of the greatest pairs of hands to ever play the game. He couldn't believe it when I told him I had never intercepted a ball in the NFL before. We went on to win the Pro Bowl game, 20-13. It felt great knowing that my interception gave us a 20-7 advantage and became the turning point of the game. Looking back, it really wasn't until that play that I felt like a real Washington Redskin. It was a great feeling to represent the franchise so well in the Pro Bowl after a losing season. Hopefully that play provided the great Redskins fans something to cheer about for the upcoming season.

STILL MAKING PLAYS

Ken Harvey was voted to two more Pro Bowls after the '96 and '97 seasons before retiring after the '98 season. During the '96 season, Harvey, the sack specialist, recorded his first regular-season interception to go with his spectacular Pro Bowl pick.

In 2002, in celebration of the Redskins 70 years in the NFL, a blue-ribbon panel selected the 70 Greatest Redskins of all time. Harvey was chosen as one of them.

"I can't tell you how proud I am to have been chosen among the greatest Redskins ever," he says. "Despite having played six seasons before I got here, I really came into my own with the Redskins. I played in an era where we didn't win a lot of games, but I think the fans know I gave it my all."

After his retirement, Harvey stayed with the team for a number of years as the President of the Washington Redskins Alumni Association.

"That was a tremendous honor," says Harvey, "especially since the great Bobby Mitchell asked me to do it. He felt I was old enough to relate to both Redskins alumni and the current team. I was just honored that Mr. Mitchell thought enough of me to think I could lead the alumni association."

As president, Harvey was instrumental in raising thousands of dollars for Caring for Kids charities for several years. He went all over the country to speak to kids about staying in school and staying off drugs. He even penned children's books.

"I had a tough time maturing as a kid," says Harvey, "so I have a special attachment to children's issues. Helping them grow up and become successful is the greatest feeling."

After leaving the alumni association in 2005, Harvey remains a focal point in the community. He regularly speaks to high schools and is even part of the Leading Authorities Speakers Bureau. Among his many charities is the National Center for Missing and Exploited Children. He currently lives with his wife and their two sons, Anthony and Marcus (his first son, Nathaniel, passed away as an infant from SIDS) in Great Falls, Virginia, and works as a motivational speaker and entrepreneur.

In 2006 Harvey became a special correspondent for washingtonpost.com, reporting on the Redskins and providing an insider's insight throughout the season. It's just one more way that his heart is still tied to the team.

Chapter 8

JOE JACOBY

It is impossible for someone to overlook Joe Jacoby. After all, when you stand 6-foot-7, weigh over 300 pounds, have the toughness of a tank and the athleticism of a boxer, there is no way to see the forest for this massive tree. Yet 28 National Football League teams looked past him during the 1981 NFL Draft. Incredulously, no personnel man, general manager, scout, or coach thought the three-year Louisville starter could play.

It wasn't until after 332 college stars with last names other than Jacoby had been selected that several teams called to inquire about signing him—as a defensive tackle.

A country boy at heart, Jacoby chose the Redskins over the other teams in part because he had never been to the nation's capitol and thought it would be neat to take advantage of a free trip. Thirteen seasons later, Jacoby retired as one of the most dominating tackles of his era; a four-time Pro Bowler, a mainstay Hog, and the owner of three Super Bowl championships.

How Jacoby was overlooked is not as important as how he made the team and became one of the most feared linemen in the league on arguably the NFL's greatest offensive line ever.

Joseph Erwin Jacoby was born July 6, 1959, in Louisville, Kentucky. The second oldest child of Erwin and Mary Jacoby, young Joe grew up in a close-knit family where athletics were second nature.

The family's closeness made a string of horrible tragedies even tougher for Jacoby to overcome. During his freshman year in high school, Jacoby lost his father. The death put an extra burden on his mother, Mary, and his two brothers and his sister, to work extra jobs to keep their heads above water.

Despite the extra pressure, Jacoby found an escape in sports. "I was taller than most kids and was pretty good at both basketball and football," says Jacoby. "Kentucky is basketball crazy, so I was in a good spot."

Truth be told, the humble Jacoby dominated both sports at Louisville Western High School. He became a high school prep All-American in both football and basketball. When it was time for the highly touted college recruit to select a university, he chose to stay close to his family and enrolled at the University of Louisville to play football.

But just as Jacoby was getting comfortable combining the rigors of college football and academics, another tragedy struck. Though he suffered from no known health issues, Jacoby's younger brother Thomas, just a high school freshman, died in his sleep.

"I just happened to be home from camp," says Jacoby. "The next morning, Thomas passed away. My mother was so devastated she didn't want an autopsy. The grief was indescribable."

With a heavy heart, Jacoby eventually returned to school. Again he found a cathartic escape in the competition and physical challenge of football. A season later, as a sophomore, Jacoby was the main cog in a powerful Cardinals offensive line. Under coach Vince Gibson, they went 7-4 for back-to-back seasons and opened holes for two 1,000-yard rushers, Calvin Prince and Nathan Poole. Then, after a 4-6-1 season in

Joe Jacoby anchored the left side of The Hogs offensive line for 13 seasons, including four Pro Bowls, four Super Bowls, and three World Championships. Not bad for an undrafted free agent.

George Gojkovich/Getty Images

'79 under Gibson, the coach was replaced by Bob Weber. Jacoby became captain. But the coaching change and Jacoby's leadership didn't translate into a winning season. While the offense was still solid, the defense slid after losing the likes of All-America linebacker Otis Wilson and defensive back Dwayne Woodruff. The team went 5-6 Jacoby's senior year.

Still, one would think that an agile 6-foot-7, three-year starting tackle at a Division I school would warrant some interest from NFL personnel gurus. But that wasn't the case.

"Back then the draft was 12 rounds," says Jacoby. "That's 12 rounds over two days. No calls."

Hours after the draft, Jacoby's phone finally started ringing. The Buccaneers called, as did the Bengals, Cowboys, Seahawks, and the Washington Redskins.

"The Redskins wanted to fly me up," recalls Jacoby. "I was a kid from Louisville and had never been close to Washington, D.C. So I took a free trip not knowing what would happen next."

JAKE GOES TO JACK'S TEAM

For an undrafted free agent offensive lineman looking to make it in the NFL, Jacoby couldn't have picked a more challenging set of coaches to impress than those of the Washington Redskins.

Joe Gibbs had just taken over as head coach and had spent his first two draft picks on offensive linemen, snagging All-America tackle Mark May of the University of Pittsburgh with the first pick, and his teammate, guard Russ Grimm, with his second. Gibbs desperately wanted to bring the glory back to the Redskins organization, so he also brought in more than 50 free agents.

"There were so many people that first day. The Redskins were signing people left and right," says Jacoby. "I remember seeing Joe Theismann and all these stars, people I watched on TV just the year before. In all, I think there were 110-120 people in camp."

Wading through the droves of players, fans, and media people, Jacoby was led into Coach Gibbs's office by assistant general manager

Dick Myers. "Joe told me that I had a great opportunity to make the club as a defensive lineman. I just looked over at Dick like, 'What is he talking about?' Turns out, someone had given him wrong information about me. I found out a few years later that the Redskins were trying to release me out of my contract because they had already signed 18 offensive linemen. I was the 19th."

According to Jacoby, line coach Joe Bugel was allowed to bring 18 offensive linemen to camp. Jacoby's signing put them over the limit, so they decided to make him a defensive tackle and have him hold a blocking bag for a couple of weeks.

"I don't think they had any intention of ever playing me," says Jacoby. "They were going to have me stand around and hold a bag, then let me know I was one of the first cuts."

But as it happens with most rags-to-riches stories, there's often a little luck thrown into the mix of talent, dedication, and determination. And Jacoby's journey was no different.

Jacoby can thank the team's number-one pick, Mark May, for helping him get noticed. May, the 20th overall pick in the '81 draft, held out for more money, prompting the need for an extra offensive lineman. Jacoby started playing more and hanging out with his new roommate, Russ Grimm. Coach Bugel must have had this vision of an unstoppable left side of the line when he watched the towering Jacoby, walking side by side down to practice with wide-body Grimm.

Once Jacoby started lining up with Grimm on the left side, it didn't take Gibbs and Bugel long to realize they fell ass-backwards into getting a once-in-a-lifetime player: a big, physical left tackle who just happened to be a rookie free agent that nobody else wanted.

But just when Jacoby thought that he was in a position to finally concentrate on football, another incomprehensible tragedy struck. While the rookie was working his tail off to make the team, Jacoby's mother, Mary, died while he was at camp.

"To think that I lost three family members before I was 21 years old is mind boggling," says Jacoby. "It inspired me beyond words and definitely made me grow up quickly."

Even with all the grief flowing through the young man's soul, Jacoby somehow managed to compartmentalize it enough to make the 1981 Redskins as an undrafted rookie.

"I was going through a lot during that first year with my mother passing," says Jacoby. "But another thing that motivated me was my competitive nature. I hated to lose. Once I was given the opportunity to make the Redskins, I was going to do everything I could to make the team."

Looking back on the Redskins historic draft of '81, it's easy to see how the Redskins were able to go to four Super Bowls in 10 years. But the most valuable rookie may have been the one they didn't draft.

ON A ROLL

As the story goes, once Coach Bugel got his brood of behemoths together and attached his legendary tag, "The Hogs," to his linemen, the group began making sure the rest of the NFL knew who they were.

Several players from that 1981 group became the original Hogs; Jacoby at left tackle, Grimm at left guard, May at right guard, Jeff Bostic at center, veteran George Starke at right tackle, and tight ends Rick Walker and Don Warren. Another key Hog was guard Fred Dean.

"We got off to a slow start that first season, but after everyone got comfortable, we started to roll," says Jacoby. True enough: the Redskins started the '81 season with a 26-10 loss at home to the Cowboys, followed by defeats by the Giants, Cardinals, Eagles, and 49ers.

Halloween was approaching and the Gibbs-led Redskins weren't scaring anyone. "We didn't get our first win until we went to Chicago and that was in October," says Jacoby. Then the Redskins began a three home-game stretch against the Patriots, Cardinals, and Lions. The young team won all three games and the following week went to Giants Stadium and won 30-27 for their fourth-straight win.

With the rushing tandem of Joe Washington and John Riggins accounting for over 1,600 yards rushing and Theismann passing for 3,568 yards, the Redskins suddenly were one of the NFL's most dangerous young teams.

By the time the '81 season ended, the Redskins eclipsed their 1-6 start by winning seven of their final nine games. The team had put themselves in a perfect situation to keep the ball rolling in '82.

THE DREAM SEASON

More than anything, Joe Jacoby had simply survived the 1981 season. Losing his mother was a tremendous tragedy on its own, but it also brought back heart-aching memories of his father and brother.

But for Jacoby there was always football. In a fan-frenzied town like Washington, where one of the biggest supporters was then-President Ronald Reagan, competing in the NFL was as good as any job in filling the large personal void.

On the field, the only void facing Jacoby and his teammates was the impending players strike. It started after the second game of the season and lasted 57 days. When it was over, the NFL decided to reduce the number of regular-season games that year to just nine.

The NFL Players Association won a bunch of new benefits, but for the Redskins, the strike meant the momentum had been stopped. They were 2-0 before the strike, but now all the discussion about winning the division to make the playoffs went out the window; there would be no division winners. The good news was that the playoffs would be expanded from four teams from each conference to eight teams, for a total of 16. Just like in college basketball, the teams were rated 1-8 based on their records.

The Redskins would lose one game that year—a 24-10 loss at home to the Cowboys. As the playoffs—or as they were known that year, the tournament—began, Dallas was in the Redskins' sights.

"It really was like a tournament that year," says Jacoby. "We had an extra playoff game and no team had byes. We faced Detroit first, then

Minnesota, and finally Dallas. Because we had the best record in the NFC, though, they were all home games. It was incredible playing all three playoff games in front of the great Redskins fans."

Once the Redskins got to the postseason, the other playoff teams found out quickly what the game plan would be: run behind the Hogs. Specifically, give the ball to John Riggins and have him run behind the Hogs. The 11-year veteran had requested the protection; with his counterpart, speedster Joe Washington ailing, Coach Gibbs responded to Riggins' plea with a resounding yes.

In the first round, the Redskins treated the Lions like they were cubs, beating them 31-7. With the Hogs leading the way, John Riggins gained 119 yards. But the team showed tremendous balance. Protected by the Jacoby and company, Joe Theismann had enough time to complete 14 of 19 passes for 210 yards and three touchdowns—all to tiny Alvin Garrett. At just 5-foot-7 and 178 pounds, Garrett caught six passes for 110 yards. But even though the crowd was into it, the team knew they would face tougher competition. The Lions, after all, had claimed the eighth playoff spot with a paltry 4-5 record.

The Redskins next faced Minnesota. Again, the Redskins played to their strengths: the massive Hogs and the efforts of Riggins. It was the most dominating ground performance ever seen in the playoffs. Riggins toted the rock an amazing 37 times and bulldozed his way to 185 yards.

"I remember we held that ball for almost the whole first quarter," says Jacoby. Riggins scored from the two on the second drive, and Theismann put the game out of reach with touchdown tosses to tight ends Warren and Garrett.

The fans at RFK Stadium were already chanting, "We Want Dallas!" Dallas outscored the Packers 37-26 at Texas Stadium the next day. Jacoby and his mates were especially looking forward to the rematch. He says of the game, "It was one of the most intense games I ever played in and definitely the most intense that year because our only loss was to the Cowboys. They were the team to beat. They had been in the NFC

Championship game two years in a row, losing to the 49ers the previous year and the Eagles before that. So they really wanted this game."

The Redskins were happy to have home-field advantage. "Because it was at our place, it was pretty emotional. The fans were incredible. It was pretty neat to see the stadium move like that during a game. . . . In the end, we walked away winning 31-17 and we were headed to the Super Bowl."

For Jacoby, who had accomplished so much so quickly in the NFL after so many personal losses, the emotions were just beginning to pour out.

GAME OF MY LIFE
BY JOE JACOBY

Of the four Super Bowls we played, the first one stands out to me. Really, the whole playoff run was special. But the Super Bowl was very special and incredibly emotional because it was held on January 30—my mother's birthday.

I remember my eyes welling up during the national anthem. Looking around, it was one of those perfect southern California days at the Rose Bowl in Pasadena. I know she would have loved to have been there. My dad too, and, of course, my brother.

But when the game started I channeled all my emotions into winning that game. My competitive nature took over. I remember we were behind before we knew it. In the first quarter Dolphins receiver Jimmy Cefalo caught a long touchdown bomb. Then we traded field goals and scored on a touchdown pass to Alvin Garrett. We had tied it up, but then Fulton Walker returned a kickoff for a score and by halftime we were losing.

After playing tough physical games in the playoffs, especially against Dallas, we were confident. We had been running well all game with Riggo. When that fourth-and-1 play came in, 70 Chip, it was a short yardage, goal line-type play. We were down 17-13 and it was well into the fourth quarter. We ran it to the left side. I blocked the guy in front of me and John knew from the way the play was set up that there'd be one guy left that he'd have to beat. It turned out to be Dolphins safety Don McNeal.

The whole offensive line did its job. I remember wingback Otis Wonsley did a great job. He chipped one guy and chipped on another and took out two more. Just as the play was designed, John still had one guy—McNeal—to beat. Riggo stiffed-armed him, and 43 yards later we were all celebrating in the end zone.

That day he carried the ball even more than he did against Minnesota—38 times for 166 yards. We Hogs and the whole Redskins team were a part of his MVP day. We had all done our jobs.

When the game was over, I couldn't help thinking about my mom. She and my dad and my brother would have been proud. Then I thought about them again at the parade. The parade was a neat thing. It was a pretty wild experience. I'll never forget it.

JUST THE BEGINNING

Jacoby's 1982 season, just his second in the NFL, was only the start of his great career. Anchoring the left side of the line along with Grimm and Bostic for the next 10-plus seasons, the Redskins would find themselves in many more Super Bowls. As Redskins fans know, they won each one with different quarterbacks and different running backs. The one constant in the ground game was The Hogs, especially Jacoby, Grimm, and Bostic.

"I blocked for several quarterbacks. People ask me which was the toughest to block for, and I say they were all challenging," says Jacoby. "We all had our jobs to do on whatever play was called. And each one had to follow us for protection. Hopefully, we did our jobs upfront to keep them clean."

What about the running backs? "Same thing. Most of the running backs adapted to what we were doing. They would watch film with us, so they understood The Hogs' tendencies, what to look for. They knew how to react because we were all in the same meeting room. Bugel and Gibbs made sure of that."

Reflecting on the Redskins' second Super Bowl victory against the Denver Broncos, Jacoby recalls that even when they were down 10-0, they didn't panic.

"We went into that game as underdogs, but we didn't throw in the towel when it was 10 zip," he says. "We just knew we couldn't keep doing what we were doing. We had to get back on track. The things that Doug [Williams] did in that game were pretty neat. That was another wild week. We had some incredible practices. A couple times that week practice was so intense Coach Gibbs had to call it because we were beating each other up so much. Once Doug got rolling, the running game opened up. I mean, Timmy Smith had over 200 yards rushing. Everyone deserved a lot of credit in that game, but our line played extremely well."

Jacoby preferred the more direct, our line against your line stuff. "But when it came to the Super Bowls, we often ran the counter trey. I didn't like it as much, because it meant I had to do some running. It was a big play for us in Super Bowls, though. We scored three times off it."

When Jacoby is asked about coach Joe Bugel he says, "The biggest things I learned from Bugel were technique and repetition. Run the same play over and over until it is perfect. Practice proper footwork for a successful play. That's what he preached."

Jacoby retired after the 1993 season, having played 170 games. Although he was named to the same number of Pro Bowls as teammate Russ Grimm, only Grimm's name has been mentioned as a possible inductee to the Pro Football Hall of Fame.

While Grimm has been nominated for the Hall of Fame a few times, just missing election this past year, Jacoby has largely been overlooked, just as he was during the 1981 draft. But all Jacoby cares about are the same things he cared about back during his youth, his years at Louisville, and his Pro Bowl career with the Redskins: family and the championships he won with teammates.

"I have no problem with the Hall of Fame committee singling out Russ Grimm over me as a candidate. Russ deserves it," he says. "When it comes to the Redskins, I think our record speaks for itself. From 1982-92, we went to four Super Bowls and won three. We still hold the Super Bowl record for rushing in a game. So I have no idea why there's not one person from The Hogs in the Hall of Fame. Would I like to be in? Yeah. Am I worried about it? No. It's out of my control."

These days, when Jacoby isn't doing his radio shows, managing his numerous auto dealerships, or keeping up with former teammates like Grimm and Bostic, he's a doting husband to wife, Jenna, and father to their two daughters, Irene and Lauren.

Both of his children are competitive swimmers. Irene is attending SMU on a partial scholarship and Lauren is wowing them in high school. The closeness of Jacoby's family matches the one he was surrounded with growing up. And, of course, so is the competitiveness.

"I have been shoveling my two kids around for the last 11-12 years and they talk about athletes' training regimens, well, there is nothing like swimming," he says. "For years we've been getting them up at 4 a.m. for morning swim practice before school. I'm thankful they've got driver's licenses now. But it's been so neat traveling around watching them compete. They swim all over—Florida to New York and beyond. They're beautiful blue-eyed blonds. And the best thing is they look like their mother!"

The closeness and support Jacoby's daughters receive from their dad would have made their grandparents proud.

Chapter 9

MIKE BASS

Mike Bass is always happy to talk about his career, especially when it means reliving one of the most unusual and exciting plays in Redskins history. But the former star cornerback has a more serious matter to discuss: the NFL pension, or more specifically, the lack of a respectable NFL pension for the majority of former players—especially those from Bass' era.

Most of the players from the 1950s to 1980s receive a monthly pension ranging from about $200 to $600, based on years in the league.

"My pension is $564 a month," says Bass. "That's absolutely ridiculous. And some of the guys don't even get $150 a month. Hall of Famers we played with aren't getting $200 a month! They are the ones that made the game of football what it is today. I'm talking about people before me. It's just a travesty when you compare what fellows are making today—millions. The benefits are just tremendous, but they don't need them. It's us who made the game what it is."

Comparatively speaking, Bass' pension is more than some, and yet it is still miniscule. Bass, originally drafted by Vince Lombardi's Packers in 1967, retired shortly before the 1976 season after a violent collision with Giants fullback Joe Dawkins. The result was a neck injury so severe that today that his neck still gives him pain. According to Bass, the Redskins were unwilling to pay him the remainder of his salary after he was hurt, so he sued them.

"The Redskins actually refused [to settle] and fought me in court," says Bass. "And still I only received benefits because of workman's compensation."

According to Bass, current players are in a position to help the older players. His and other generations were the ones who went on strike and won better benefits in 1974, 1982, and 1987. But so far, today's players are unwilling to set aside any money for the men who paved the way. Bass says they just don't understand or appreciate what the older players have done for them.

"They're young and think they're invincible," says Bass. "And that nothing will ever happen to them, when indeed for the majority of them their playing careers will be less than five years. As a result, the extent of injuries doesn't start appearing until you're in your 40s and 50s. You take a look at the Hall of Fame ceremonies each year. The majority of guys can't walk now."

In the past year there have been numerous articles and TV reports about the gross inadequacies of the NFL pension plans for these former greats. Bass has been one of the leaders of this effort. He's worked hard to get the media and the NFL to address this horrific cause.

The lessons of never giving up and speaking up for what you believe in were instilled in him at an early age. They were lessons his parents had taught him, and later, coaches like Don James and the great Vince Lombardi emphasized them. It molded him into the candid, thought-provoking leader he is today.

RUNNING SMART

Born March 31, 1945, in Ypsilanti, Michigan, just east of Ann Arbor, Michael Thomas Bass was the eldest of three children born to Thomas and Louise Bass. His father was a doctor, his mother a teacher.

Originally drafted by the Green Bay Packers and Vince Lombardi in 1967, **Mike Bass** was eventually cut, and he struggled to make it in the NFL for a couple seasons. Then in 1969, Lombardi joined the Redskins and gave the young cornerback another chance. *NFL/WireImage.com*

"My parents emphasized education over everything else," says Bass. "They thought it would be good to become a doctor over anything else."

However, what his parents discovered was that their son was an excellent athlete. At Ypsilanti High School, Bass became one of the state's best running backs. His mother became a huge football fan and attended all his games. He also was an excellent basketball player and more than held his own running track.

"I didn't do too badly in high school, so I had a choice of accepting an athletic scholarship or not," says Bass. "I chose Michigan even though it was just seven miles away."

At Michigan, Bass's coach was not Bo Schembechler but his predecessor, Bump Elliott, who coached the Wolverines from 1959-68. As a freshman at the University of Michigan in 1963, Bass showed off his running skills, but the coaches weren't happy with his blocking. So Don James, an assistant at the time who would become the legendary coach at the University of Washington, convinced him to switch to cornerback.

"I had a good relationship with Don," says Bass. "He convinced me that I would be a good defensive back, so I made the move and started as a junior. I remained there the rest of my career."

During the mid-1960s, the Wolverines were a talented club. In 1964 they went 9-1 and won the Big 10 title, where they beat Oregon State in the Rose Bowl. "We had some great players," recalls Bass. "Tom Mack, a great lineman who's in the Hall of Fame; linebacker Frank Nunley, and defensive backs, Rick Volk and John Rowser."

As a senior, Bass earned an invitation to the 1967 College All-Star game. That didn't mean he was going to be selected in the NFL draft, but he was more than willing to get the extra exposure. The '67 draft was the first common draft. Before the common draft, both leagues could draft the same player and that player could choose the team he wanted to sign with. But because of the impending merger between the AFL and NFL, the bidding wars were now over.

A LEGEND CALLS

Bass was hopeful someone had noticed his outstanding Big 10 play and was planning to give him a shot. So you can imagine his surprise when, after 11 rounds, the one team that decided to take a chance on him was the world champion Green Bay Packers.

Lombardi made Bass the 314th player selected, choosing him in the twelfth round of a 17-round draft. The problem was that the Packers were loaded at defensive back, and Lombardi had picked Bass' teammate, John Rowser, nine rounds ahead of him, and another defensive back, Dick Tate, in the fifth round.

"I was excited to have an opportunity to play for Lombardi, but I was realistic, too," says Bass. "On top of drafting Rowser, they had Hall of Famers Herb Adderly, Willie Wood, plus Tom Brown and Bob Jeter."

Though a long shot, Bass performed well enough to be on the cusp of making the team. But, in the final cut, the Packers chose their third-round pick, Rowser, over their twelfth-round selection, Bass.

"It would have been better to be cut two or three weeks earlier, so I could land with another team," says Bass. "Even though I was down, Coach Lombardi gave me confidence by pulling me aside and telling me, 'You can play in this league. Don't give up.' That kept my spirits up."

Unfortunately, as the last cut, the only team that was willing to pick him up was a perennial losing organization, the Detroit Lions. There he basically rotted on the taxi squad for two seasons. "They had me play more receiver than defensive back," says Bass. With just two weeks to go in the '67 season, Detroit's premier receiver, Pat Studstill got hurt and the team activated Bass for the final two games. Unfortunately, the league required that a player be active for at least three games to be credited with a season. Bass missed it by one game. The next season, the Lions deactivated Bass for all 14 games.

"They had some good players, such as Lem Barney, Mel Farr, and Charlie Sanders, but the team never translated their talents to the football field. In my opinion, the Lions leave a lot to be desired. Everything starts at the top, and winning organizations are winners from the top to bottom. A lot of that affects the attitude of the players."

Bass realized he would never get a chance to play. So he pleaded for his release. As the 1968 season ended with bench splinters being the only thing marring Bass' pristine Lions uniform, Bass was eager for another chance. His prayers were answered when he got another call from a familiar friend.

LOMBARDI CALLS . . . AGAIN!

In the spring of 1969, Bass finally got redemption.Coming out of retirement, Vince Lombardi, the new coach of the Washington Redskins, remembered his former 12th-round selection and wanted to give him another opportunity.

"I jumped at the chance to come to Washington when Coach Lombardi asked me," says Bass. "You don't know how happy I was to get away from the Lions."

Reunited with Lombardi, Bass had an advantage over long time veterans like Sonny Jurgensen and Sam Huff. He had already been through a Lombardi camp two years earlier with a championship team. He was ready for the name-calling, the fear, and the pure exhaustion.

"There are a lot of stories about Coach Lombardi that quite frankly affected us all," says Bass. "He was a father figure who was very stern. But he was a fellow of great, great integrity. And great, great support for the players. His way was the only way, and we didn't mind that. In that day and age, we know he treated everyone fairly. This was at a time when there was a de facto limit to the number of black players on a team, and that never entered into his decision-making process."

Bass says that there was an unwritten rule in the NFL that you always needed an even number of black players, so they could room with each other without having a Caucasian with an African-American roommate.

"The Redskins were notorious in the early days for having only white players. It took Bobby Mitchell in the early 1960s to break that barrier on the Redskins, and Lombardi didn't care about race or color; he fielded the best players."

To prove that Bass was worthy of playing for Lombardi, he had to perform when that window of opportunity opened. He had waited two years for a second chance, and he got his opportunity during the first week of camp.

"I replaced a guy named Aaron Martin who had been a defensive starter the year before," says Bass. "That first week he missed a tackle and Coach Lombardi screamed, 'Get in there, Mike.'"

Bass started the next 104 games, never riding the bench again. In his first season as a starter, Bass picked off three passes. According to him, the secret to his success was never taking huge chances and doing what the defensive schemes asked him to do.

As everyone knows, Lombardi only coached the Redskins that one season. But in that time, Bass secured a coveted place as one of his starting corners for his solid play. His most proud moment playing for Lombardi was a big day he had against the NFL's top receiver in 1969—Roy Jefferson of the Pittsburgh Steelers, a player who would later become a teammate.

"In my opinion, Roy Jefferson is one of the most overlooked Redskins," says Bass about the clutch receiver who joined the Skins in 1971. "He was a great talent and an incredible receiver. When we faced Pittsburgh in '69, Roy was leading the league in yards."

In 1968, Jefferson led the NFL with 1,074 yards. He would surpass that mark in 1969 with 1,079 yards. But on one day in Week 5, the first-year starter would shut him out, as the Redskins won 14-7.

"I was so afraid of someone catching a pass on me that I did everything I could to shut him down," says Bass. "That was the crowning point of my career, shutting down the great Roy Jefferson."

THE FUTURE IS NOW

After Lombardi, George Allen took over the team and put the onus on defense. After watching tapes of his two bookend corners—Bass and another overlooked star, Pat Fischer—Allen had no intention of finding replacements.

"George changed the whole mind-set," says Bass. "Everyone knew that defenses won championships. So it was great when George Allen put an emphasis on defense and turnovers. It made defenses popular. His schemes were unlike any I had seen before and they worked. It made our job easier. We didn't feel like we were sitting back and taking the blows. We were in a position to give the blows. It emphasized the benefit of having a coordinated defense."

Bass says that as a result, players didn't have to have exceptional ability. They just had to be intelligent and disciplined. "They had to be smart and know where they were supposed to be," he says. "We had to know the defenses inside and out. We had to know where our help was coming from. But all of these played to our strength. As a result, it made our defense so much better."

The former Michigan star who had struggled to make the Packers and Lions had finally found a home in Washington. Because he was a fundamentally sound player who didn't like to gamble, he became the perfect player for Allen.

"The difference between teams a lot of times is very small," says Bass. "What lost games boil down to is mistakes made. I was never overly fast, so I prided myself on fundamentals and techniques. I never made mental mistakes. In my entire career at Washington I gave up maybe five touchdown passes. I'm very proud of that."

After intercepting a team-high eight passes in '71 with one going for a score, he snagged another three during their Super Bowl season in '72. Another area in which Bass was fundamentally sound was special teams, which was just slightly lower on Allen's list of important ingredients to a winning team. Allen was so dedicated to special teams that he hired the NFL's first special teams coach, a gentleman by the name of Marv Levy.

"Special teams were something I always played," says Bass, who returned a blocked field goal 32 yards for a touchdown during the '72 season as a precursor to his Super Bowl heroics. "George was the first coach to really emphasize it, and we practiced everything—especially blocking kicks. When we got to Super Bowl VII, we knew special teams could play a big part."

GAME OF MY LIFE
BY MIKE BASS

When it comes to that blocked kick returned for a touchdown in Super Bowl VII against the Miami Dolphins, there's a bit of an ironic twist that people don't realize. Dolphins kicker Garo Yepremian and I were on the cab squad years before back in Detroit. So I knew him. When I left Detroit, he left Detroit. I went to Washington and he went to Miami. At the time sidewinders, as we called them, were not prevalent in the league. So we didn't consider them real athletes. That's why it was a little ironic to see Garo trying an athletic move like throwing that pass in the Super Bowl.

I had always been on special teams, and Marv Levy, our special teams coach, had worked on blocking such a kick. The block generally came from the opposite side and I was always lined up opposite. My job was that of the spy man, the one that actually got there in case the kick was blocked. My job was to try to grab the ball. I had scored a couple of touchdowns in my career from blocked kicks, blocked field goals. I had scored in '71 and I think the prior year. So we knew what to do at the Super Bowl.

It was the fourth quarter and the Dolphins were up 14-0 and were about to try a field goal to make it 17-0. Time was running out. Yepremian kicked the ball and Bill Brundidge, who was 6-foot-5, blocked the kick. It popped back up into Garo's hands and when I saw that my first thought was, "Here's my chance to nail a kicker." That's the way I looked at it. So I bore down on him thinking I would get a good lick on him, never thinking that he didn't want to touch the ball. That ball was a hot thing coming after him.

Garo thought he could pass it and it slipped out of his hands. Then he batted at it. If he had batted it down, there wouldn't have been any chance to take it back. Instead he popped it back in the air. I jumped as high as I could and caught the ball, thinking "I can't let a kicker tackle me." So I started to break away. Then I saw Earl Morrall, the backup quaterback and holder. So I gave him a little fake and thought, "I can't let a quarterback tackle me."

After that, my old running back skills came into play and I headed down the sidelines for a touchdown. I've been told it was 49 yards. It happened so fast and all I could think was, "Now it's 14-7. We have a chance."

It turned out to be our only touchdown of the game. Unfortunately, it wasn't enough. But I'll never forget it.

HITS AND MISSES

For a consummate professional like Bass, the play that gives him the most nightmares is one that has long been forgotten by the media. It's a play that Bass thinks could have won Super Bowl VII for the Redskins, even though he had already made the play of the game minutes before.

"It was later in the fourth quarter, when the Dolphins were trying to run out the clock. Miami quarterback Bob Griese attempted a short pass to Paul Warfield, and I hesitated to try to go after the ball. I always played about seven, eight yards deep. For some reason I hesitated instead of going after the ball, probably because I was concerned they were going to try an out-and-up pass. I dream about that play. Had I been able to break on that short out, I may have been able to intercept it and take it in for a touchdown and a tie."

But had Bass broken on the ball, he also could have easily missed it by a half-second and Warfield could have turned and scored easily, similarly to the quick out catch by Chiefs receiver Otis Taylor in Super Bowl IV where Vikings defensive back Earsell Mackbee missed the tackle for the deciding touchdown.

As the next few seasons passed, Bass remained an integral part of Allen's defense. He led or was tied for the team lead in interceptions three times: 1970, 1971, and his final year in 1975. When he retired prior to the 1976 season due to his lingering neck injury, Bass was third all-time in interceptions with 30, just behind Brig Owens, 35, and Sammy Baugh, 31. Today Bass is fourth all-time with Darrell Green leading the way at 54. Three of Bass' picks went for touchdowns, including another from a fumble recovery.

Looking back at his career, Bass is happy that he was chosen as one of the 70 Greatest Redskins. It means a great deal that fans still remember him. He also relishes the great times and big wins he enjoyed with his teammates.

"I played with a lot of great guys," says Bass. "I enjoyed playing with [linebacker] Chris Hanburger on the right side. He and I knew where the other was at all times. I also admired Pat Fischer so much. He and I were very close and still are. Neither of us had blinding speed, exceptional size, or anything of that sort. But we were consistent and played well as a team. I'm very close to Brig Owens as well."

When asked who was the best receiver he ever faced, Bass doesn't hesitate to answer. "Bullet Bob Hayes," he says emphatically. "He should have been in the Hall of Fame years ago. It's a travesty he's not."

Still, he has a soft spot for his teammate and one-time foe, Roy Jefferson. "I played against and with some of the best receivers to ever come along. Charley Taylor is in the Hall of Fame. But one of those who never gets the recognition, and yet should, is Roy Jefferson. He was a receiver's receiver. As far as I know, he never dropped a pass. He was extremely independent, arrogant like receivers should be, and very talented. I think his not being listed as one of the 70 Greatest Redskins, well, the panel missed the boat on that one."

After retiring, Bass continued to have operations on his neck and knees. All told, he's endured close to a dozen surgeries. He waited until after his playing days to start a family so he could devote quality time in raising them. A few years after retiring, they moved to the Bahamas where he owned a hotel. Bass and his family returned to the mainland in the mid-1990s and moved to Gainesville, Florida, where he became a student counselor.

Today, Bass is an entrepreneur who owns KimLou Global LLC, a consulting firm that specializes in Project Funding and Travel. KimLou Global is named after the two most important people in his life—his daughters, Kimberly and Louise. His travel company is KimLou Global Travel, a full-service online travel company.

Reflecting on his career, Bass summarizes it by saying, "When you come out of college and you don't make the Packers, then you can't make the Lions—the perennial losers in pro football—in two years of trying, it can batter your ego a bit. I did, however, pride myself in my own reliability and consistency over the years I played. I wanted to leave a mark and leave the game on my own terms. Unfortunately, like a lot of players, injuries caused me to leave the game sooner than I wanted, but I've moved on.

"Now, if we can get the pension problems straightened out so that guys who gave their hearts and souls to the game can get the medical care they deserve, it'll be a start on the right path."

Thanks to the perseverance of Mike Bass and other former players who continue to speak out over the injustice, the NFL pension problems are finally beginning to be addressed.

Chapter 10

RON McDOLE

When it came to football, Ron McDole fooled them all. Even though he was a big guy, measuring 6-foot-4 and weighing 265 pounds, he didn't exactly consider himself an imposing figure.

"I certainly wasn't a body builder," he laughs. His pro career spanned an incredible 18 seasons. "The biggest thing was I never got hurt—physically. The doctors tell me they want to examine me when I die to see how I withstood 18 NFL seasons. I was lucky, really. I never tore a knee up. The only thing I really did was separate my shoulder the last game in my last year with the Bills. I once cracked an arch, but I played anyway."

McDole says his special "body type" prevented him from receiving a big injury. "I was fortunate," he laughs, "I guess you can't pull fat or break it!"

Born September 9, 1939, in Chester, Ohio, near Toledo, McDole grew up in an area where football ruled. He was a naturally big kid and after a stellar high school career at Thomas DeVilbiss High School in Toledo, he was recruited to play at the University of Nebraska.

"I went to Nebraska back when Oklahoma dominated the Big 8," he says. "I didn't know much about the area, but I decided I would go anywhere to play football. There I met a little guy who was actually from Nebraska. We ended up captains and were drafted by the same team, the St. Louis Cardinals."

His name was Pat Fischer, a small but tough-as-nails defensive back that pound for pound was one of the toughest players in the NFL. With a height differential of a good seven inches, McDole and Fischer became unlikely friends.

"We still keep in touch today," he says. "I always kid him that I never got the big scholarship or contract. Instead I was given a Nebraska kid to take care of. We started out at Nebraska, then went to the Cardinals together, and then both ended up with the Redskins. He doesn't live too far and we still get together to do things."

ADAPTING TO THE PRO GAME

While McDole and Fischer both began with the Cardinals in 1961, their careers went in different directions. Fischer would stay with the Cardinals for seven seasons while the beefy defensive lineman was traded to the Houston Oilers, who had won the first two AFL Championships in the upstart new league.

The Oilers, with George Blanda at quarterback, played the Dallas Texans for their third AFL Championship in '62 and McDole, unfortunately, felt the sting of losing his first championship.

"It went into overtime and became the longest game in NFL history at the time," says McDole. The game also featured one of the all-time gaffes in pro history. Dallas running back Abner Haynes won the toss, but got a miscommunication from the sidelines. Instead of receiving, he elected to "kick to the clock," with the wind. By rule, however, the team that loses the ball gets to elect which side they want to defend. The Oilers, of course, chose to have the wind at their backs, so Haynes' decision to kick proved costly in two ways.

"It was one of the biggest blunders of all time," says McDole. "But somehow they won anyway."

The following year, the Texans moved to Kansas City and became the Chiefs. McDole was cut by the Oilers and had a try out with the Vikings. When that failed, the Bills picked him up.

Ron McDole was an all-time fan favorite. Maybe it was because of his terrific play, or his nickname, "The Dancing Bear." Or perhaps it was his self-deprecating humor: Asked how he played 18 seasons without a serious injury, McDole quipped, "I guess you can't pull fat or break it!"

Nate Fine/WireImage.com

"I started getting discouraged," says McDole. "I knew I could play. But I had been getting these migraine headaches, which kept me from playing a lot. I must have gone through dozens of spinal taps. With the Cardinals I spent the last few games my rookie year playing offensive tackle. I didn't like blocking and getting smacked in the head. That didn't help my headaches. I liked defense better because I could do it to someone else. When my migraines persisted with the Oilers, they just released me after a while. I think they were afraid to keep me."

The Bills, with new coach Lou Saban at the helm, needed a defensive end and gave McDole a chance. In fact, he along with fellow end, Tom Day, and tackles Jim Dunaway and Tom Sestak, became one of the best D-lines in either league.

"We made the playoffs four years in a row and played for the AFL Championship three of those years. We won back-to-back championships in 1964 and 1965."

Much of the credit went to the Bills defense. Joe Collier, who would become the Broncos' defensive coordinator during the 1980s and resurrect the Orange Crush defense, was the genius behind the Bills explosive, stunting defense.

"Lou Saban and Joe Collier were two great coaches," says McDole. "Saban had the ability to evaluate talent and move some people around a bit. He's the one who moved Tom Day from guard to defensive end. Collier was extremely smart. He developed a lot of different packages for our defense. We played San Diego in '64 for our first championship and won pretty handedly [20-7]. Then we played them again for the '65 championship, and Lou and Joe were afraid they would figure us out. So we stunted like crazy, played a three-man line. Heck, I even went back into coverage on a few plays. We confused the hell out of them."

The Bills shut out the Chargers 23-0 for the team's second-straight championship. McDole and company so dominated the contest that San Diego's high-octane offense, led by Lance Alworth and AFL rushing leader Paul Lowe, never reached the red zone.

McDole credits the two championships to having teammates that played hard for each other and to having a coaching staff dedicated to winning. McDole himself became one of the best defensive ends in the AFL. He was voted to two AFL All-Star games in 1965 and 1968 and intercepted an incredible six passes during his eight seasons—almost unheard of for a defensive lineman. As always, McDole downplays his achievements.

"One of those All-Star games, our whole team made it," says McDole. "They decided to have the AFL champions play the rest of the all-stars. We thought we'd kill them because we were a team. But we lost [30-19]."

The following year, 1966, the Bills again made it to the AFL Championship game but lost to the Chiefs.

"They went to the first Super Bowl after that game," says McDole, "That could have been us, but we didn't play very well."

The Bills championship teams broke up, and a philosophy to go for younger players became the charge. Saban had left after the final championship and coached at the University of Maryland before returning to coach the Denver Broncos in 1967. McDole stayed with the Bills through the 1970 season with John Rauch and, finally, Collier coaching the team.

"We had a lot of great players on those Bills teams and I loved playing for the Buffalo fans. But they were rebuilding, and I don't think I was in their plans. I was 32 years old, which is when a lot of linemen think about hanging 'em up. If it wasn't for George Allen, I don't know how much longer my career would have lasted."

BOUND FOR WASHINGTON

According to McDole, George Allen's justification for his famous "Over the Hill Gang" was that he preferred players with experience. "George loved the older guys," says McDole.

McDole was the perfect fit for Allen's complex defense. Allen had been a defensive coordinator for the Bears when they won their 1963 championship and he learned from the best—George Halas. He wanted guys who could think, not just react. By assembling experienced defensive players like McDole, Verlon Biggs of the Jets, and players from his old Rams team, he had some of the best and most experienced players in the league on one unit.

"He liked us because we were like coaches on the field," says McDole. "We could change our defense anytime we wanted during the game. We had so much experience . . . we were all involved. The system was very difficult. There were a lot of check-offs in that system. Most of us had lost a step here and there, so we knew we had to outsmart them. We could check out of a defense as a group, or individually and make a play."

By respecting his players and giving them ownership in a system, playing became fun again for McDole and the defense.

"I think he would have been happy if we had won every game 7-0," laughs McDole. "He didn't care. I think he thought the offense was there just to give us a rest."

McDole says he was fortunate to work with some great coaches, the two best being Saban and Allen.

"They were a lot alike," says McDole. "Both had the ability to motivate people and move them around to become a good fit. Lou would yell and scream, but you knew where you stood with him. I liked that. Players like to be treated like men, and both George and Lou treated their players like men."

PLAYING FOR MORE CHAMPIONSHIPS

Beating Dallas and going to the Super Bowl in 1972 was perhaps the biggest highlight of McDole's career.

"We had a great defense and a great offense," says McDole. "Our offense wasn't flashy, but we had a good ground game and our defense made sure we didn't need to score a lot of points."

In the first round of the 1972 playoffs, the Redskins defense shut down the Green Bay Packers easily and won 16-3 on Christmas Eve. In that game, Allen instituted a five-man defensive line and shut down the Packers' powerful ground game. Pro Bowl running back John Brockington rushed for a paltry nine yards on 13 carries. The Redskins scored on a 32-yard touchdown pass from Billy Kilmer to Roy Jefferson and kicker Curt Knight added three field goals.

The next week the Redskins faced their nemesis, the Dallas Cowboys, for the right to face the undefeated Miami Dolphins in Super Bowl VII.

"That game became our Super Bowl," says McDole. "That was a big thrill. Everyone played well. George used to give out prizes back then. He was giving out color TVs for the most valuable player in a game."

The Redskins dominated the Cowboys on every level in the 1972 Championship. The defense decimated the Cowboys' vaunted offense to such an extent that quarterback Roger Staubach was sacked for 25 yards in losses and passed for only 73. The final 26-3 thumping is considered one of the greatest victories in Washington Redskins history.

"We came into the meeting room the week after that win and George looked at us with this huge ice-cream wide grin and said, 'Well, everyone played so well we've decided to give everyone a color television set,'" says McDole. "He had Sylvania come down from Botavia, New York with all these TV sets. When we hit the field for that practice there was something like 47 color television sets stacked up on the field. It was like Christmas!'"

GAME OF MY LIFE
BY RON McDOLE

I've always been a team guy, so it's difficult to pinpoint an individual game that I can look at and say, "Yeah, I made a difference in winning or losing." But one game that sticks out was that Viking game in 1975.

That season was a struggle. We made the playoffs four straight years, but had some injuries in '75. By the time we faced the Vikings we were already 6-4 and struggling for our lives for a playoff spot. Minnesota, on the other hand, was undefeated. They were something like 10-0.

We came out like we were on a mission and jumped ahead 21-0. It was great because we were at home and we were finally giving the hometown Redskins fans something to cheer about. The Vikings came back on us and actually took the lead, 30-24. We were shocked.

I was playing against Vikings tackle Ron Yary that day, a great player who was elected to the Hall of Fame a few years back. Once Minnesota got ahead of us, our defense knew we couldn't allow any more points. I remember roughing up quarterback Fran Tarkenton on one play, and he was so mad that Diron Talbert, of all people, actually had to restrain him from coming after me. Now that's something you don't see old Diron do too often!

We managed to get the ball back for our offense and, boy, Billy Kilmer led this great drive the length of the field. He tied the game up at 30, throwing a touchdown pass to Frank Grant with about 30 or 40 seconds left. Then Mark Moseley kicked the extra point to give us a 31-30 advantage. There was only time for maybe a kickoff and a couple plays. We thought the game was pretty much over and were pretty excited on the sidelines to knock off the undefeated Vikings.

But wouldn't you know, the Vikings get the ball and Tarkenton zips a bunch of passes like it's practice. Suddenly Fred Cox, their old straight-ahead kicker actually has the opportunity to win the game with a 45-yard field goal. I was on the field goal block and extra-point teams. And, again, I lined up on Yary. The whole game I was going hard inside, hard inside against Yary, always trying to set him up for when I really needed to fool him. Well, this was it—a field goal to win the game on the last play.

They snapped the ball and I took a half step inside. Yary bit on it, and I stepped right around him and got good penetration and leaped up and blocked the kick. The ball squirted away and we won. As a defensive end, you don't get very many opportunities to win a game. But that time I did. It was one of the few times where I was responsible for the exact outcome of a ball game. We won 31-30. We didn't make the playoffs that year, but we had knocked off the last undefeated team in the league.

STILL ROLLING STRONG

Just as McDole got the best of one of the NFL's all-time great tackles that day, his unassuming approach belies the fact that he was one of the game's most consistent players. In 18 seasons, McDole played an incredible 240 games. He also intercepted 12 passes. To put this achievement in perspective, Jim Marshall, a fellow defensive end who holds the NFL record for games played with 282, intercepted just one pass in his 20-year career. McDole also recovered a fumble for a touchdown.

McDole thinks the secret to intercepting so many passes might be in his facemask. He was the last lineman to wear the old two-bar facemask, which gave him instant throwback status.

"I was an offensive end in college in the beginning and wore the old two-bar. As I got bigger I ended up playing tackle. I didn't switch to the cage because I never liked wearing the thing. It made me feel confined. In the pros I started out with a two-bar as a rookie and they moved me to offensive tackle with the Cardinals because we had a bunch of injuries. I didn't like getting hit in the face, so I put a cage on for a while. But when I moved back to defense, I used a single bar, then a double-bar from then on.

"I liked being able to seeing what was going on. I could keep my eyes open and it may have helped me intercept all those passes. I did break my teeth once, but it was a freak thing. A running back's heel caught me up in the mouth, but that wasn't enough for me to switch to a cage. I wore that old double-bar until the day I quit."

Even though he retired nearly 30 years ago in 1978, Redskins fans still hold McDole dear to their hearts, maybe because he seemed like them: a hard working guy who loved his job. Maybe it was his ever-present big smile peering out of that old two-bar facemask. Or maybe it was his popular nickname, "The Dancing Bear."

There are many accounts on how McDole got that name. Some say Sonny Jurgensen gave it to him. Others say the Buffalo press gave him the name years before joining the Redskins. But only McDole himself has the real story.

"A bunch of us were downtown at some bars with [Tom] Brookshier and [Pat] Summerall after a game one time. We had won and I was out on the dance floor joking around. Those guys asked me to dance on a table. So of course I did it. They were laughing hysterically and said I looked like a dancing bear. And because they were calling games then, they took it up in the press box and started calling me that in front of the nation. Nicknames happen that way."

After retirement, McDole continued his off-season job as an industrial shop teacher. Later he began his own woodworking manufacturing business, supplying furniture for libraries in the Winchester, Virginia area.

Now, semi-retired, McDole calls himself a "Guest Worker." He lives in the Winchester area and helps out his four children and four grandchildren whenever he can. "My oldest son has a cabinet shop in Roanoke and I help him out sometimes. Basically, I work when I feel like it."

After McDole's extraordinary 18-year career, he deserves to do whatever he wants.

Chapter 11

DON BOSSELER

The 2006 Redskins featured a number of stars from the University of Miami. Clinton Portis, Santana Moss, Sean Taylor, and the Redskins' top 2006 draft pick, Roger "Rocky" McIntosh, are a few in the long line of incredibly talented players from Miami who have donned the Burgundy and Gold. Yet 50 years earlier, another celebrated player, running back Don "Bull" Bosseler, was one of the first in that line of tremendous backs from Miami.

Bosseler came out of college even more heralded than Portis, Moss, or Taylor. As the Redskins first pick in 1957, Bosseler was selected higher than any of them. He became the ninth overall pick in a legendary draft that would include nine future Hall of Famers.

He spent his entire eight-year career with the Redskins, playing during some of the more grim years in franchise history. Yet in spite of the average sporting cast, Bosseler was considered one of the best running backs in the league—always near the top of the rushing totals. In his eight years, he never led the NFL in rushing, but that was because of another back drafted the same year; Jim Brown led the league in rushing eight of his nine seasons.

Still, Bosseler was the Redskins star, and he delivered every week. He was named one of the 70 Greatest Redskins nearly 40 years after he retired.

Born in Weathersfield, New York, on January 24, 1936, Bosseler grew up in Batavia, New York, a small town southwest of Rochester. He was a natural athlete, excelling at baseball, basketball, track, and football. Scouts from all over the country knew about him, and he was eventually recruited to play football at the University of Miami. He became a four-year starter at fullback. During his 1956 senior year, the team went 8-1-1. Bosseler was named All-America and voted MVP of the Senior Bowl.

In the Senior Bowl, Bosseler helped his draft status by spearheading a South team that accounted for a jaw-dropping 370 yards rushing. He scored two fourth-quarter touchdowns, and the South won 21-7. Bosseler routinely ripped off large chunks of yardage in the game. On one drive after the North jumped to an early lead from Purdue's Len Dawson touchdown pass, Bosseler gutted the North's defense with runs of 32 and 12 yards before teammate Del Shofner of Baylor punched it in to tie the game.

ONE OF THE BEST NFL DRAFTS EVER

Following the game, Bosseler's name was mentioned along with some of the other elite college prospects in the upcoming draft.

"It was a tremendous draft," recalls Bosseler from his home in Miami. "Paul Hornung was the top pick of the Packers. Then Jon Arnett, a star running back from USC, went second to the Rams. Quarterbacks John Brodie, Len Dawson, tackle Jim Parker, and a guy named Jim

---

Fullback **Don "The Bull" Bosseler** was one of the top backs in the league during his eight-year Redskins career. Known for his bruising downhill running, Bosseler retired as Washington's all-time leading rusher and was selected as one of the 70 Greatest Redskins. *Nate Fine/WireImage.com*

Brown, a pretty good running back from Syracuse, were drafted just ahead of me."

With the ninth pick, Redskins coach Joe Kuharich and owner George Preston Marshall chose the hard-charging, 6-foot-1, 212-pound fullback.

"I don't think I was a very flashy running back," he says. "I was big and I could get the tough yards. But I could also block and catch some too."

The Redskins, in dire need of offensive punch, used their top four draft choices to upgrade the offensive backfield.

"Joe Walton, an end from Pittsburgh, who became the head coach of the Jets, was the second pick," says Bosseler, "followed by two more running backs, Eddie Sutton and Jim Podoley."

The young backfield, led by veteran quarterback Eddie LeBaron, became popular with the fans and the media. A beat writer for the Redskins nicknamed the infant trio "The Lollipop Backfield." Bosseler shakes his head when he thinks about it. "I didn't particularly like the name," he smiles. "I thought it was childish. I wanted to get rid of it. But sportswriters came up with the name because we were all rookies. There wasn't much we could do about it."

So the big back and his rookie teammates showed fans and the rest of the league that they were a lot tougher than their hard-candy namesake.

The Lollipop Backfield of Bosseler, Sutton, and Podoley combined for 1,522 yards rushing in 1957, with 673 yards and seven touchdowns coming from the crew-cut-wearing Bosseler.

Rushing for 673 yards may not compare to the massive yards that running backs put up today, but they only played 12 games, and it was good enough to give Bosseler the NFL's third highest rushing total that season, behind fellow rookie Jim Brown's 942 yards.

Bosseler quickly discovered that, with Brown and a team like the Packers around, he would not be fighting for any NFL championships or rushing titles. Still, he became a star, one of the team's go-to guys on a squad that would scratch and claw to reach the .500 plateau.

"Our backfield was young, but LeBaron was a great quarterback," says Bosseler. "He was a little guy, about 5-foot-9, not quite 170 pounds. But he was very smart, a good play caller. I never understood how he could throw the ball over those big linemen. Even when he used the jump pass, he still had to get the ball over these guys who were 6-foot-4, 6-foot-5. People didn't realize he had a great throwing arm. He didn't think twice about taking off and running. He'd drive Kuharich crazy with his runs. Eddie was stocky but really gutsy."

BEST OF THE BEST

During Bosseler's early pro days, the NFL was far from the 32-team mega league it is today. The AFL hadn't been born yet, and three teams from the All-American Football Conference (AAFC) in the 1940s—the Colts, the 49ers, and the Browns—had already been absorbed into the NFL. That meant there were only 12 teams in the NFL during his first season in 1957.

To play in the NFL you had to be the cream of the crop. The number of players fortunate enough to receive paychecks from the NFL back then was just a fraction of the players now. The total number of NFL players then was about 480. Today there are about 1,700. The 1957 Redskins had just 38 players on the team. As a result, players knew each other because they lined up often. As they do today, the Redskins played in the Eastern Conference, which then consisted of the Cleveland Browns, the New York Giants, the Pittsburgh Steelers, the Philadelphia Eagles, and the Chicago Cardinals. The Western Conference included the Detroit Lions, the San Francisco 49ers, the Baltimore Colts, the Los Angeles Rams, the Chicago Bears, and the Green Bay Packers.

"I remember my rookie year well," says Bosseler. "Don Shula was on our team. He had played a few years with the Browns, the Colts, and now was on the Redskins. Shula, Joe Walton and I used to hang out. We were all single then, so there were plenty of things to do here in D.C."

The Redskins went 5-6-1 the one year with Shula on the team. The next year, Shula retired and went into coaching, and the Redskins went 4-7-1; in 1959, they went 3-9.

"It got even worse," says Bosseler. "In 1960 and 1961, we only won one game a piece. I was in my fifth season and with my third head coach! I guess we didn't have the overall talent of other teams in the league and it was driving the owner, George Preston Marshall, crazy.

"One day Mr. Marshall came over to my locker and cornered me, asking if I'd come over for lunch one day," recalls Bosseler. "The first thing I thought was, 'What did I do?' He could be a volatile guy, so I had no idea what he wanted. I was nervous as I dressed the next day and didn't want to be late. I hurried over to his place at noon, this huge mansion, and knocked on the door. Well, this butler answered and stared at me. I told him who I was and he looked at me dumbfounded. 'Mr. Marshall is still in bed,' he replied. I couldn't believe it. I didn't know what to do, but the butler told me to just wait and that a third party would be joining us. I was thinking it was Marhsall's wife, Corinne Griffith, who was a beautiful former movie star. Finally, after standing around forever, Marshall came in with a familiar-looking gentleman and said, 'Do you know Arthur?' I looked over and it was Arthur Godfrey, the famous broadcaster who hosted his own show, *The Arthur Godfrey Show*. The three of us sat there and had this tremendous lunch. I was shocked."

It was in Bosseler's humble nature to not realize that he was a star in his own right. "It didn't occur to me that Mr. Marshall just wanted to invite one of his more familiar players over for lunch with one of his famous friends."

Despite the brushes with celebrity, Bosseler felt more at ease on the gridiron. "We played 12 games then," says Bosseler. "We played everyone in our conference twice, and then played two other teams from the Western Conference. I got really comfortable playing teams in my conference."

Bosseler usually had his best games against conference rivals. Of his three career 100-yard-plus games, two were against the Steelers and the other against the Eagles. He also tied a Redskins record by rushing for three touchdowns his rookie season versus Philadelphia.

GAME OF MY LIFE
BY DON BOSSELER

I don't know what it was about the Eagles, but I always seemed to play better against our rivals from up the highway. I know it really has nothing to do with how I played, but I always found it interesting that my older brother, George, went to the University of Pennsylvania. I used to go watch him play football at Franklin Field, which, of course, is where the Eagles played. I was very familiar with that field; I felt at home there. But I played well against the Eagles here at Griffith Stadium, so I can't explain. The Colts were closer, but maybe we always got up for the Eagles because they were in our division.

When I was a rookie in 1957, we had lost in Philadelphia the first time, 21-12, and we were determined to win at home. I scored three touchdowns in the rematch, tying a team record, and we won 42-7. The next season we split the games again.

In 1959 we were 2-3 at the time and headed for what would be a terrible 3-9 season. The Eagles were a fast-improving team and would win the NFL Championship the following season. We were hungry and determined to play well. Even with their great team, and guys like Chuck Bednarik, Marion Campbell, Tom Brookshier, and Ed Khayat (a former Redskin, who would return to the team in 1962) on defense, we were confident we could run on them.

I always felt our line was pretty underrated. Guys like Don Boll, Ray Lemek, Johnny Miller, Jim Schrader, and Red Stephens, took a lot of pride in their unit and they opened up some beautiful holes for me, especially that day.

I was having a pretty good year, and I sensed I was going to have a big day. Back then you never saw the large gaping holes that you see today. Defenses were allowed to do so much physically to you back then that you really had to be tough on offense. I guess I was what you would today call a "downhill runner." I was a fullback, so I was never confused with Hugh McElhenny. I usually made my one cut and hit the hole.

Well, I had over 100 yards and two touchdowns going into the fourth quarter. But that didn't really matter to me. The only thing I cared about was that we were losing, 30-23.

But then on our final drive, Eddie LeBaron connected on some nice passes, and I had a couple long runs to get us down near the goal line with time running out. We had a second-and-goal at about the 3-yard line. So they decided to give it to me three straight times. The first try I was near the goal line when, for some reason, the whistle blew. The referee was waving his arms and pointing to the ground that the play was over. I didn't understand because I was pretty close to the goal line and I felt like my momentum was still going forward.

So we tried again. I took the ball and lowered my helmet. I could see that I had just gotten into the end zone. Again, the referee blew his whistle and said, "No, you didn't get in!" I couldn't believe it. I was really upset and determined. I looked over and saw Bednarik even more fired up.

We huddled up again and this time LeBaron called my name again, "The Bull!" Having been stopped twice, I was a little surprised to hear my number called again, but I took on the challenge. LeBaron stuck the ball in my gut and I immediately saw the Eagles defense swarm to where I was. A group of them met me head-on and stopped me cold. That was it. Game over.

I think Sonny Jurgensen came on and ran out the remaining few seconds for the Eagles. I was crestfallen. After the game, teammates congratulated me on my big day. I had rushed for 168 yards on just 23 carries and scored two touchdowns. Later we looked at film and saw I had clearly scored on my second try. But what could you do? This was years before instant replay. It made me feel a little better, but not much. It was my biggest day as a pro and a game I'll never forgot it, mostly because we lost.

PRO BOWL BOUND

Following the 1959 season, Bosseler was voted to his only Pro Bowl. He played five more years with the Redskins and retired in 1964. At the time of his retirement, Bosseler became the Redskins all-time leading rusher and had led the team in rushing three seasons, 1957, '59, and '60. He posted three 100-yard games: two against the Steelers, with 145 yards and two touchdowns in 1958, and 136 yards in 1959; and 168 yards and two touchdowns in that infamous contest against the Eagles in 1959.

His career numbers were great: 3,112 yards on 775 carries for a career 4.0 average. And he snatched 136 passes for 1,083 yards and scored 23 career touchdowns.

In 1990, Bosseler was inducted into the College Football Hall of Fame. His alma mater, Miami, retired his jersey. In 1999, he joined Ottis Anderson, Bernie Kosar, and Burgess Owens in the team's Ring of Honor. His name displayed for all to see at the Orange Bowl.

Finally, in 2002, the blue-ribbon panel named Bosseler one of the 70 Greatest Redskins, an honor that he says is one of his proudest moments of his life.

"I think playing in the NFL for eight seasons is a big accomplishment," says Bosseler, "and being named as one of the 70 Greatest Redskins, well, I can't tell you how proud that makes me."

Bosseler has had his share of inspirational people contribute to his success. "I had some good role models in my life. My brother George, [and] a guy by the name of Danny Vandetta, who was my high school coach."

Since retiring in 1964, Bosseler has made his home in Miami, Florida. He works as a stockbroker.

"I've been married for 43 years to my wife, Marcia, and we have four grown children who all live here in Florida. I'm blessed with five grandchildren," he laughs. "I've had a wonderful life and am happy with my contribution to the Redskins history and the great Redskins fans."

Chapter 12

PAT FISCHER

Pat Fischer grew up not knowing he was too small for football. One of nine children and the second youngest of six boys, Pat was raised in a small town in Nebraska where everyone played football; size never occurred to him.

"For me, my brothers weren't any bigger than I was . . . I could tackle people, and when I hit them, they fell down."

That simple truth inspired the 5-foot-9, 170-pound cornerback to excel in high school, then at the University of Nebraska.

"When I was growing up I thought the world was made up of nothing but football players," he recalls. "I thought everyone played football. And in the little town that I grew up in—all the kids did play football. You got in the backyard and that's what you did."

Pat had plenty of competition in his own backyard. His four older brothers were great football players, as was his younger brother, Jerry. One older brother, Kenny, became his first football coach. The oldest Fischer boy, Cletis, who also was 5-foot-9 and 170 pounds, played a season for the New York Giants, and another brother, Rex, was drafted by the 49ers.

"Football was a wonderful thing for the Fischer family," he says. "I think sports taught us competition, which prepared us for all the great challenges of life."

Born January 2, 1940, in St. Edward, Nebraska, Fischer and his family moved to Oakland when he was 11, then later after his sophomore season playing for Kenny, they moved to Omaha and he became an All-State running back at Westside High School.

Even though he was vertically challenged, he played like a linebacker. He wasn't the type to run out of bounds or try a lot of fakes. Fischer often lowered his shoulders and beat bigger players with leverage and sheer determination.

He had interest from a few schools but none of them had a chance. For kids growing up in Nebraska, there was but one school. And the Fischer boys all dreamed of playing for the University of Nebraska. All six lived the dream.

BORN TO BE A CORNHUSKER

One of the first people Fischer met at Nebraska was a tall tight end from Toledo, Ohio, who would later make a name as a stalwart defensive end and become one of his closest friends—Ron McDole.

"Ron and I have known each other since we were teens," says Pat. "He's always been a good friend and a great competitor."

By the time Fischer got to Nebraska, the team's all-time rival, Oklahoma, was dominating college football and had gone undefeated during a three-year period, 1955-57. Fischer's coach, Bill Jennings, never fielded a winning team and never won more than four games a season. But with players like Fischer and McDole, they did something that no other team was able to do for several years. In 1959, their Nebraska team halted Oklahoma's 74-game conference winning streak with an improbable 25-21 win.

At 5-foot-9 and 170 pounds, **Pat Fischer** was perhaps pound for pound the toughest defensive back to ever play. Despite his size, Fischer played 17 seasons and lay wood to much bigger receivers who dared to catch a pass in his territory. *NFL/WireImage.com*

"That was a big thrill," says Fischer. "We beat them again my senior year."

Fischer nearly scored on a 70-yard punt return in the game. As a sophomore, he zigzagged his way to a 92-yard touchdown against Penn State. Whether he was playing defensive back, quarterback, halfback, or returning punts or kickoffs, Fischer was all over the place. Along with McDole, he was the team's captain and led the squad in all-purpose yards each year.

Still he never made All-America or All-Conference. So after winning his last game at Nebraska and knowing he had excelled at everything his team asked him to do, Fischer thought he'd reached the end of his football career.

"I thought my days of playing football were over until I was invited to play in the [North-South] All-Star game and played well," he says. "It was the first time I thought, 'Wow, I might get drafted.'"

MR. IRRELEVANT

In today's draft, the last player selected gets the moniker "Mr. Irrelevant." They throw a parade for him and everything. And even though Fischer wasn't close to being the last player drafted in the 1961 draft, the St. Louis Cardinals waited until the 17th round to select the halfback. In fact, St. Louis thought so little of him that he was the sixth halfback and 232nd player drafted that year.

Going from Nebraska to the NFL isn't considered a huge leap, but when the team has trouble finding equipment small enough to fit you, it doesn't fill you with a lot of confidence. Luckily for Fischer, there was a familiar face in the sea of unknowns. His buddy, Ron McDole, had been drafted by the Cardinals in the fourth round.

It wasn't until the team finally found some equipment to fit Fischer that he got the opportunity to show his worth. During a camp scrimmage, Fischer found himself in the open field trying to tackle 1957 Heisman Trophy winner John David Crow. At 6-foot-2 and 200 pounds,

Crow would be considered big even by today's standards. Back then he was huge.

As Fischer began to take aim on Crow, it didn't occur to him that the second player chosen in the entire 1958 draft had rushed for over 1,000 yards the season before. It didn't occur to him that he had averaged a blistering 5.9 yards a carry, much of that earned after initial contact. Or that his mere presence, which included nerve damage on one side of his face that made him look even more menacing, scared his own teammates.

When the two players crashed into each other, it resembled a mouse trying to catch a cat. Fischer hit Crow low, wrapping his arms around Crow's legs. Crow landed on his back. The mouse, Fischer's new nickname, had won.

"I remember tackling him and everyone made a big deal about it, but I didn't think much about it," he says. "Tackling is something I always did. I liked that contact."

Head coach Frank "Pop" Ivy kept Fischer, who made his mark on special teams. As a rookie, he returned punts and kickoffs, averaging 25.1 yards a return. His second season, he boosted his average to an impressive 26.7 yards. Fischer became a starter that 1962 season and had three interceptions after four games, but he tore his hamstring and missed the rest of the season. By then, McDole was playing for the Houston Oilers and later enjoyed several years with Buffalo.

By the time he finished his third season, Fischer was an emerging star for St. Louis, having plucked eight interceptions. New coach Wally Lemm was the beneficiary of some good draft luck. Better yet, with players like Fischer and tackle Luke Owens on defense, and with quarterback Charley Johnson, receiver Bobby Joe Conrad, and tight end Jackie Smith scoring points, the Cardinals had improved from 4-9-1 in '62 to 9-5 in '63.

In 1964, Fischer became a legitimate star. He notched 10 interceptions and returned two of them for scores. The media finally started noticing this 5-foot-nothing, 170-pound dynamo. Naturally, they played up his lack of stature.

"I didn't know I was too small until a few years after I was in the league when people started writing about it because I had played successfully," he recalls. "It never entered my mind that I was too small, because I could tackle people."

Fischer remembers two of the greatest running backs he had to tackle. Both played on the Cleveland Browns. His rookie year, he got a chance to tackle Bobby Mitchell and Jim Brown.

"When I went to tackle Bobby, the first thing that went through my mind was that if I hit him I might not be able to get him down. But when he got close to the line of scrimmage, I just grabbed him and threw him down before he got momentum. I got penalized for it, but it gave me confidence. Jim Brown was another story. He was an incredibly physical runner. The greatest runner I ever played against. I'm happy to say I did get to tackle him a few times."

Fischer's final season with the Cardinals was in 1967. A salary dispute and some defensive lapses that were blamed on the secondary got him put on the trading block. In 1968, Fischer was sent to the Washington Redskins for a couple of draft picks and his whole world changed.

THE BURGUNDY IS GOLDEN

Though a Midwestern boy who spent seven pro seasons in a Midwestern city, Fischer adjusted easily to the Washington scene. Head coach Otto Graham was happy to have one of the top cornerbacks in the NFL.

In seven seasons, Fischer had snagged 29 interceptions and made more than a few receivers and running backs pay the price. He was brought in to add toughness to a Washington defense that was one of the league's biggest sieves.

"When I first came to Washington, people would go to the games and they knew they would see some exciting offensive plays," he says. "We had an incredible offense of Hall of Famers: Sonny Jurgensen, Charley Taylor, Bobby Mitchell, and a great tight end in Jerry Smith.

They scored a lot of touchdowns but [because of the defense] the fans never expected us to win."

After another poor season in '68 in which the team went 5-9, Graham was fired. When the new coach was announced on February 7, 1969, legend has it the clouds opened up and it was sunny in D.C. for the next year.

"Even though I had played in the NFL all those years, when I heard Vince Lombardi was going to coach the Redskins my first thought was just making the team," remembers Fischer. "His reputation preceded him everywhere he went. Looking back, I'm proud to say that I made the team under Coach Lombardi. That's saying something. He could have cut me. But I made a team that he coached."

Lombardi was one of the first Redskins coaches in a long time to care about fielding a great defense. Linebacker Sam Huff even came out of retirement to play for Lombardi. Fischer proved to be valuable player. He and linebacker Chris Hanburger were the only defensive players voted to the Pro Bowl. Better yet, the team enjoyed its first winning season, 7-5-2, since 1955.

Tragically, the Lombardi era ended after one glorious season, after which he succumbed to cancer. Assistant Bill Austin took over in 1970 and the team dipped to 6-8. The organization finally came to the conclusion that in order to win, they needed a coach who'd focus on defense. They went out and got the right man.

BRING US YOUR OLD, HUNGRY VETERANS

Hiring George Allen changed the fortune of the Redskins forever. The former coach of the Los Angeles Rams preached teamwork, hard work, and defense. Like Lombardi, Allen also liked Fischer's humble, blue-collar, lunch-pail mentality.

"George appreciated guys who worked hard. And I worked hard and practiced every day for him," says Fischer. "He brought together guys who are now my friends and we won a lot of football games. I appreciate that he kept me on the team and he united me with people I liked and would go to war with at anytime."

Allen wasn't into aerial shows even though he had Jurgensen, Taylor, and Smith. He preferred a tough running game and a winning defense. So he began trading draft picks for established pros, creating the famous "Over the Hill Gang."

"Winning under George Allen became a great lifestyle for our fans and became a great thrill for us," says Fischer. "Our fans became real fervent fans. He may have come in and announced the future is now, but that became true.

"You have to look at that team and say we were all good friends. That was an example of unity. That was an example of a team. That group was comprised of guys coming from different places. George Allen brought them in and we all fell into the same mold. We'd get supercharged from one another. Did we like one another? Of course we did; we had to. But it was also easy for us to like each other."

In seven seasons, Allen never had a losing record. Fischer looks at the 1972 NFC Championship game against the Cowboys as perhaps the most memorable. But for him, all the playoff games were equally memorable, especially the celebrations afterwards.

"There was never anything that compared to those playoff games because everyone in that locker room was part of it," he says. "There was not a moment that will ever compare to it. . . . [We] were all heroes. And that's where you realize what it means when you have a total team commitment to something. It's all about guys doing their jobs and mine was covering receivers."

GAME OF MY LIFE
BY PAT FISCHER

There wasn't a game we played with the Redskins that was as significant a win as that 1972 victory over the Cowboys. But they were all exciting. If you weren't happy to be there playing for the Redskins, then you didn't love football as much as we did. Every win was exciting, running out of that tunnel in front of those fans, knowing you were going to play in front of that crowd.

Still, when I look back at my career, I realize I never played games; I played against people. I played against receivers like Gary Collins of the Cleveland Browns, Bob Hayes of the Cowboys, and Harold Carmichael of the Eagles. I didn't prepare to play against a whole bunch of people. That would have been overwhelming. I'm glad I didn't have to play against them all.

I'd say Collins, Hayes, and Carmichael were the toughest receivers I ever went up against. Collins was 6-foot-5, a good athlete, and he could really catch the football. When you played against Collins, you also had to keep an eye out for the likes of Brown, Mitchell, and Leroy Kelly. The Browns had quite a package of players who'd won the NFL Championship in '64. When they faced the Colts for the title, it was Collins who scored all the touchdowns in a 27-0 win.

Another tough guy to cover was Harold Carmichael. What a challenge. The guy was 6-foot-8. I was 5-foot-9. He was almost a foot taller than me, so that was always a tough matchup.

But probably the best receiver I went up against was Bob Hayes. He was a sprinter, which meant you had to leave early when covering him. And by early I mean that when they broke the huddle, I started my backpedal.

It's not that Hayes was the best receiver, but the Cowboys were always tough to beat, so a lot of times it came down to one or two plays. Our mental state was different playing against the Cowboys than a team like, say, the Eagles. So when I played against Bob Hayes and the Dallas Cowboys, every play counted. He could convert a short play into a long gainer. In a game like that, individual plays make the difference between winning and losing. I'm glad to say we won our share against the Cowboys.

17 FOR 17

It's fitting that Pat Fischer remained a Redskin for as long as George Allen coached the team. Along with Talbert, McDole, Kilmer, and some others, Fischer was a true Allen player. Tough, unselfish, and humble, he was dedicated to restoring a winning mentality in Washington. When Allen left after the 1977 season, Fischer called it quits, too. The little "mouse" who wasn't drafted until the 17th round played an incredible 17 NFL seasons and 213 games, a record for a cornerback when he retired. He also played in three Pro Bowls, intercepted 56 passes, returning four for touchdowns, and scored another on a fumble recovery.

A decade after he retired, NFL Films named Fischer the Redskins all-time "Tums" neutralizer. When asked about the award, Fischer laughs and recalls one of his more memorable plays.

"We were playing the Cowboys one year and Kenny Houston had just intercepted one of Roger Staubach's passes. Immediately, I was looking for someone to block," he laughs. "I saw Staubach out of the corner of my eye and realized this might be the only time in my life that I would have a clear shot at him. This was back when there were no cornerback blitzes, so I never had a chance to really hit a quarterback.

"Well, I must have run past three or four Cowboys just so I could get to Staubach. That's the funny thing. When I got to him, my face lit up and I dove right at his feet and knocked him down. He was so upset he got up and kicked me and it was right in front of an official. Not only did we get the ball, but they flagged Staubach with a 15-yard unsportsmanlike penalty. Of all the players who got upset at me, I got Staubach!"

Since then, those players from the Redskins and Cowboys have met a few times during charity flag football games. "The first time, Staubach came up to me and I didn't know what he was going to say," says Fischer. "Well, he smiled and put his arm around me and said, 'Pat, you're the only guy that caused me to get a 15-yard unsportsmanlike penalty in my whole career.'"

In the 30 years since he left the game, Fischer continued working at the same off-season job he held during his playing days. "I worked as a stockbroker all the years I played," he says. "Now I'm a real estate agent."

Fischer says the toughest thing about transitioning from pro football to retirement was finding ways to stay competitive. He enjoyed the regiment of being on a schedule where everything led up to the game.

"When you're working you want to remain competitive some way," he says. "But nothing compares to playing in the NFL. Everything we did was to prepare for Sunday. We didn't have to make any decisions. We knew in July we had to be somewhat in shape. So we started running in June. We'd report to training camp. We all had jobs doing different things, so we had to work around that. During the season you're on a schedule. You have to be at practice at this time. You practice for two hours, you meet afterwards, then you go home. Saturday night comes along you meet at the Marriott and get ready for the game.

"That Sunday after the game you go out and have a little party, win or lose. So what decisions are you making? You've got a little money in your pocket. Everyone's excited to see you; people are friendly. They tell you what they think of the game. It's tough to duplicate that."

But life is good for Pat Fischer. He stays in touch with many of his teammates, especially his closest friends, Talbert, Kilmer, and McDole. Last year was especially good. His son got married, and his daughter gave Fischer his first grandchild.

Without a doubt, the proud grandfather, in remembering his own football-centered childhood, will surely make football part of his grandchild's life.

Chapter 13

JEFF BOSTIC

In the summer of 1980, Jeff Bostic, an undrafted free agent with the Philadelphia Eagles, thought he had endured all the football he could take. After six weeks of grueling two-a-days under the perfection-demanding eye of coach Dick Vermeil, Bostic was one of the team's last cuts. The results-focused Vermeil, then in his fifth season as head coach, had no need for a rookie free agent center. He was primed to take his group of hand-selected veterans to the Super Bowl that season, and he would do it without the unknown youngster from Clemson.

"I remember calling my parents and telling them I'd been cut," says Bostic, who thought he would get a lot of sympathy for his valiant effort and almost making a super-caliber team. "My dad said, 'You should call that guy from the Redskins and see if you can get a tryout.' I told him, 'No, I'm done.' I had spent six of the toughest weeks I can remember playing my heart out. But my dad was persistent. Heck, my older brother Joe was already playing football for St. Louis [Cardinals, before they moved to Arizona], and I guess my dad thought if Joe could make it, I could too."

Bostic's dad, Joe Sr., persisted. "Just drop by the Redskins. You're going to drive right through there anyway. It's on the way," he told his son. The geography lesson in hand, Bostic called Redskins scout Mike

Allman and asked if he could drop by for a workout. What followed is now part of Redskins history.

Fourteen years after that visit, Bostic retired with three Super Bowl rings and one Pro Bowl appearance. Not bad for an undrafted, undersized, unwanted kid whose career began by deciding which way to drive around the Washington Beltway. When asked about how making all the right turns on that journey home changed his life more than 25 years ago. Bostic says, "I was the guy who had preparation meet opportunity, and [I was] in the right place at the right time."

Born September 18, 1958, in Greensboro, North Carolina, Jeff Lynn Bostic was the second of two boys born to Joe and Sharon Bostic. Like many kids growing up in the rolling hills of the old republic, the Bostic boys competed in nearly every arena.

"We played everything," says Bostic, "football, basketball, baseball. I got into wrestling and my brother, Joe, was a genetic freak."

Joe was 6-foot-2 by the time he turned 12. In Junior High, he caught up with his height by filling out to 260 pounds. "That wasn't me," says Bostic, "I never got as big as Joe. If I was going to be good at football, I couldn't do it on brute strength."

So Bostic honed his gridiron skills on the wrestling mat. "I loved football and baseball, but I think wrestling was my best sport," he says. "Wrestling taught me the essence of sport: physical confrontation. It's one on one. There's nobody else. I learned the importance of leverage, pressure points, stamina, and fighting through things."

He also learned conditioning, something that years later would allow him later to survive Vermeil's training camp, and 14 more with the Redskins. "Anyone who's ever wrestled knows it takes tremendous conditioning. Football has breaks after each play. But wrestling can be non-stop for up to six minutes."

Jeff Bostic may have been the smallest interior lineman on The Hogs, but the undrafted free agent proved to be one of the most valuable. In 14 seasons, Bostic anchored the line for four Super Bowls and three world championships. He also served as the team's long-snapper.

George Gojkovich/Getty Images

After following his older brother to football stardom at Ben L. Smith high school, Bostic continued to embrace Joe's shadow and matched his decision to go to Clemson. Both Bostic boys manned the Clemson offensive line.

While Joe was 6-foot-4, 255 pounds in college, Jeff was a small chip off his brother's shoulder; a 6-foot-1, 220-pound sophomore. His Clemson teammates included some future big names: a young Dwight "The Catch" Clark, All-America receiver Jerry Butler, and quarterback Steve Fuller. By the time Bostic played his final game at Clemson, he had been a three-year starter at guard and center, tipping the scale at a mighty 237 pounds.

Though he wasn't named All-America like his brother, Joe, he did show enough consistency to be noticed by NFL scouts. As a smallish but athletic lineman, Bostic prepared for the NFL draft as if he were a Top 10 pick. In 1980, the draft was comprised of 12 rounds, not seven like it is today. For sure, he thought, he would hear his name called.

As the second day of the draft came to a close and Bostic was not one of the 333 players called, he began to think about the strong possibility of life after football.

The only two teams that called about signing him as a free agent were the Eagles and the Redskins. Bostic chose the Eagles, who had lost the previous year in the playoffs to the Tampa Bay Buccaneers. The Redskins had just missed the playoffs, losing a heartbreaker in the final game of the season to the Cowboys, 35-34, as quarterback Roger Staubach engineered two touchdowns in the final minutes to win.

"I was a 13th-round pick in a 12-round draft," says Bostic. "But I thought I had a chance to make the Eagles. Vermeil was a good man who put on a tough camp."

Every undrafted rookie needs something to make him stand out, and Bostic's extra something was his versatility. He was quick enough to play both guard and center. Plus, he was a talented long-snapper.

"They used to cut you by flying a paper under your door at 3 a.m.," says Bostic. "I sat there in the dark as the team trimmed its roster to 60. My roommate had already been cut, so I sat there by myself."

Bostic would survive another cut and make it to 50. In today's NFL, being among 50 players would have meant making the team. Back then, however, there were fewer teams and fewer jobs. NFL rosters were 40 players, plus a few on the "taxi squad," later named "practice squad." When the team trimmed its roster to 45, Bostic received the slip of paper under his door and knew it was time to leave.

"I was so tired by then I just wanted to go home. I mean six weeks of two-a-days in West Chester, Pennsylvania. It could have been any town. Just the day-in and day-out struggle was a lot." But Bostic adhered to his father's wishes. He looked at the success that Joe was having and decided to give it one final try.

"So I called the guy, Mike Allman, a personnel guy for the Redskins who had called me before the draft," recalls Bostic. "I asked him if he minded if I came by and worked out for him. He said, 'Sure, I saw you got released.'"

Bostic had no idea what was going on with the Redskins. George Allen was long gone and Jack Pardee, a former Redskins great, had been the coach for the past three seasons. Bostic ran and did speed and agility drills for them, including the broad jump and the high jump.

"I also did some long-snapping for them. When I finished the workout, he said, 'You know, we've been having trouble with our long-snapper. If he has a bad snap in the next game, we'll call you.'"

Bostic didn't think much of it and went home to North Carolina. When the Redskins played their next preseason game, he was able to watch it on the TV. "This was before the Carolina Panthers and Jacksonville Jaguars," says Bostic. "We got Redskins games, because at the time they were the closest team."

Just as the Redskins coach had predicted, the long-snapper sailed his first attempt over the punter's head and Bostic suddenly was a Washington Redskin.

"I got to town on a Saturday, and nine days later we were opening up the season on *Monday Night Football* against the Dallas Cowboys."

In one bad snap, Bostic went from an unemployed 22-year-old thinking hard about going into the construction business, to playing a nationally televised game for the Redskins against their hated arch-nemesis.

Even with Bostic's great long-snapping prowess, the 1980 Redskins struggled mightily. When John Riggins took a year sabbatical, Pardee's record slipped to 6-10 and he was fired. For Bostic, a new coach meant starting over to prove himself.

"Joe Gibbs came in and brought a whole new coaching staff. Suddenly everyone was starting from ground zero," says Bostic. "I went into camp fourth string. I didn't know there was fourth string in the pros."

But Bostic proved to be a tenacious battler, often going up against guys who outweighed him by 50 pounds. Using the leverage he'd learned many years earlier as a wrestler, he started to prove he belonged. After a week at camp, he was third string. A week later, he was second.

"Then one day during stretching, Joe Bugel came up to me and said, 'What do you think about starting?' I was so naïve, I said, 'Starting what?'"

Bugel smiled at him and replied, "You're going to be my starting center when the season starts."

THE HOGS

Building championship teams sometimes comes down to everyone from the coach, players, and administrative office being on the same page.

"We had a lot of young, talented guys assembled in very close proximity in their careers," says Bostic. "We were fortunate enough to have a guy like Joe Gibbs coaching us. And the staff he put together was as good as any in the league."

With an all-star coaching staff that included Richie Petitbon, Larry Pecatello, Emmitt Thomas, Tory Torgensen, Dan Henning, and Joe Bugel, Gibbs had a coaching staff that matched his young, talented team.

Gibbs looked at the NFC landscape—at Dallas' tough pass rushers, Harvey Martin and Ed "Too Tall" Jones, at the Eagles' Carl Hairston, and at Giants linebacker Lawrence Taylor—and developed a powerful, one-back offense to offset the division's dominating defensive players. The key to the Redskins' offensive success would be the guys upfront.

Going into his second year with the Redskins, the 6-foot-2, 265-pound Bostic was joined in 1981 by top draft picks tackle Mark May, 6-3, 310, and guard Russ Grimm, 6-foot-3, 295. The team also added an intimidating 6-foot-7, 320-pound mountain of a man, not through the draft, but as an undrafted free agent—tackle Joe Jacoby.

"I can see how I might have been overlooked," says Bostic, "But how did a guy 6-7, 300-plus pounds go undrafted in a 12-round draft? It's mind-boggling to me."

Along with 300-pound veteran George Starke, the Redskins' offensive line was the biggest in the league, even with the smallish Bostic manning the middle.

The first time Bostic heard the name "The Hogs" was sometime during training camp.

"Bugel was talking to Grimm one day," says Bostic, "He said something like, 'It's time for your Hogs to hit the sleds.' You didn't really catch it at first. It was during training camp. We're in Carlisle, Pennsylvania in the month of July. Not where you want to be. He started calling us 'The Hogs.' It kind of gave us a rallying call, kind of like a fraternity."

For Bostic and his linemates, being one of the "The Hogs" was fun at first, but success brought other challenges. "Then you start winning, and the next thing you know there's pressure to perform," says Bostic. "Suddenly there are T-shirts, pig noses, guys dressed up as the Hogettes. It goes from some quirky cliché in training camp to something that's survived 25 years. But what I think it did was give a young offensive line something to bond to and, ultimately, it gave the viewing public some idea as to what the success of a football team really comes from, what the engine is that drives your team."

A LINE OF CONSISTENCY

The Redskins' offensive line didn't change much over the next 10 years. Bostic, Grimm, and Jacoby remained entrenched engines, as all encompassing as snarled traffic in D.C.

More Hogs arrived during the late 1980s. R.C. Thielmann, Raleigh McKenzie, Jim Lachey, Ed Simmons, and Mark Schlereth joined them, but the premise remained the same: a power running game built on simple physics—force equals mass times acceleration. The Hogs' massive, quick-footed linemen proved to be an unstoppable force regardless of the quarterback or running back behind them.

In Super Bowl XVII, when the Redskins were down 17-13 in the fourth quarter and they were on fourth-and-1, the play came in "I-left, tight wing, 70 chip on white." It was the Hogs who made it possible for John Riggins to make the most historic play in Redskins history.

The next year, during the '83 season, the Redskins went to their second straight Super Bowl after putting up a record 485 points. Not a point would have been possible without The Hogs. In '86, the Redskins found themselves trailing the Denver Broncos 10-0 in the second-quarter of Super Bowl XXII. By halftime, the Skins had blown by Elway and company, 35-10. Quarterback Doug Williams threw for 340 yards and four touchdowns, and an unknown running back named Timmy Smith became the only back to ever rush for more than 200 yards in a Super Bowl. Again, thank the Hogs for the decisive 42-10 victory. During the '91 season, the Redskins went 17-2 and scored 585 points, winning their third Super Bowl with another quarterback, Mark Rypien, and two new backs, Ernest Byner and Gerald Riggs.

The one constant through it all was the Hogs. Bostic, Jacoby, Grimm, and friends were there, as always, leading the way.

GAME OF MY LIFE
BY JEFF BOSTIC

If there's one game that really exemplified our football team it was a 1990 game we played in Detroit. It was a weird game. The Lions were running the Mouse Davis run-and-shoot offense with Rodney Peete at quarterback. Barry Sanders had scored on a long touchdown run and was making us look bad.

Our quarterback that day was Stan Humphries. Mark Rypien was hurt, so Stan started and was having a bad day. He threw three interceptions with one returned for a touchdown. We were getting crushed, 35-14.

So with about 10 minutes left in the third quarter, Gibbs put in our third-string quarterback, Jeff Rutledge. Now, Jeff was a great pro. He had been in the league for a long time with the Rams and Giants. He was primarily our holder for kicks. In fact, Jeff was a heck of a holder. He was probably the greatest holder I ever saw. But I don't think he'd thrown a pass in a regular-season game in two years.

Well, he came into the huddle and didn't say much. He was a veteran and didn't have to, he just started throwing the ball and we did all we could to protect him. Jeff led us on a couple scoring drives, but the Lions answered and still held a huge lead going into the fourth quarter.

Even with the game seemingly out of reach, we never quit. We kept fighting. We kept coming back and scored 17 points in the fourth quarter with most of those points coming at the very end. I remember Jeff tied the game on a quarterback draw with just seconds left. Then Chip Lohmiller won it in overtime with a 40-something-yard field goal for a 41-38 victory.

We were so exhausted. I remember being slumped on a chair in the locker room, unable to get up. I found out later that we held the ball for something like 51 minutes of a 70-minute game. We also had more than 600 yards of offense. Jeff threw for over 300 yards in about a quarter and a half.

But that was us. It didn't matter who the quarterback was, or who was running the ball. We weren't going to quit. We were resilient and believed in ourselves the whole time. That game typified our team.

We went to four Super Bowls in 10 years with three different running backs and three different quarterbacks. The offensive line was the constant. It didn't matter who drove the car; the engine was always running.

AN ERA OF GREATNESS

When looking back at all the seasons during the first Gibbs era when the Redskins enjoyed riding the Hogs, Bostic believes the '91 Redskins may have been one of the best of any era.

"As a team we were solid everywhere," says Bostic. "We played 19 games and lost just two, each by less than five points. Our defense allowed just 224 points, while our offense scored 485. And in 19 games, we gave up just nine sacks."

The nine sacks is probably the greatest stat signifying the cohesion, tenacity, and competitiveness of the famed Hogs line. "Rypien was a very good quarterback, but any quarterback at that level who can play 10-12 games and know they're not going to get hit is going to put up great numbers," says Bostic. "I'm not talking sacks; I'm saying you're not going to get hit. No one is going to put a glove on you. That's the kind of line we had."

He also points out that the beauty of that '91 line was its unbelievable depth. "Our bench consisted of guys like Russ Grimm, Ed Simmons, Ray Brown, and Mark Addicks."

Grimm was hurt for most of the '91 season, and after collecting his third Super Bowl ring, he retired to coaching. Bostic and Jacoby continued playing for another two years, even after coach Gibbs retired and Richie Petitbon took over for one season.

"We probably scored 60-70 more points in 1983, but our defense wasn't as good as our '91 team. I mean, when you call your defensive backs 'The Pearl Harbor Crew,' like we did in '83, that might give you some indication about their coverage problems."

When Bostic finally retired after 14 memorable years, the one thing he clearly wouldn't miss was training camp. "It's the monotony of it all that got to me," says Bostic. "6 a.m. wake-up call; 9 a.m. breakfast; you hit the field for two hours; then you're off the field, and you shower and get treatment. You got lunch from 12:30 to 1 p.m. Then, 1 p.m. meetings until whenever they get over. Back on the field at 4 p.m. You're off the field at 6:15 p.m. Meetings at 8 p.m. Curfew at 11 p.m. Get up the next day and do it again."

All in all, Bostic says he spent 17 months of his life toiling in training camp. During those 14 seasons, he also experienced numerous aches and pains that would be considered injuries to most people. He's undergone five surgeries so far: three for his knees and two for his shoulder.

For all his troubles, Bostic was elected to the Pro Bowl just one time. But what's missing from the description of his workmanlike consistency as a mainstay Hog was that he also spent 10 years as the team's long-snapper. That's a lot of extra punishment, especially since it was years before the new rule that forbids defensive players from lining up head to head with the snapper.

"That's the story of my life," laughs Bostic. "Fifteen years too late for that rule. As a long-snapper, I used to get killed out there. Our guards were taught to interlock their legs and stick their head inside to block on field goals and extra points, so there really wasn't anywhere for centers to go. You couldn't get your legs out. Today there are long snappers who play a long time because that's all they do. If you believe in reincarnation, you want to come back as a kicker or a snapper. But you want to be a good one. The only time they hear their name is a bad snap."

Bostic looks back on his days with the Redskins fondly. He remains great friends with several former teammates, especially Jacoby, Grimm, and Don Warren. But when he thinks of his legendary linemates, the thing that irks him is the shock that there is still not a single Hog in the Hall of Fame.

"I don't know what [the Hall of Fame selectors] think we were doing it with, smoke and mirrors?" asks Grimm incredulously. "There wasn't anything smoke or mirrors about our football team. We won three Super Bowls with three different quarterbacks and three different running backs. That offensive line was the engine. If you're really going to do that group justice, that whole line should go into the Hall of Fame together."

He also can't believe some of his offensive mates aren't in, like Art Monk. "He only retired at the top in career receptions. I must be missing something." Then there are guys he played against that he scratches his head over. "I played against [Bears defensive tackle] Dan Hampton. He's in the Hall of Fame, are you kidding me?"

Still, to him the ultimate tribute isn't the Hall of Fame, chosen by pencil-wielding scribes who never played the game. It was being chosen one of the 70 Greatest Redskins.

"It's all hard to fathom," says Bostic. "I was a kid that was too small to make it in college. I went to college and by my second year I was starting. I couldn't even fathom that I'd be going to play in the pros. By the luck of the draw, I somehow ended up with the Redskins after going through Philadelphia. The next year they fired the coach, brought in Joe Gibbs. Preparation and opportunity meet. The stars, the moon, and everything else are aligned. I end up playing for a storied organization like the Redskins and get named one of the 70 greatest players. It's hard to fathom."

Now living in Georgia, with his wife, Lynn, and three daughters—two of which go to Clemson—Bostic and his brother Joe have a construction business, and he stays in the Washington scene during the season broadcasting games for Comcast and CBS Radio.

One of his biggest thrills as a player came early on in his career and it turned out to be humorous redemption for those exhausting six weeks he spent as an undrafted rookie free agent in Philadelphia.

"It was after the 1983 season and I was chosen as North Carolina's professional athlete of the year," says Bostic. "Guess who the emcee was—Dick Vermeil! When he introduced me he said, 'The guy we're honoring tonight for professional athlete of the year, I cut him in 1980. That shows you what kind of coach I am.'"

Vermeil may have been one of the first, but definitely not the last, to kick himself for overlooking one of the greatest Redskins ever.

Chapter 14

JOE THEISMANN

When Joe Theismann showed up at the Washington Redskins camp in 1974, he didn't fit the typical George Allen résumé for success. For one thing, Theismann wasn't a grizzled veteran. He was young. He wasn't experienced, having spent the past three seasons in Canada. Theismann also wasn't the typical quiet rookie. He was brash, confident, and in his own words, "a real jerk."

On top of that, the players didn't think they needed him. The Redskins already had enough quarterbacks. The popular Billy Kilmer, who two seasons prior had led them to the Super Bowl. And future Hall-of-Famer Sonny Jurgensen, at 40 years old, still had a lively arm and was by then Redskins royalty. So when Allen sent the Miami Dolphins, who'd originally drafted Theismann in 1971, a number-one pick for his rights, there was a lot of head scratching in D.C.

"Here I come in, a kid out of Notre Dame," Theismann recalls. "I had never thrown an NFL pass and I've already got my own TV segment. I'm doing commercials. I came rolling into town and my first comments were, 'I didn't come here to sit, I came here to play.'" Theismann had also written a book entitled *How to Play Quarterback*. It didn't sit well with Kilmer and Jurgensen, or his teammates or the fans. Little did fans know then that this brash, young, motor mouth of a man would someday propel the Redskins to their first Super Bowl Championship.

Born September 9, 1949, in New Brunswick, New Jersey, Theismann grew up in a working-class town called South River. He was athletic from the start. Despite his size, he excelled in baseball and football, though football was the sport he was most passionate about. "We lived close to some schools, so there were plenty of fields," he says. "I was always out playing."

While his father worked seemingly around the clock, Joe's mother often played catch with him. She knew he loved football most but didn't want him to play for fear he would get hurt. "She didn't want me to play football. Afraid I'd break something. But by the time I was 12 and saw how well I could throw the ball, well, she let me play."

A natural leader with unbridled enthusiasm, Theismann played quarterback from the get go. "It wasn't the simplest of roads. I was always skinny. My senior year in high school I was about 5-foot-10, 148 pounds," he says. But Theismann did have some help on his high school team. His backup was a player who would go on to become a Pro Bowl receiver with his archrival team.

"Drew Pearson was a heck of a player for our high school team," says Theismann. "We were tough to beat." In fact, South River went undefeated in Theismann's senior year and he got a lot of attention from recruiters: "I actually signed at North Carolina State and then changed my mind to Notre Dame," he says. Intent on playing as early as possible, Theismann volunteered to return punts just so he could get on the field as a sophomore. Soon he was the starter.

"Even as a sophomore at Notre Dame I had supreme confidence in my ability," he recalls. "One game against USC, Sandy Durko intercepted a pass and ran it back for a touchdown. I remember walking by Coach

Although a self-described "jerk" when he first joined the Redskins in 1974, **Joe Theismann** proved to be a tough, enthusiastic team player. He led Washington to its first Super Bowl Championship in 1982, and he was named the NFL's MVP the following season. *Jonathan Daniel/Getty Images*

Parseghian and saying, 'Don't worry. I'll get it back.' He says it's the last time he ever worried about me."

By the time Theismann was a senior, all the talk around South Bend, Indiana, was about the Heisman Trophy. According to Theismann, Notre Dame's PR Director, Roger Valdiserri, had heard it mispronounced as "Thize-man" early on and remembered it later. From that, a campaign for the Heisman began. "My senior year he calls me in his office and asked how I pronounced it," he says. "I told him, Thees-man, and he said, 'No, we're going to pronounce it Thize-man' and all of a sudden the Theismann for Heisman frenzy was built."

Jim Plunkett, who led Stanford to the Pac 10 Championship and a Rose Bowl victory, won the Heisman in 1970 as Theismann finished second after a career record of 20-3-2 at Notre Dame. "I believe in my heart of hearts that it was the campaign in part that caused me to lose the Heisman Trophy," he says. "I don't believe the balloters wanted a campaign to determine whether or not someone won the trophy. That's taking nothing away from Jim [Plunkett], he certainly deserved it, but I don't think it helped my cause."

OH, CANADA

Even though he finished second in the Heisman voting, once the 1971 NFL Draft came around, Theismann was nowhere near the top of the prospects. Teams have always been enthralled by measurables. The quintessential quarterback prospect back then was 6-foot-3 and weighed 210 pounds.

So it wasn't surprising that the early first round went like this: the New England Patriots selected Jim Plunkett from Stanford, 6-3, 220-pounds; the New Orleans Saints picked Archie Manning, Mississippi, 6-foot-3, 212-pounds; and the Houston Oilers chose Dan Pastorini, Santa Clara, 6-foot-2, 210 pounds. Theismann was also passed up for Ken Anderson and Lynn Dickey, plus two relatively unknown quarterbacks, Leo Hart and Karl Douglas—all of whom enjoyed a fraction of the success that Theismann had at Notre Dame.

Standing an even 6-foot and weighing 188 pounds, Theismann knew the reason he was selected in the fourth round and as the 99th overall pick by the Miami Dolphins was because of his size. On top of being drafted later, Theismann wasn't guaranteed a spot on the field. The Dolphins were a Super Bowl team, fresh off a 24-3 loss to the Cowboys in Super Bowl VI. Starter Bob Griese was just 26.

A month later, Theismann signed with the Toronto Argonauts of the Canadian Football League. "I went to Canada and we went to the Grey Cup my first year," says Theismann brightly. "It was the Super Bowl of Canada." Theismann played well in Canada, passing for 2,440 yards and 17 touchdowns as a rookie. In '72, he broke his ankle in the first game and missed seven games, but still put up 1,157 yards and 10 touchdowns. When he walked away for the NFL after three seasons, Theismann was considered one of the best quarterbacks in Canada and had been a two-time all-star.

STARTING OVER

At 25, Theismann was starting all over again as a rookie in the NFL. But just like he had done in Miami, Theismann arrived overflowing with confidence, which rubbed the tight Redskins team the wrong way.

"I arrive in Washington where Sonny Jurgensen was a Hall of Fame quarterback. And Billy Kilmer was one of the toughest guys to put on a uniform," says Theismann. "The city absolutely loved them, and the first thing I said was, 'I didn't come here to sit; I came here to play.'" Rookies didn't typically talk like that back then, especially on a team like the Redskins that had a lot of veteran players.

"I was a Jerk," says Theismann. "Those comments pissed off Sonny and Billy. They were tolerating the radio and TV shows [I did], but then I wrote a book about quarterbacking, which I had never done in the National Football League, and I think that might have been the straw that broke the camel's back."

Theismann says sometimes people create friendships based on mutual hatred of someone else. But the friendship that grew between

Kilmer and Jurgensen was especially unusual because they'd never gotten along that well; both were vying for the starting job.

"The way I hear the story is, Billy and Sonny were down at the Dancing Crab and made a pact that it no longer mattered which one of them started as long as 'He' didn't,'" says Theismann. "I was referred to as 'He.' There was a genuine dislike for me by them and the other veterans." Kilmer and Jurgensen continued to split time in 1974 as the team won the division but lost in the first round to the Los Angeles Rams. Theismann was able to contribute to the team as a punt returner, taking back 17 punts for 162 yards over two seasons.

Frustrated with his lack of playing time, Theismann's mouth got him in more trouble during the 1976 season. "Rusty Tillman had one of those Monday meet-and-greet [fan shows] where you talk about the game and they have guests and all that. So I got up to speak about the game and all of a sudden I said, 'Hey, I don't play for George Allen, I play because I love the game.' The next morning the headlines read, 'Theismann doesn't play for Allen.'"

Even though it only appeared in a little paper, Allen got wind of it and sent one of his assistants to have Theismann come in to talk to him. "Well, I had seen the headline and my wife was giving me a hard time because she just hung the drapes in the house," says Theismann. "She said, 'We're going to get traded, we're going to get cut. You should have kept your mouth shut.' I had said it truly out of frustration."

As Theismann made his way to Allen's office, one of Kilmer's closest friends on the team, safety Jake Scott, had some parting words. "I'm walking by Jake's locker to speak with George and he looks up at me and says, 'I hope you get your fucking ass traded to Green Bay.' I mean, this is one of my teammates. So there was never a lot of love on that football team for me."

Theismann sat down with Allen and explained to him that his words had been said out of frustration. He asked to be traded to one of the new expansion teams, Seattle or Tampa Bay. "I told him to trade me and then think about having me come back when I'm old because he didn't like young players," says Theismann. "Thank God he didn't trade me."

Following the '77 season, Allen retired and new coach Jack Pardee finally made Theismann the starter as Kilmer became the backup. "I started great," says Theismann. "We were 6-2, toast of town. I was on the cover of the *Sporting News*. Then we went 2-6 and finished 8-8. In '79 it came down to the season finale against the Cowboys for the division crown and the playoffs. Tony Hill made that catch and the clock operator cheated us out of three seconds near the end. But those are the kinds of dramatics that went on whenever George Allen and Tom Landry played each other."

Despite Theismann's three seasons of solid play at quarterback, the Pardee era didn't last long. He was replaced on January 13, 1981, by San Diego's offensive coordinator, Joe Gibbs, and everyone had to show the new guy they belonged.

WHO IS THIS GUY?

Joe Gibbs doesn't come across as a tough, hardened NFL coach in the mold of a Bill Parcells or Mike Ditka when you first meet him. "Joe was very quiet, almost introverted," says Theismann. "He had those huge glasses, I used to call them fog glasses. He appeared almost nerdish, but you found out right away he was extremely bright."

Most of all, Theismann was excited to have a coach from a high-octane offense like San Diego. "I was thinking, 'Man, this is like a quarterback's dream. I could be like Dan Fouts throwing for thousands of yards,'" says Theismann. "Well, we got through the first part of that season and we were 0-5 and it was my understanding that there was going to be a deal with the Detroit Lions, me for Eric Hipple. Eric had a terrific game on a Monday night against the Giants, and the deal never went down. The next week we lost to the 49ers. And I wound up driving to Joe Gibbs' house and having a sit down with him for two hours."

Theismann says Gibbs had some concerns about his many outside interests away from home, the TV shows, the endorsements, and so on.

"I had felt that Joe and I never really had the chance to connect early on," says Theismann. "He had a preconceived notion that my outside activities took precedence over football, and I wanted to explain to him that that was not the case. I would do anything to show him how much I loved football. I told him I'd sell all my interests, give up my shows, if that's what he wanted me to do. I told him to just give me a chance to be his quarterback."

From that day on, things were different. The Redskins went 8-3 the rest of the year. Then in 1982, they won their first two games just before the strike. When play resumed, the Redskins won six of the next seven regular-season games to finish 8-1.

Due to the strike the playoffs were expanded from five teams in each conference to six. Behind the strength of the Redskins defense, the leadership of Theismann, and the running of John Riggins behind the Hogs offensive line, the Redskins crushed their first two opponents, Detroit 31-7 and Minnesota 21-7. Now they faced the hated Cowboys for the NFC title and the right to go to Super Bowl XVII.

GAME OF MY LIFE
BY JOE THEISMANN

The 1982 Championship game against the Cowboys is the game that sticks out most in my career. The Cowboys and the Redskins were the preeminent teams in the NFC at the time. It was during the '82 strike, when there were so many things that really played against anybody going anywhere. We were in a wildcard situation in the playoffs and there were going to be four playoff games. In the first round of the playoffs, Redskins fans kept chanting, "We want Dallas." Then all of a sudden the day came: our archrival on our home field, and the winner goes to the Super Bowl. The reason why this game is so near and dear to me, more so than the Super Bowl itself, is because it was at home. There was so much at stake, and the game was in our building in front of our fans.

That whole game was as hard hitting a game as I've ever been around. I remember rolling out and throwing a ball up the field and Ed

"Too Tall" Jones hit me so hard he darn near separated me from my teeth. I remember the intensity and the speed of the game. The hitting was like nothing I had experienced before.

The part of the game I'll never forget was how much we enjoyed running the ball near the end. Randy White was probably one of the more hated guys on the Cowboys. He was such a great football player and a painful thorn in our sides. I was in the huddle in the last drive. We'd gotten the ball on our 40-45 yard line and Joe Gibbs had called the play. I repeated it in the huddle and Russ Grimm said to me, "No."

I said, "What do you mean, no?"

"I want to run the ball over Randy," he said. That play was called 50 Gut.

"Okay, fine," I said. "50 Gut!"

Riggins got 5-6 yards. Gibbs signaled in the next play. I called the play and Grimm again said, "No."

I said, "What now pray tell?"

"I want to run 50 Gut over Randy," he said. So I said that was fine.

We got a first down. After that I didn't even look at the sidelines. I just looked at Russ and the smile across his face. I think we ran 11 straight 50 Guts and they were all designed to punish Randy. It was our way of basically saying, "Look buddy, this is it!"

The score was 31-17 when the Cowboys got the ball back with 27 seconds left in the game. I was standing on the sidelines and one of my teammates said to me, "We're going to the Super Bowl." But I still didn't realize that the dream was coming true. I told him, "No, not yet." I mean, what was going to happen in 27 seconds? In my mind, I didn't want to give myself a chance to relax. Then all of a sudden the ground beneath my feet shook.

At RFK stadium we had aluminum seats on the field. Everyone was stomping their feet on those aluminum seats and the ground beneath me was shaking. I'll never forget that as long as I live. It was absolutely unbelievable. Even the way the game ended was surreal. We ran a play on fourth down with four seconds to go. Everyone ran into the locker room.

Well, the officials went into the Cowboys locker room and had to get 11 players to come out and take the final snap. We had to do the same and get 11 guys to play defense for that one play.

As a matter of fact, the circumstances of that last play constitute one of those trivia questions that no one gets right. The question is, what two guys were high school teammates and played quarterback against one another in a NFC Championship game? The answer is Drew Pearson and me. Drew actually came out and took the last snap as quarterback. It was one of the most bizarre endings to a football game.

To me that was the game. Of course, the Super Bowl was a culmination of everyone's dreams. But that was in Pasadena; this game was in front of our fans.

AFTER THE FANFARE

In the Super Bowl, the Redskins overcame an early deficit on to win 27-17, securing their first Super Bowl Championship. Theismann's stats didn't garner him Super Bowl MVP honors, which went to Riggins, but he made perhaps the second biggest play of the game, knocking down a blocked pass near the goal line that would have been an easy interception for Miami defensive end Kim Bokamper.

The following season, the Redskins put together perhaps their greatest offensive team in franchise history. Theismann completed 60 percent of his passes for 3,714 yards and 29 touchdowns and a gaudy 97 rating; Riggins rushed for 1,347 yards and an NFL-record 24 touchdowns. Receiver Charlie Brown snagged 78 passes for 1,225 yards and eight scores. Theismann was named the NFL's MVP.

In 1984, Theismann led the Redskins to an 11-5 record, but the up-and-coming Bears beat them at home. The following year, the Redskins were 5-5 when they met the New York Giants on *Monday Night Football*. Theismann and his team struggled and, at 36, he started hearing some chants for the young gunslinger, Jay Schroeder, who had one of the strongest arms in the league.

Every football fan in the world knows what happened that night. For many, the slow motion replay of Theismann's leg snapping like a tree in a tornado still nauseates people. Theismann has his own take: "The funny thing about my life, and you hear it with any older quarterback, like Drew Bledsoe and Brett Favre, is when you overstay your welcome. As much as you did for a city or as much as people like you, they tend to start to really not like you. So in my case, Super Bowl champs in '82, MVP of the league in '83, and back to the Super Bowl that year and the playoffs again in '84—then I'm in the middle of a season where I'm struggling in '85 and all of a sudden, I basically cheat the hangman with that gruesome injury."

"What happened to me kind of pre-empted what a lot of people wanted to do to me during that '85 season, which was hang me out to dry. You wind up with this catastrophic injury that people talk about 20 years later. All of a sudden, it's like, 'Well, we never had a chance to roast the guy.' For me it all worked out for the better."

Today Theismann is as visible and audible as he was at anytime in his football career. After 18 years of broadcasting ESPN *Sunday Night Football*, Theismann was elevated to the dream job of any football announcer: *Monday Night Football*. Teaming up with broadcaster Mike Tirico and *Washington Post* sportswriter Tony Kornheiser, Theismann made up last year's *Monday Night* trio.

Unfortunately, it took too much time for the trio to jell, and after one season, Theismann was replaced by Ron Jaworski. Still, this was a small setback compared to the uphill battle he'd overcome on the gridiron. ESPN quickly offered Theismann an analyst job to broadcast college football games, but with his many interests and charities, he was still undecided.

Theismann spends part of his time as a motivational speaker. He makes about 50 speeches a year. "I love being able to share my story with people," says Theismann. "Maybe there's something I can share with them that'll give them a shot at dreams they'd like to come true, or maybe gives them a chance in a relationship that allows them to enjoy both their own life and share in other people's lives."

He is also committed to charity work, such as research for Alzheimer's disease, and cleaning up the environment. He also does extensive work for children's hospitals. Sports-wise, Theismann stays competitive with golf, playing on the Champions Tour and several Pro-Am and Celebrity Players Tour events.

Of course, one of the more striking things about Theismann is his eternally youthful appearance. Even now, nearing 60, he still looks like he could lead the Redskins offense to another Super Bowl. But the reality is that old No. 7 has seven grandchildren. His three children, Joe Jr., Amy, and Pat, are in their late 20s to mid-30s. Theismann has been married for more than 10 years to his wife, Robin.

He's in a state of post-football bliss, and he hopes his speeches and insight into the game will motivate a new generation.

Chapter 15

MIKE NELMS

Mike Nelms always had dreams beyond the football field. Even at an early age when he dreamed about being a professional football player, it wasn't for the glory or the fame; it was for the money. He wanted to make enough to buy a dealership and become an entrepreneur. He knew, of course, that in order to make it in the NFL he had to be great. The challenge was that everyone—including his parents—thought the real athlete in the family was his brother.

Still, Nelms became a football star, got drafted, and made it in the NFL as one of the best kick returners and special teams players in the modern game. He played in Super Bowls, starred in championship games, and enjoyed his share of Pro Bowls. The journey to get there, however, was as twisted and complicated as some of his returns.

Michael Craig Nelms was born April 8, 1955 in Fort Worth, Texas. Growing up in a football-crazy state like Texas, it's not surprising that Nelms and his brother loved the gridiron game. Their parents, Alfred and Betty, shared their sons' love for athletics and went to many of their games.

"My brother, Alfred, was a very good athlete," says Nelms. "He was significantly better than me. Everyone was surprised when I went to the pros instead of him."

In addition to football, Nelms starred in track as a high jumper. But his real passion was football because he felt it was his best chance to be successful for life. Even at a young age, Nelms was focused on the future. He was an earnest, methodical planner who never let his goal of becoming a success stand in his way.

"I had decided early on that I was going to become a professional football player and save enough money to become an entrepreneur," says Nelms. "Everything I did was with that in mind. Sometimes I would tell people I knew that we could no longer be friends, because they were doing stupid things. I knew hanging out with them would keep me from accomplishing my goals."

Nelms is the first to admit that he's not perfect. But all it took was a simple backyard tackling game to convince him that football was his way to achieve all his dreams.

"I was in the third grade and we were playing a game called run-through," says Nelms. "The game was exactly as it sounded. Everyone was at one side of the field and I was at the other. I'd get the ball and have to run through everybody just like a kick return. There were no blockers, just you against everybody. I loved it."

If coaches had been watching the fearless tot channel his way through the throng of tacklers, they would have said he was a born kick-returner. Soon football became his favorite sport and the local team—the Dallas Cowboys—his favorite team.

"I grew up a Cowboys fan until about the sixth or seventh grade," says Nelms. "Then some things happened on the team that made me start to look at other teams besides the Cowboys."

Nelms had started hearing negative things about "America's Team." He'd heard that the team didn't always treat their players well and dismissed them rather harshly when they got hurt. In addition to things

During the early 1980s when the Redskins were rich with stars, no one proved more exciting than **Mike Nelms**. In five seasons, Nelms earned three Pro Bowl appearances as one of the NFL's top returners. His ability to make big plays earned him the honor of being named one of the 70 Greatest Redskins. *Ronald C. Modra/Sports Imagery/Getty Images*

he heard on the radio and read in newspapers, Nelms had read a book, *North Dallas Forty*, by Peter Gent, a former Cowboys receiver. The novel was about a fictitious dysfunctional football team from Dallas, and the character of the coach was a dead ringer for Tom Landry.

So while most of his friends and family cheered for the Cowboys, Nelms became just a fan of football instead. When he starred at O.D. Wyatt High School in Forth Worth and the recruiters came calling, Nelms chose to attend a small NAIA school called Sam Houston State that was 200 miles south of the Dallas-Fort Worth area.

While at Sam Houston, Nelms proved to be a great player. Not only did he excel at defensive back, but he also broke the Bearkats' record for the longest punt return—87 yards against Sul Ross. Unfortunately, after a couple seasons, for reasons that were never completely understood, Sam Houston's coach contacted Nelms' father, Alfred, and told him that he thought it would be better if Nelms played elsewhere.

Nelms chose to transfer to Baylor University in Waco, a bit closer to his Forth Worth hometown. But in order to transfer and play right away, Nelms needed to complete his associate's degree. To make it happen, Nelms had to go to a junior college, Tarrant County JC, for two semesters following the football season.

Keeping his dream of making it in the NFL in mind, Nelms tirelessly took the extra coursework to complete the degree in time for the following season. "I just looked at it as a necessary challenge," says Nelms. "I was going to accomplish my goal by any means necessary even if that meant taking extra courses."

Nelms starred at Baylor for two seasons, 1975-76, and quickly became known for his dangerous playmaking ability. The Buffalo Bills, a disastrous 2-12 in 1976, were in desperate need of a playmaker. Bills coach Jim Ringo, a Hall of Fame center with the Green Bay Packers and Philadelphia Eagles, selected Nelms in the seventh round of the 1977 draft.

QUICK EXIT

The 170th player chosen, Nelms knew that he had to prove his worth as a defensive back as well as a return specialist to make the team. But a lot of his teammates felt that because he could play defense and special teams, he had an advantage over other rookies.

"The other DBs were telling me I had it made," says Nelms. "I wasn't so sure. Next thing I knew, they kept those guys and got rid of me."

Nelms just shrugged off the setback and looked for the next opportunity. That opportunity came from the Great White North. "Someone literally knocked on my door, woke me up, and offered me a three-year contract to play in Canada for the Hamilton Tiger-Cats in the CFL."

Although it was never his dream to play in the CFL, it was professional football and he could begin to make a decent living and start investing his earnings. Crazy as it sounds now, Nelms was given a chance to play defensive back, but not to return kicks. With Canada's extra wide fields, it would only seem natural that the return games were off the charts. And what better return man than Nelms? "I pleaded for them to let me return kicks. I played mostly defensive back and wasn't given a chance to take any back," he says. "When Hamilton finally gave me a chance, a guy fell on the back of my heel and my big toe smacked out of its socket."

Even for a seasoned trainer, the sight was gruesome. "At halftime I took off my shoe and saw my toe just dangling, so I put my shoe back on and finished the game at corner and returned kicks with a broken big toe—and today you've got guys complaining about turf toe."

Nelms missed only about a month of playing time. "I had been so close and wanted to show them that I could play," says Nelms. "Yes, this was a setback. But look how quickly I came back!" Hamilton, however, showed little tolerance and cut Nelms the day he came back. "I think they got rid of me because they were concerned about future injuries."

Once again, his pro dreams seemed as cold as the Canadian wind. But Canada is not the NFL and Nelms was nothing if not fast. The Ottawa Rough Riders wanted his speed. They were on their way to the playoffs, so they picked up his contract for $100.

On that team, as with his previous one, Nelms played mostly defensive back and rarely returned kicks. At this point, however, all Nelms cared about was that he was still playing professional football. There was still a chance to save enough money to be an entrepreneur.

Nelms quickly discovered that the CFL was the place of second chances. The star quarterback of the league at the time was Jerry Tagge, a highly regarded All-American at Nebraska, who played briefly with Green Bay. Marv Levy, the Redskins special teams coach in the early 1970s, left to be the head coach of the Montreal Alouettes, where he coached five seasons and won three Grey Cups before returning to the NFL as the head coach of the Kansas City Chiefs and later the Buffalo Bills.

"When I saw Coach Levy have success in the CFL and return to make in the NFL, I thought I could, too," says Nelms. "You have to have confidence in yourself. It helped to see people make it happen."

In 1979, Nelms got the Canadian credentials to go along with the incredible plays. He made the '79 All-Star team as a defensive back and kick returner. "I also set records for interceptions," says Nelms. With his stellar play, Nelms felt like it might be time to try the NFL again.

FAREWELL, OH, CANADA!

Now almost 25, Nelms hired his father as his agent and they started auditioning for teams. "We flew to 15 teams—Minnesota, Denver, the Saints, everybody." Nelms and his father quickly learned that negotiating for an NFL contract was not only difficult, but extremely frustrating.

"A lot of teams wanted to sign me, they just didn't want to pay me," says Nelms. "Everyone kept low-balling me. I saw that the average NFL contract was $100,000 per year and a $100,000 signing bonus. I didn't want to haggle with money, so I said, 'Just give me what you gave him and let's get it done.'"

Instead, teams were offering Nelms half that amount. Some teams even asked him to do comparison shopping for them. "I told one team, 'I'll sign right now if you give me this amount.' It wasn't unreasonable. He said, 'Go somewhere else, come back with their offer, and we'll do better.' I didn't want to do that. It was crazy."

Finally, Nelms decided to try two of the higher-echelon teams to see if they would buck up. So he visited the Dallas Cowboys and the Washington Redskins. "Dallas offered me twice as much, but they set it up in such a way that I wouldn't get my last check until 2001. At the time, it was 1980! My whole goal was to make money, save it, and become an entrepreneur. How can I do that with my money all tied up? So I told them no."

Luckily for future of the Redskins, Nelms had a friend inside the organization. "My father used to know Willie Wood, the former Packer great," says Nelms. Wood knew Bobby Beathard. I liked Bobby because he was a straight shooter. He saw the value and play-making ability I could bring to the team and offered me the contract I wanted without all the foolishness. I just looked at him and smiled. 'Yeah, I'll sign' and that was that."

HAPPY RETURNS

Knowing that he no longer needed to focus on playing just defensive back, Nelms was able to turn it on immediately in the NFL. As a first-year player in 1980, Nelms returned 48 punts for 487 yards, and 38 kickoffs for 810 yards. The Redskins loved his return style: quick and decisive, just like his life plans.

His impact was immediate and he made the 1980 Pro Bowl. The kid who had gotten cut by the sorry Buffalo Bills in '77 and had spent three seasons in Canada begging for a chance to return kicks was hanging out in Hawaii at the Pro Bowl with teammates Walter Payton and Randy White.

In 1981, Joe Gibbs became the new Redskins coach, but there was still no stopping Nelms. He returned 45 punts for 492 yards and two touchdowns, and led the NFL in kickoff returns with 1,099 yards and a league-high 29.7 average.

Nelms, however, almost didn't get the chance to play. "I missed a couple games with a broken thumb," says Nelms. "When I broke my thumb they put it in a cast, it looked like one of those oversized foam hands that fans bring to the games." Gibbs took one look at the gorilla mitt Nelms was wearing and said, "There's no way in the world you can play with that." Nelms persisted, but in the end Gibbs won, until the next game.

"He put someone else in and they didn't do well," says Nelms. "So Gibbs came back to me and said, 'Are you sure you can work with that thing?' I told him yes." After demonstrating for his coach, he was allowed to return kicks. "There's even a [Topps 1982] football card that shows me sitting on the bench with this big cast on my hand. I was just determined to have a great year."

Nelms always had a high tolerance for pain. "It's just a little pain and discomfort," says Nelms. Watching Nelms return kicks, the word that comes to mind is fearless. He hardly ever signaled for a fair catch because of his supreme confidence. "I never liked to fair catch, because I always thought I could return one for a touchdown," says Nelms. "A lot of guys wouldn't fair catch because they cared about their average. I never cared. I just wanted to do what I could to get the ball closer to the goal line."

In an important home game against the Patriots, Nelms showed the 50,000 fans at RFK stadium what he meant. The Redskins had lost their first five games under Gibbs. They were 1-6 when they faced New England. Washington needed a win badly, and when a team is desperate for a win, the spark sometimes comes from a big play.

"I was back to catch a punt when I saw this guy coming at me," says Nelms. "He had his ears pinned back. As soon as I caught it I knew he was going to blast me. Of course, I didn't think about fair-catching. My concern was he was so close I didn't have room to maneuver. So the moment I fielded the punt, I ducked my head and he slammed into me like a train. I had fielded so many punts I turned my head and let his momentum sling him off. Then, I went straight at everyone and kind of cornered a few guys. Then I hopped and skipped through and popped clean."

The result was a 71-yard blur that defied logic. "I got a TD on that one," laughs Nelms.

Best of all, the Redskins won the nail-biter 24-22, the first of a four-game winning streak. Because of Nelms' superior play, Washington went 8-3 the remainder of the season. Nelms was named All-Pro. But it bothered him that he was the only Redskin selected to the Pro Bowl. As the 1982 season approached, the best was yet to come.

THE MAGICAL SEASON

By the time he was in his third NFL season, Nelms was one of the most recognizable names on the Redskins. But Nelms was never about recognition. He was too busy saving his money and trying to get better. He wanted the team to enjoy the same accolades that he was getting.

"It was strange being at the Pro Bowl by myself," says Nelms. "Joe Montana was there, Tony Dorsett, James Lofton, and Lawrence Taylor. But I would have rather had my teammates sharing it with me."

Nelms got his wish in 1982. Despite a strike-shortened season, the Redskins went 8-1 and held the top seed in an eight-team playoff tournament. Nelms delivered with 32 punt returns for 252 yards, and 23 kicks for 557 yards. Again, he was named to the Pro Bowl team. But this time there were more Redskins: former Canadian star Joe Theismann and receiver Charlie Brown. Strangely, no offensive linemen made it.

"The Pro Bowl was great, but I wanted to win," says Nelms. "I wanted to make plays for my team when it counted." As Nelms looks back on the '82 season, he couldn't have picked a more important or ironic game to do it in.

GAME OF MY LIFE
BY MIKE NELMS

The long return I had against the Dallas Cowboys in the NFC Championship game is one that I'll never forget.

It was a crazy, intense game. They scored early with a long drive and a field goal. Then we came back with a touchdown. By halftime it was 14-3. Then, like the Cowboys always do, they came back. Gary Hogeboom came in and drove the team all the way down the field for a touchdown. Now it was 14-10.

As I stood back to receive the kickoff, the crowd started cheering and encouraging all of us. At this point, I was pumped full of adrenaline. I took the ball and went straight up through them for 76 yards. I took it back deep into Cowboys territory to the 20. I didn't score, but that play took the wind out of their sails. The best thing was, we won the game, went to the Super Bowl, and became world champions.

But when I think of that game, I realize it taught me a lot of things outside the game of football. Mostly what it taught me was not to judge someone by what you hear. Growing up, I heard things about the way the Cowboys treated players that I didn't like. Because of that I didn't always see Coach Landry in a positive light. I watched him with that stony exterior and that fedora hat on the sidelines, his arms folded and that stern expression, and I formed opinions about him.

Well, after we won the Super Bowl, I was at the Pro Bowl and, as usual, the coaches are from the losing conference championship team. Tom Landry was my coach!

I was in the locker room getting dressed, and Landry was on the other side and looked over at me. He got up and started walking toward me. I was sitting on the bench by myself. I saw him, then looked to my right and my left, and thought, "Why is he coming over here?"

He said, "Hi Mike, how are you doing?" Before I could say anything, he sat down next to me and we started having a conversation. He told me he always appreciated me, and the way I ran the ball. He congratulated me—and the Redskins in general—on the Super Bowl win and for having such a great year. Then he told me that he thought the turning point of that game had been my kick return. We talked some more and by the time the conversation was over and he'd left, I felt shocked. I met him a few times after that, at Baylor and at other events. He was the same gracious, personable man each time. The opinions I had about him before had been wrong. He was a warm, welcoming guy.

When I think about that return, I think about Tom Landry more than what that kick did to change that game. I saw *North Dallas Forty*—that's not the guy I knew. I never played for him, only against him, but from my experience with him, I have no stones to throw.

THE ULTIMATE DREAM

In the Super Bowl, Nelms stepped up again. He returned six punts for 52 yards and two kickoffs for 44 yards. When he retired two years later, he had become one of the most prolific return men in NFL history, with 175 kickoffs for 4,128 yards and 212 punt returns for 1,948 yards and two touchdowns. He also intercepted a pass in one of the few opportunities he got to play defensive back.

But for Nelms, the big picture wasn't about becoming an NFL star, it was about becoming a success in life. He found it in the automobile business.

"I got into the General Motors dealers academy and trained to own and operate a dealership," says Nelms. After for years of training, Nelms bought a Chevrolet-Toyota dealership in Culpepper, Virginia, and named it, "Mike Nelms Champion Chevrolet Toyota."

Nelms took all the life lessons he had learned on the football field and applied them to his business. He also never lost sight of the most important thing: family. He and his wife, Michele, have four children, three girls and a boy. All of them play sports. His oldest daughter ran track at University of North Carolina and now works for ESPN. Another plays basketball for a small school, and the other goes to Columbia. His son is in high school.

Nelms still keeps in touch with former teammates Doc Walker, Art Monk and, especially, one of his closest friends, Joe Washington, one of his heroes growing up.

"Joe is cool people. In my mind he was a legend," says Nelms. "When I was at Baylor and my brother played for Oklahoma State, I saw a game and noticed that Joe taped his ankles up real high. So I thought I'd do the same. Man, I couldn't wait to tell him. Talk about pain and discomfort. All the way up to my calves. I don't know how he ran with all that tape. But he was tremendous. He ran back a kick one time against OSU and he caught it and started walking. It caught everyone by surprise, they misjudged him and he was gone."

Even though he accomplished so much in just five NFL seasons, Nelms doesn't like to dwell on the past. He was named to the 1980 All-Decade Team, and a few years ago he was named one of the 70 Greatest Redskins. For Nelms, the thought of attaining so many honors after being challenged throughout the course of his life is a bit overwhelming.

"I try not to think about those things too much," says Nelms, as humble as ever. "You do and you stop walking on the ground. You start floating. I prefer to keep both feet on the ground."

Chapter 16

JOE
WASHINGTON

Joe Washington was born to go the distance. The broad borders of his home state of Texas weren't big enough to hold him back, even though he was just 5-foot-10 and175 pounds. During his distinguished career, no one lit up the scoreboard quite like Joe Dan Washington, Jr.

After burning up the high school fields in Texas, he bolted across the state line to play at Oklahoma and rushed them to back-to-back national championships. He raced into the NFL as the first-round pick of the San Diego Chargers. There, he got sidetracked with a phantom knee injury. Then it was on to the Baltimore Colts, where he electrified a national audience in one of the most memorable Monday Night performances of all time. Next, he took his incredible talents to the Washington Redskins, where he helped catapult the team to national prominence with two Super Bowls. Finally, he would end his career in Atlanta, just as the number of devastating knee injuries began to match his number of runs.

Joe Washington was born September 24, 1953, in Crockett, Texas. Soon after, the Washington family moved four and a half hours south to Bay City, Texas, near Houston. They lived there until young Joe was in the fifth grade, then settled east of Houston in Port Arthur, home to other famous Texans like former Cowboys coach Jimmy Johnson and legendary rock singer Janis Joplin.

For Washington, the boundless fields of Texas meant an endless playground for him and his brother and sister. "My dad, Joe Sr., was my high school football coach and [school] athletic director," says Washington. "So for my brother, Kenneth, and sister, Pat, it was like living in a candy store."

Because they personally knew the coach, the Washington kids had access to all the sporting facilities. "Up until I was in the fifth grade, my dad even operated the swimming pool during the summer. You couldn't beat it. Get up, have three squares, play all day."

At Lincoln High School, the Washingtons gave opponents double vision. With his sophomore brother at quarterback and him playing tailback, the duo was easy to identify and impossible to stop.

"The funny thing is, as good as we were, I think my sister was the better athlete," he says. "She was 5-foot-9 and faster than you can imagine."

Even with his slight build, Washington dominated the high school competition. Not just in football, but in baseball and basketball as well. Like most Texas kids, Washington's dream was to play for the Texas Longhorns in Austin. Being recruited by countless schools meant Washington had his pick.

"Texas is where I wanted to play," he says, "but I ended up crossing the border to play at Oklahoma University." To say Texas and OU are rivals is like saying the Dallas Cowboys and Washington Redskins don't see eye to eye. Why choose the bitter enemy? The Washingtons were close to a high school football coach named Wendell Mosley, who'd just become the backfield coach at Oklahoma.

"I knew Wendell Mosley ever since I was a kid," says Washington. "Being a coach's son I had been through the southwest conference and met most of the coaches through my dad. The thing about playing in

During Joe Gibbs' first era, the Redskins' running game always got a jolt of lightning whenever **Joe Washington** was in the game. His combination of speed, moves, and pass-catching abilities made him one of the NFL's most dangerous playmakers. *Ronald C. Modra/Sports Imagery/Getty Images*

Texas is you ride a bus to all weekend games. I wanted to travel a little bit. Oklahoma allowed me to fly to some games, which was a thrill."

Oklahoma's head coach during Washington's freshman season was Chuck Fairbanks, who would leave for the NFL after Washington's sophomore year to coach the New England Patriots. But along with Mosley, the person that most influenced Washington was senior running back Greg Pruitt.

Washington quickly identified with the small, fleet-footed All-American. At 5-foot-10 and 190 pounds, Pruitt rushed through opponents out of the Wishbone offense better than any back before him. Despite his size, he finished second in the 1972 Heisman race and went on to play 12 seasons in the NFL with the Cleveland Browns and Los Angeles Raiders. Washington was all that wrapped, incredibly, in an even smaller package.

As Pruitt began lighting up the NFL, Washington showed he was more than an able replacement. After rushing for 630 yards as a freshman, Washington scorched the Big 8 his sophomore year with 1,173 yards. Unfortunately for Nebraska, Colorado, and the rest of the conference, he was just getting started. He exploded his junior year with 1,321 yards, plus another 512 yards in kick returns, and 14 touchdowns. He was the clear difference maker in the Sooners powerful offense. Against Colorado, Washington carried the ball just 19 times—but that was good for 211 yards and four touchdowns. He was everybody's All-American and finished third in the Heisman. But beyond all the accolades, the most important thing for Washington was Oklahoma's undefeated season and their first national championship since 1956.

The next year, Washington's final season, the Sooners won their second consecutive national title. "We had an unbelievable team," says Washington. "We lost just two games my entire college career, one as a freshman and one as a senior. But the biggest thrill was being a part of those back-to-back national championships in '74 and '75."

Just as Pruitt had passed the torch to Washington, Washington had motivated the next class of stars: Elvis Peacock, Horace Ivory, Kenny King, and future Heisman winner Billy Sims.

"Playing running back in the wishbone at Oklahoma was a glamour position," says Washington. "I think people could relate to me because I wasn't the biggest guy out there."

CHARGED UP

The impact of Oklahoma's back-to-back national championships lasted all the way to the 1976 NFL Draft, as three Sooners were among the first 15 players chosen.

"That just showed you how great our team was, to see so many Sooners going in the first round," says Washington, who was selected fourth overall by the San Diego Chargers. Playing in the tough AFC West, Washington was excited to go up against some of the best defenses in the league—Oakland, Denver, and Kansas City.

Tragically, Washington never got the chance his rookie season. Playing for charismatic Chargers coach Tommy Prothro and an offensive coordinator named Bill Walsh, Washington was eager to show his versatility. So he volunteered to return kicks during the preseason. His first time was against the Patriots and his former college coach, Chuck Fairbanks. In a flash, with no one around, Washington tore up his knee in what he describes as the "phantom tackle."

"I never missed a game in college due to an injury," says Washington. "Then I get to the pros and I'm returning a kickoff, and both my inside and outside cartilage goes. No one touched me. It was a phantom sniper in the 85th row."

Doctors only repaired Washington's inside cartilage. Apparently, they did not notice that the outside cartilage had been damaged as well. Not wanting to waste his rookie season, Washington rehabbed vigorously to return from surgery in six weeks. "Even when I came back from surgery after six weeks, I knew something was wrong," says Washington, who couldn't cut like he had before.

Washington believes the outer injury was a previous one and that's why the doctors had missed it. "I think part of my outside injury was an older injury from college that went undetected," he says. "Because of the tissue tear and the blood on the inside area, they didn't check outside."

It would be a whole year until Washington got a chance to show why he was a Top 5 pick. Playing behind starter Don Woods, and splitting time with rookie Clarence Williams, Washington showed his versatility whenever he got a chance. Playing mostly on third down, and carrying the ball just 62 times all season, Washington rushed for over 200 yards. And his 31 receptions for another 244 yards were third on the team.

"I thought I made a good impression [on the Chargers]," says Washington, who continued to return kicks. "I didn't get to play much, but felt like the NFL game was made for me."

TRADE WINDS

Even with limited playing time, Washington made more of an impression on the rest of the NFL than he'd imagined. Right before the 1978 season began, Baltimore Colts coach Ted Marchibroda shipped Pro Bowl running back Lydell Mitchell to the Chargers for the young playmaker.

After being shut out and embarrassed in an opening-day loss to the Dallas Cowboys, 38-0, then again the following week to the Dolphins, 42-0, the Colts faced the New England Patriots on *Monday Night Football*.

In a deluge of rain that hasn't been seen in the NFL since, Washington defied the flooded conditions and slippery Astroturf of old Foxboro Stadium to register one of the most talked about performances in *Monday Night Football* history.

Down by more than two touchdowns in the fourth quarter, Washington threw for a touchdown and caught a touchdown pass. Then, after the Patriots suddenly scored to tie the game with seconds left, Washington fielded the final kickoff amidst the river of wetness and zigzagged his way 90-plus yards for the winning score—all while swirling winds and hurricane-like conditions slammed the field.

When it was all over, the drenched, stunned crowd poured themselves into their vehicles as they tried to comprehend the 34-27 loss, and the Sayers-like explosiveness of this 5-foot-10, 175-pound missile.

"The thing I remember about that game was that all my scoring was done in the fourth quarter," says Washington. "That kickoff return gave me the perfect setting to show people what a 175-pound guy could do if given the chance. I loved playing for Coach Marchibroda. He didn't care that I wasn't 6-foot-1, 200 pounds. He knew what I could do and gave me a chance."

Washington made the most of his opportunities. In '78 he nearly eclipsed 1,000 yards rushing by pounding the ball 240 times for 956 yards. He also caught 45 passes for 377 yards, and returned punts and kickoffs for another 536 yards.

Washington had his best NFL season production-wise in 1979; he was a one-man show in Baltimore. Despite missing a couple games due to injuries, he rushed for 884 yards and led the NFL with 82 receptions—more than any wide receiver—for another 750 yards. He also scored seven touchdowns. For his efforts, Washington was named to his first Pro Bowl.

Washington wasn't just a dual threat. He was a threat every time he touched the ball. "I guess that's how the game has changed," he says. "You've got guys who run the ball and when it's a passing down, you put in someone who's a receiver. Since I could do that, they didn't need to substitute me."

In 1980, due to recurring knee problems, Washington began splitting carries with rookie first-round pick Curtis Dickey, a prototypical tailback at 6-foot-1, 215 pounds from Texas A&M. Washington still managed to put up nearly 1,000 yards from scrimmage and register four touchdowns.

Although the two backs complemented each other, Washington wasn't happy. He wanted to be a full-time starter and knew if he could just get past his knee problems, he could continue to prove his worth. He got his wish on draft day 1981, when Marchibroda traded Washington to the Redskins.

WASHINGTON CALLING WASHINGTON

April 1981 was a defining time for the Washington Redskins. The firing of Redskins coach Jack Pardee following the 1980 season marked the first time GM Bobby Beathard and Joe Gibbs would sift through the more than 300 pro prospects to compile their draft wish list. What came out of the meeting marked the foundation for three future Super Bowl teams.

While the '81 draft yielded the likes of Mark May, Russ Grimm, Dexter Manley, Larry Kubin, Charlie Brown, Darryl Grant, and Clint Didier, the team also secured free agent tackle, Joe Jacoby. But perhaps the biggest steal was getting one of the NFL's most talented playmakers.

"That first year was exciting," says Washington. "John [Riggins] had sat out the year before under Pardee, and had come back to play for Gibbs. I got hurt the second play of the second game against the Giants. After the 0-5 start, I got healthy and we got things turned around and finished 8-8. We jelled as a team and even though I missed some games, I was able to put up some good numbers."

Washington's use of the word "good" is a big understatement. In his first season with the Skins, the former Colt bolted for 916 yards rushing with four touchdowns and a 4.4 average. He caught 70 passes for 558 yards and another three scores. He was the only back to be among the top 15 in rushing and receiving. When Washington wasn't in the game, Riggins added to the assault with 714 yards.

"I had gone from starting on the Colts to starting for the Redskins," says Washington. "I showed that despite my size, I could be an every-down back who could run, catch, block, and throw the half-back option."

Eager to duplicate his feats in '82, Washington was instead sidelined for most of the season with more knee injuries.

"Once again, no one touched me," he says, still frustrated by the setback all these years later. Washington suffered a torn ACL, meniscus, and more cartilage damage. When the Redskins got into the playoffs, Washington tried to come back. He carried the ball just four times and caught three passes during the Redskins' playoff wins over Detroit, Minnesota, and Dallas.

Frustrated with his bashed-up knees, Washington decided not to suit up for the biggest game of his pro career. When Super Bowl XVII kicked off on January 30, 1983, Little Joe was standing with his team on the sidelines in street clothes.

"I thought I could play, but the knee wouldn't respond," says Washington. "For me, I knew I couldn't go out and perform the way I was accustomed to and I didn't want to be a detriment to the team."

Washington's selfless act no doubt added to the bright luster of the Redskins' first Lombardi Trophy. Despite the numerous injuries and setbacks, Washington was even more determined to help the Redskins return to another Super Bowl. At 30 years old, Washington felt the upcoming 1983 season was the perfect opportunity to show his incredible resiliency and endless talent.

GAME OF MY LIFE
BY JOE WASHINGTON

That whole 1983 season is really memorable for me because of what I had to do just to get back on the field. I'd had three knee surgeries the year before. That's got to be some kind of record. Naturally, because of my injuries, John Riggins had become the starter. I wasn't happy with that, but I've always been a team player, and I certainly wasn't going to jump off a bridge because of it.

When the Los Angeles Raiders came to town, they were one of the AFC's top teams. We were 3-1 at that point and we knew it was going to be tough. It was one of those sweltering days in D.C., too, the first week of October. Plus, we had scored at least 20 points or more in each game, so we knew the game was going to be exciting.

I had started the season well with a couple 100-yard games, and I was ready to play. The Raiders game was special because I was able to help bring us back from the brink. We were down 17 points in the fourth quarter and they decided, in order to put more points on the board, they were going to sit John and let me do my thing.

What was really exciting about it was that my friend Greg Pruitt was playing on the other side. He had been in the league since 1973 and was still doing it all—running, receiving, returning kicks. We were up 17-7 at halftime, and I thought we were in good shape.

Then all of a sudden Jim Plunkett started throwing touchdown passes. We had a decent drive going and when it stalled, we thought we'd punt it and put them deep in their territory. Well Greg, at age 32, was back to return the punt and fielded it at his 3-yard line. Unbelievably, he returned it 97 yards for a touchdown. Now, we're down 35-20 with only five or six minutes left.

You always want to play well going against your buddies. So I got my chance to show what the other Oklahoma back could do on the next series. Joe Theismann tossed me a screen pass on the right side, and I just started speeding down the sideline. I got a great block from Jeff Bostic and bolted for 70 yards. Charlie Brown scored a few plays later and we were down 35-27.

We got the onside kick and turned that into three points, 35-30. Now there was hardly any time left, maybe a minute or two, and our defense came up big. They stopped the Raiders and we got it back. Theismann threw passes to me and Charlie Brown and suddenly we were at the Raiders six-yard line with just 33 seconds left.

Coach Gibbs called a play where I was the lone guy in the backfield and I was lined up behind the left tackle. The Raiders were in a man-to-man defense. I truly believe everyone in the stadium knew I was going to get the ball. They knew our plays, our tendencies down in that area. I had done it hundreds of times. I was going against Raiders linebacker Rod Martin.

When the ball was snapped, Rod tried to chuck me, but I slid off and ducked inside. Despite breaking off him, his coverage was tight and Joe lobbed me the ball. I know I must have stretched my arms out to grab it, but I just remember catching the ball.

Once we scored, pandemonium broke out. RFK was such an intimate setting with all those seats so close to the field. And when we won that game 37-35, the whole place shook. The Raiders needed a miracle to win, but they were too exasperated. It was one of the most intense, hard-fought, exciting games I'd ever been in.

I had a lot of injuries in my career, but coming back to play well during the 1983 season and especially that Raiders game is a moment I'll never forget.

STILL GOING THE DISTANCE

Even with more knee injuries than Joe Namath and Gale Sayers combined, Washington would come back from those three off-season surgeries to finish the 1983 season with 772 yards rushing and a blistering 5.3 average. He also snagged 47 passes for 454 yards and six touchdowns.

"I wasn't the same player I was before, but I don't think the fans could tell," says Washington. "I had a good season, but I got banged up as the playoffs approached and wasn't close to being 100 percent."

Washington did, however, get to play in his first Super Bowl, although not enough to make an impact. In the 38-9 drubbing by the Raiders, Washington carried the ball just three times and caught three passes.

During the 1984 season, his ninth, Washington was only healthy enough to play in seven games. In '85, his 10th season in the NFL, Joe signed with the Falcons and registered 538 yards from scrimmage.

"At that point, I'd had so many knee injuries and surgeries I knew the old grey mare wasn't what she used to be, so I retired," says Washington.

Even though he played just four seasons with the Redskins, Washington's impact was immeasurable. In 2002, he was named one of the 70 Greatest Redskins.

"Looking back now, my time was short on the Redskins, so to be voted as one of the 70 Greatest Redskins was really a great honor, probably more of an honor than any game I've played."

Even with all the setbacks, Washington has no regrets. "Who knows what I could have done without all the injuries," he says. "I feel pretty good about my career. I proved I could be an every-down back. That one season I carried the ball 240 times. That was a full load for a 175-pound back. I never got a thousand yards, but I didn't get the carries that a lot of those 1,000-yard rushers get. But not too many of them caught the ball as much as I did. I had 18 receiving touchdowns. And I even tossed three TD passes," he says with a laugh.

Today Washington is a stockbroker with Wachovia Securities and lives in Maryland. He and his wife, Meadow Lark, his high school sweetheart, have been married "for 50 wonderful years" and have a daughter, Brandy, who recently graduated from the University of Pennsylvania.

"I still see a lot of the guys from time to time," he says. "Doc [Walker] and I are good buddies, and no one comes any better than another good friend, Mike Nelms." He also stays in touch with Art Monk, George Starke, and long-time trainer Bubba Tyer.

Washington also hasn't forgotten the Redskins fans. He does autograph shows whenever he can, especially when his good friend Nelms is on the docket. Also, he runs a football camp during the summer to help kids improve their speed and quickness.

"I enjoy doing it to help kids and it keeps me in shape. Plus, sometimes fans might hear me on the *John Thompson Show*," he says. "Doc will call me up and ask me on the show. It's fun talking about the Redskins and all the good times we had."

Especially the times when the hosts bring up the legendary exploits of the little big man, Joe Washington.

Chapter 17

DEXTER MANLEY

During the 1980s, no one rushed the quarterback better than Dexter Manley. You can throw in Lawrence Taylor's name if you want, but how often was he one on one with a big offensive tackle? Manley put the thrill back into watching two giant linemen sparring to get the sack.

"There's no question that there was no one in the NFL more talented than I was," says Manley today, a year after surviving a 10.5 hour brain surgery to remove a colloid cyst, the result, he says, from his NFL days. "There were players more versatile, like Reggie White. But no one could rush the passer better than me. Not one soul."

The man has a point. Not including his rookie year in 1981 before the NFL started keeping official stats on sacks, Manley notched an incredible 64.5 sacks from 1982-86. Taylor, the more publicized sack master, recorded 61.5 during that time. Manley finished his career with 97.5 sacks, most of them during a seven-year stretch.

Manley relishes thinking back to his NFL days. They were happy times and he was one of the league's top defensive players on one of the league's best teams. But that was a long time ago. Manley knows it. For him, every day is a fight to stay clean from alcohol and drugs.

He says it started innocently enough. "It was a regular-season game. I wasn't sad or depressed like some people might think. It was the opposite," says Manley. "I was celebrating. We were winning and I was just enjoying being in the league."

Just 25 years old at the time, Manley had no idea the power of booze and drugs. "You can't compete with drugs and alcohol because they work," says Manley. "I had no idea what I had gotten myself into—I felt powerless to stop it."

Manley continued to use drugs and alcohol and watched his promising career go from leading the NFL with 18.5 sacks in 1986, to 8.5 during the strike-shortened '87 season, and nine sacks in both '88 and '89. Still impressive, but not close to what he was before.

In 1989, he failed a drug test and the NFL suspended him. Feeling his life begin to slide, he felt the need to come to terms with some of his innermost secrets, including the fact that he was functionally illiterate. According to Manley, he decided to confess his problems and his illiteracy to a woman while on an airline flight. Little did he know that she was a reporter for *USA Today*.

"I've never told anyone this," says Manley about coming forward about his illiteracy, "I was running from the National Football League because I had a urinalysis [I needed to do]. I was working for home-team sports, which covers the Orioles, and I'd been invited to spring training. So I was on a plane flying down there and felt depressed and bad morally. This was when George Bush Sr. was running for president . . . at the time, the talk was about banning Pete Rose from baseball. There was so much turmoil in sports. I was feeling remorseful. I just felt compelled to stop wearing the Boy George makeup and tell people who I was.

"The next day, I see this huge headline saying I'm functionally illiterate. Then all of a sudden, people asked me to come forward." Manley eventually went before congress to admit it. He began being

---

Dexter Manley typified the passion and talent of the Redskins' swarming defense in the '80s. Although off-the-field problems curtailed a possible Hall of Fame career, Manley was arguably the best pass-rushing defensive end of his era. He retired with 97.5 sacks. *Focus on Sport/Getty Images*

tutored and a short time later he was reading and writing at a tenth grade level. It was a small victory in a sea of problems.

The next year, the Redskins dropped him from the team. He played a year with the Arizona Cardinals and the Tampa Bay Buccaneers before failing a second drug test in 1991.

Manley then played in Canada for two years before his world collapsed. From November 1994 to July 1995, Manley was arrested four times for possession of crack cocaine. Even though they were small quantities, he served 15 months of a four-year sentence. He was paroled in 1996 and appeared to have turned his life around, until he was busted in 2001 for cocaine, caught while trying to swallow it. He was charged with evidence tampering and served two more years before being released in March 2004.

HOUSTON, WE HAVE A PASS RUSHER

Manley's life didn't begin in such a whirlwind. Born in Houston, Texas, on February 2, 1959, he was the youngest of four kids born to Carl and Jewellean Manley. His parents were hardworking and stern, but not overly strict.

"My father worked for an oil company, and my mother was a nurse's aid at a hospital. They provided a steady income growing up, but the community itself was dysfunctional," says Manley.

Manley lived in a section of Houston, he says, where a lot of bad things were going on. "Many were underprivileged and disenfranchised," he says. "Luckily, my parents instilled in me good intrinsic values. That carried me a long way. I may have grown up functionally illiterate, but having good intrinsic value helped me build that bridge."

A terrific career at Jake Yates High School led him all the way to Oklahoma State. But shortly before leaving for college his mother passed away, leaving the young man to make the journey with a heavy heart in the summer of 1977.

It was a tough time. Luckily his first coach at Oklahoma State was Jim Stanley, a tough but compassionate coach that Manley says was in the mode of Paul Bear Bryant.

"Jim cared about me and I cared about his family. He was a beautiful guy," recalls Manley. His next coach went by the name of Jimmy, as in Jimmy Johnson; long before he coached the Dallas Cowboys, Johnson coached the other Cowboys at OSU.

"He was a great motivator, a great recruiter, and a great defensive coach," says Manley. "He knew how to pick talent and players. That's what I liked about Jimmy Johnson."

Johnson, who is known for treating players differently, always pushing their buttons, decided to motivate Manley with reverse psychology.

"Jimmy Johnson told me I wasn't going to do anything," says Manley. "But I didn't take it as a negative. It motivated me. It made me work harder and become the player I was and it's motivated me now. People usually don't tell you what you're not going to do. So I just flipped the switch. I didn't get down on myself or fall back on the race card. It motivated me."

By his senior year, NFL teams knew all about the 6-foot-3, 253-pound defensive end with the powerful legs and lightening-quick moves. Manley says any misgivings about his ability had to do with character issues he suffered while at OSU. He had been on probation.

He was passed over by every team for four rounds before the Redskins nabbed him in the fifth as the 119th player selected. The 1981 draft would become one of Washington's all-time greatest drafts. They chose tackle Mark May in the first round, guard Russ Grimm in the second, Manley in the fifth, receiver Charlie Brown in the eighth, defensive tackle Charles Grant in the ninth, and tight end Clint Didier in the 12th and final round.

MR. MANLEY COMES TO WASHINGTON

On the surface you probably couldn't pick two guys more different than these two rookies, first-year pro Dexter Manley and first-year head coach Joe Gibbs.

Gibbs was quiet, studious, and, in the words of Joe Theismann, "almost nerd-like" in his mannerisms. Manley was loud, boisterous, and loved having a good time. But on the field both Gibbs and Manley were intense, competitive, and difficult to beat.

Manley sees it this way: "You know how Steelers great Mean Joe Greene came in with Chuck Knoll when he was in his first year with Pittsburgh? That's what it was like with Coach Gibbs and me. There's no question that he is one of the great NFL heroes. I was fortunate to be there with him from the beginning. I am grateful to him and GM Bobby Beathard. They both believed in me. We had some great times and some challenging times."

In the beginning, the great times outnumbered the bad. Even though the Giants had drafted Taylor, big defensive end Leonard Mitchell had gone to the Eagles, and the Cowboys nabbed pass rusher Glen Titensor in the third round from Brigham Young, the Redskins felt like they got a steal with Manley.

"When I got to the Redskins, I kept remembering what Jimmy Johnson had said to motivate me: that I wasn't going to amount to anything. I knew what he was doing, but I just wanted to prove everyone wrong. I was hungry and ready to work when my plane arrived at Dulles."

The first season Manley started in nine games, but he began the season watching and learning from the great Coy Bacon. By the second year, in 1982, Manley was fully entrenched as the starter at right end. In a strike-shortened season, the Redskins went 8-1. Due to an expanded playoff forum, they had to win three playoff games to get to Super Bowl XVII. They did so with a combined 83-21 over the Lions, Vikings, and Cowboys.

Over 103,000 fans packed themselves in the most awe-inspiring stadium of them all—the Rose Bowl in Pasadena on January 30, 1983— to watch the Redskins battle the Miami Dolphins. In the words of Yogi Berra, it was déjà vu all over again; the two teams met 10 years earlier in Super Bowl VII, also in Los Angeles.

The Dolphins, three-point favorites, held a 7-0 lead early in the game with a 76-yard touchdown bomb from Miami quarterback David Woodley to receiver Jimmy Cefalo. When they got the ball back after a Redskins punt, Dexter Manley showed the millions watching why he was the league's most talented young defensive end. While Woodley took a deep drop and tried to repeat the play, Manley crushed Woodley and caused a fumble. Redskins defensive tackle Dave Butz recovered and Washington narrowed the score, 7-3.

"It was great to make a major contribution during that Super Bowl," says Manley. "They say defense wins championships and we had a heck of a defense."

Woodley and the Dolphins sure thought so. The young quarterback completed only four of 14 attempts in the game. Thanks to constant pressure from blitzes and a ferocious front four led by Manley, Butz, Mat Mendenhall, and Darryl Grant, Woodley missed his last eight passes in the second half. Then he was replaced by veteran Don Strock, who went 0 for 3.

After that game, the team enjoyed a huge party in Los Angeles. The Redskins PR department told Manley that NBC wanted him on the *TODAY* show. "They were going to pick me up at 3 a.m.," says Manley, who was scheduled to appear on CBS before that. "We were in Costa Mesa, and this limousine comes and picks up Joe Jacoby and me and we took a helicopter from CBS to NBC at 3 in the morning. It was the first time I really thought, 'Hey, I'm somebody.'"

Once Manley went to his first Super Bowl, he wanted to go every year. "Once you get a taste of that first one, it's all you think about as a player," he says. "The next year we had a great team, but we lost to the Raiders. Then a couple years later we played the Broncos. I remember no one really gave us a chance in that game. Everyone thought John Elway was going to be the great white hope. They forgot they had Dexter Manley on defense and a lot of other great players too. Dave Butz, Darryl Grant, Charles Mann. Defenses win championships, and that's what we had."

GAME OF MY LIFE
BY DEXTER MANLEY

There's not one game that really stands out, as *The Game*. I enjoyed them all, and even though the championships were special, being a part of the Redskins organization meant the most. So for me, sacking the quarterback was *The Game*.

I liked to sack all of the QBs, especially the ones in our division. They all presented their share of challenges. Randall Cunningham was probably the toughest to sack, because he ran around so much. You had to put on track shoes. I found out in the Super Bowl that Elway was tough. People forget, but even Joe Montana could run when he first came into the league. Doug Williams was pretty fast, too. Luckily, he was on my team. But I didn't have a problem getting any quarterback because I always had the desire.

To be a great pass rusher, you have to study the game and the opponents. The key is having the ability to do a couple things. A lot of players are one-dimensional. They have speed, but no power. You have to have speed and power to beat the guy in front of you. Then you need the muscles to get over him and run around him, and the power to get the quarterback. That's what I had. I had the speed and the power. I could go inside or outside. I could run around the corner, or set them up on the outside and just run them over.

And, of course, there were some great linemen standing in my way. I'd say the greatest run blocker and pass blocker was Bears tackle Jimbo Covert. He was outstanding. So was Minnesota tackle Gary Zimmerman. But the best pass protector in the league was a guy who was overlooked, I think: Luis Sharpe of the Cardinals. He was tough, strong, and quick.

Mike Kenn of Atlanta was solid, too. Those guys were kind of light, but good on their feet. But I could work them. They were kind of light in the britches so I could run right over them.

The toughest quarterback, without questions, was Phil Simms. He could take a lick and was physically strong. You could hit him hard and he would get right back up, come back and do it again. But there were also some players who quit on you. I won't mention their names, but let's just say their hearts pump piss.

Another tough guy I played was Jim Kelly. It was in 1987 and we beat them 27-7. I don't know how many sacks I had, but I beat the crap out of Kelly.

I never felt like I got the recognition I deserved. I should have made the Pro Bowl more than one time (1986). The first four years when they started charting sacks, I had more sacks than anyone in the league. I was the premier pass rusher from 1982-1986 and was voted to just one Pro Bowl. When you look at all my sacks during that period and see how my performance along with the great performance of our entire defense contributed to the overall success of the team with two world championships, I should have gotten more recognition.

STILL FIGHTING THE TOUGH FIGHT

Perhaps no Redskins player signifies the resiliency of life's everyday struggles more than Dexter Manley. After his playing days were over and his well-publicized battles with drugs and alcohol became a sad epilogue to his outstanding career, he recently faced another battle.

Just two years after serving time, Manley was hospitalized on June 16, 2006, with an enlarged colloid cyst that he says he had been aware of since doctors found it in 1986.

"Back then, doctors told me it was too small and there was no growth to it at the time," Manley says. "But after a while it began to grow and block some ventricles in the brain. If fluids backed up you could die because the brain swells. Over the years, I realized it was getting worse. I found myself unconscious driving my car. When it happened in June, I talked to someone who called 9-1-1 and I went to the hospital. Then I was taken to Georgetown hospital and it was emergency surgery."

Manley endured 10 and a half hours of surgery and pulled through. But to his amazement, the miracle was the outpouring of good wishes from Redskins fans.

"The Redskins asked my wife, Lydia, to give them an email address and we got over 10,000 emails," he says. "It's not what a person has to go through to overcome something. It's what he's got inside. I've gone through the rain, the wind, and the storm. I've had a lot of obstacles. But I kept getting up, wouldn't quit. It's all of God's grace and mercy that I'm talking to you right now. I've been able to stay sober and clean. That's what's really important."

Today Manley works for First Guardian Mortgage in Gaithersburg, Maryland, as as a business development manager. He also developed a foundation, Dexter's Team, a non-profit organization with a four-fold purpose: to support drug and substance abuse prevention, encourage recovery, promote literacy, and facilitate parent education. He's also launched his own website: www.dextermanley.com.

Manley still keeps his mind in the game of football, too. His son, Dexter Jr., was scheduled to begin his senior season at the University of Oregon. "He's one of the best pass rushers in the country," Dexter Sr. says proudly. He also has another son, Derek, and a daughter, Dalis. But the person who he says has been with him through all the toughest times is his wife, Lydia.

"We've been together 19 years and been married nine. She's hung in there with me and I've hung in there with her," he says. "The good thing is, Lydia is lucky to have me. But I'm very fortunate, too. Most women would run out on a man like me."

Says Lydia: "I have no tears for yesterday, no fears for tomorrow. I'm just full of gratitude and glory for today."

In addition to his new life, Manley plans to do more public speaking to inspire youth who have been sidetracked. "Three things are going to happen with addiction: recovery, insanity, or death. Those three things are guaranteed. You're going to recover, go insane, or die. And I wanted to live.

"The thing is, despite some broken dreams, it's still a beautiful world. I can be cheerful; I can start to be happy. The low point is because of my ignorance. I didn't know anything about drugs. I didn't start using drugs until I was 25 years old. It took me to a place I didn't want to go. I didn't realize, in my stupidity, that I lost control. I was powerless. Now, I'm back."

Chapter 18

LEN
HAUSS

As a former offensive lineman, Len Hauss has always looked at football games from a different perspective than the average fan or the well-intentioned sportswriter. When asked to recall the game of his life, the former Pro Bowl center can't help but chuckle.

"I was an offensive lineman," he clarifies, still laughing. "For any fan or media person to think, 'Gosh, that game Len Hauss had was wonderful'—I mean, my greatest days were Sonny's or Billy's greatest games, or Larry Brown's and Charley Taylor's. I was a part of that. For an offensive lineman to say he had a great day against the Broncos—I don't know how you say that."

Even when he's watching NFL games today, Hauss sees the game a little differently than most people. "I've been watching the Colts offense with Peyton Manning, and that guy is just incredible." Most people would assume he's talking about Manning, but Hauss goes on to clarify. "Sure Manning is a great quarterback, but I'm talking about the other guy, their center, Jeff Saturday. I think he's the best center in the league."

Saturday was only two years old when Hauss finished his 14-year Pro Bowl career in 1977. But if Saturday had ever seen the 6-foot-2, 235-pound center play, he would have been equally impressed.

Born July 11, 1942, in Jesup, Georgia, a small town just south of Savannah, Hauss and his sister grew up understanding the value of hard work, honesty, and never thinking you're too big for your britches. "My parents were Leonard and Ida," he says. "Dad was a signal maintainer on the Atlantic Coast Railroad. Both of them worked extremely hard. I enjoyed living in a small town and still do. In fact, Jesup is where I live today."

Like most kids growing up during that era, playing sports was something they did for entertainment. Not too many families in rural Georgia had television sets. The Hauss household was no different. "I played football, basketball, ran track—the usual things," he says. "I don't think we got a TV until I was in the tenth grade."

Hauss had always wanted to attend his state school, the University of Georgia. He got his wish. At Georgia, Hauss was quick off the ball, but he was still one of the conference's lesser-known prospects. At just 215 pounds he was undersized, even for back then.

"I don't think anybody knew who I was, except I was the guy who hiked the ball to our quarterback, Larry Rakestraw," he says. That all changed, however, when Georgia played the University of Miami during his senior year.

"Miami had a quarterback named George Mira, who was considered the best quarterback in the country at the time," he says. "Because of Mira, there were a lot scouts at the game. As it turned out, Larry had a tremendous game and we won (31-14). So a lot of the scouts noticed Rakestraw and because we gave him good protection and he broke some records, longtime Redskins scout Tim Timmerera told me later that they decide to draft me. All because of one football game."

The Redskins must have known what they were doing. Of the 10 centers drafted in the 1964 NFL Draft, Hauss played in more games and went to more Pro Bowls than any of them.

During his 14-year Pro Bowl career, center **Len Hauss** spearheaded two different offenses. During the '60s, he and his linemates protected an unstoppable aerial attack. Later with George Allen, Hauss and Co. established a crushing run game that sent the Skins to Super Bowl VII.
Pro Football Hall of Fame/WireImage.com

But the road wasn't easy. The year before Hauss joined the team, Washington went 3-11 under second-year head coach Bill McPeak. He decided a drastic change was necessary. Prior to the '64 draft, he traded quarterback Norm Snead to the Philadelphia Eagles for Sonny Jurgensen. Then he traded Dick James to New York for All-NFL linebacker Sam Huff. After bringing in talent on both sides of the ball, McPeak and his staff drafted a tailback named Charley Taylor from Arizona State, a ball hawk defensive back named Paul Krause, and a self-proclaimed one-game wonder—center Len Hauss, the 115th player selected in the ninth round.

"Bill McPeak was what you expected a coach to be back then," says Hauss. "He was rather stern, offense-minded, and an all-around good guy."

Unfortunately, that didn't translate into very many wins. "We were never .500 with Coach McPeak and we didn't have a winning record for the first five years," says Hauss. After back-to-back 6-8 records, McPeak was replaced by another offensive guru, Hall of Fame quarterback Otto Graham.

"Graham was another good coach," says Hauss. "He was very offense-minded and we scored a lot of points. We had this dynamic offensive, but we didn't win a lot of games."

Still, along with the notable skill players, linemen like Hauss and guard Vince Promuto began to get recognized and garnered Pro Bowl recognition. Hauss earned his first invitation after the '66 season, and Jurgensen and Taylor were also selected.

Graham's four-year record was unlike anything he'd ever experienced as a winning quarterback under Cleveland legend Paul Brown: 7-7; 5-6-3; and 5-9. But all that changed in February 1969, when the Green Bay Packers legendary coach, Vince Lombardi, was hired to resurrect a team that hadn't had a record better than .500 since 1955.

DOG DAYS

As Hauss sits at his desk and patiently answers questions during a fall 2006 interview, he knows the question is coming. Everyone wants to know about Lombardi and the magical 1969 season. Hauss is ready to answer, but when talking football with him, the policy is always honesty.

"That one year with Lombardi," Hauss begins, "well, it was the most miserable year I ever had in football." After a pause, he continues: "I guess Jerry Kramer or Henry Jordan coined the phrase, 'Lombardi treats us all alike. He treats us like dogs.' Well, that was true. Some people responded to that mentality, but not me. I was in my sixth year and I was having a pretty decent career. It was hard being treated like a dog. To be yelled and screamed out when you were giving 110 percent."

With two Pro Bowls under his belt and a reputation for being one of the quicker, more tenacious centers in the league, no one worked harder or was more dedicated than Hauss. He didn't need a legendary coach yelling at him to try even harder.

"If the guy next to you was loafing, or the tackle or end, he screamed at everybody. That was his method of getting the team together. But it was hard on a guy from Georgia who always felt like he gave 110 percent," says Hauss. "To be called a rotten, quitting dog just because some guy was out there who never had a work ethic and he was a loafer, well, I didn't like it."

One player who absolutely loved Lombardi was Jurgensen. Hauss remembers one day after a typical dog-day practice at camp the two of them shared opposing views on the Lombardi method.

"We were sitting there one day and Sonny said, 'Isn't this great! Lombardi kicks everyone in the ass and makes them give 110 percent. I looked at Sonny and said, 'Yeah the bad thing about that is you need a kick in the ass; I don't. He's kicking me too, and I don't appreciate it.' I told Sonny that Lombardi didn't have to make me give my all, because I was doing it anyway. His approach affected people in different ways."

Under Lombardi, the Redskins improved to 7-5-2, and Hauss enjoyed his third Pro Bowl. The team seemed poised to turn the corner, but then they learned that Lombardi was dying of cancer. After the coaching great passed away, Lombardi's assistant Bill Austin became head coach. Austin lasted one season before the organization decided to go in yet another direction. This time they were going to bring in someone who could elevate their defense to play at the same level as their explosive offense.

THE FUTURE IS NOW

A year before Lombardi's death, the Redskins also said good-bye to the only owner they'd ever known—George Preston Marshall, who died August 9, 1969, at age 72. Taking over ownership of the Redskins was a Canadian entrepreneur named Jack Kent Cooke.

In 1961, Cooke had purchased a 25 percent interest in the Redskins. Now he was cashing in on his investment. He also bought the Los Angeles Lakers in 1965. Cooke knew of a fine NFL coach in Los Angeles named George Allen who believed defense won championships. When George Allen became the fifth Redskins coach in eight years, the emphasis on defense was so sudden that Hauss had this early observation: "After George became coach it wasn't difficult to see the power shift," he says. "Number one was defense, number two was special teams, number three was the fans, number four was the equipment, and offense was number five."

Allen believed an offense should emphasize two things: running the ball and maintaining possession. It's debatable whether he cared much about the offense actually scoring; he had the defense and special teams for that. Allen's focus on building a strong defense seemed to be met happily by everyone except by one person—the team's top superstar, Sonny Jurgensen. "I think early on, Sonny may have been a little too flamboyant and may have been a little too offense-oriented for George," says Hauss.

According to Hauss, when Allen first came to town he went out with a real estate agent to buy a house. They ended up driving by Mount Vernon. "The story goes that George [Allen] said, 'Oh, what a great house. This is the house I want to buy.' The realtor said, 'You can't buy that house. It belongs to Sonny Jurgensen.' He knew right away there was going to be a little competitiveness."

Even for team guys like Hauss, the transformation to George Allen football was, at times, peculiar. He cleaned house, especially on the defensive side, and brought in so many Ex-Rams, the media dubbed them the Ramskins.

"It really was a different thing," says Hauss. "Basically, he traded for the Ram defense. These Rams players already knew what George liked and the kind of atmosphere he brought."

The "atmosphere" was something that took a no-nonsense pro like Hauss a little while to buy into completely. One thing's for sure; he wasn't used to the rah-rah cheering and clapping after wins.

"I remember that first year George was here, Walter Rock, a great offensive tackle, and I watched everyone jumping around and screamin' and hollerin' after winning a game," says Hauss. "Walter and I were thinking, 'What the devil is going on here?' The next week we won and they were doing the same thing. Walter and I again just stared in disbelief. Well, we won our first five games that year. So about the fifth time we got into the locker room after the game, and we finally start jumping up and down screaming like idiots."

Perhaps adding to the strain, Allen traded for the Saints veteran quarterback Billy Kilmer, not to backup, but to compete with 37-year-old Jurgensen. Kilmer, five years younger, possessed the intangibles that Allen liked. He was a great leader, a tough competitor, and he didn't care about putting up monster stats. He just wanted to win. He was the perfect quarterback to manage Allen's ball-control offense.

"Both Billy and Sonny were leaders," says Hauss. "I played with Billy for seven years and Sonny for eight or nine. They were both very competitive. Billy was more outwardly competitive—the fired-up type. Sonny was into doing the right things, but wasn't as fiery. But the fact remains Sonny did not get along as well as George and Billy.

"You have to look at the history of the Redskins though. George was a great coach and a great guy. We loved him. I loved him. He had a great record with the Rams when he came to Washington. And who was the number-one sports figure in Washington? It was Sonny Jurgensen. Does that matter? I don't know. If you take the human element out of it, it doesn't matter. But if you put it back in, it does matter."

It's difficult to argue with Allen's choice to bring in Kilmer. In 1971, Allen's first year as Redskins coach, Kilmer started nine games to Jurgensen's five, and the team went 9-4-1 and made the playoffs for the first time since 1945. By 1972, the team had realized that the guy tossing the ball had fallen much lower on the totem pole when compared to the running game.

RUSHING TO GLORY

With an offense predicated on the run, the men responsible for opening the holes during the Larry Brown era were the Redskins offensive line. The 1972 Redskins line included Hauss, guards John Wilbur and Ray Schoenke, and tackles Walt Rock and Jim Snowden. George Burman, Terry Hermeling, and Paul Laavag also played. Unlike the Hogs, not one of them was even close to 300 pounds. "None of our offensive linemen were big," says Hauss. "Our guards were about 245 and our tackles maybe 255-260. And that's as big as you got."

Hauss, on the other hand, was a different story. He had bulked up from his 220-pound college weight and was a solid 235. Unfortunately, the Redskins brass wanted a bigger center, but Hauss had long devised a plan.

"I went to Washington at 220 out of college," says Hauss. "All these guys would be weighing in wearing just their jockstraps, because they were trying to weigh in as light as they could. I would weigh in wearing my sweatpants, a sweatshirt, and I'd tape a two-and-a-half-pound weight to each ankle so I could get an extra five pounds. I felt like they didn't think I was big enough to play. I figured I could add 10 pounds."

Of course, all that mattered to the defensive linemen in the league was that Hauss was good. Hauss and company were the immovable force behind Larry Brown's and fullback Charlie Harraway's incredible ground game. Brown led the NFL in rushing in 1970 with 1,125 yards and was named the

MVP of the league in '72 with 1,216 yards. Harraway averaged over 500 yards a season during his five-year tenure with the Redskins.

"Back then quickness and speed were more important for offensive linemen than size," says Hauss. "We had to block the middle linebacker or get the outside linebacker on a blitz. You'd have to be quick enough to pull out and do things. There were different blocking schemes."

Linemen also had to keep their hands and forearms close to their chest, all while having to contend with the likes of Deacon Jones head-slapping them silly. But Hauss thinks it's important to discuss the advantages offensive linemen had, too.

"Sure we had to deal with the head-slap, but I can't imagine playing without the cut blocks," he says. "I was notorious for cutting a guy's legs. If a guy was running in, I'd chop block him. Nothing wrong with it and I don't think there's anything wrong with it today."

Hauss points out that it's a different game now with 300-pound centers going against 320-pound defensive tackles. Trying to chop block a 320-pound defensive tackle can be more serious.

Hauss' most memorable games involved him facing up to challenging defenses and allowing the skill players he protected to have great games.

GAME OF MY LIFE
BY LEN HAUSS

The game that sticks out—other than the '72 Cowboys game—was the one earlier that year in New York, when Larry Brown had that incredible day rushing. That would qualify as one of my best games, because Larry had a great day.

The Giants played an odd defense and they had a tackle named John Mendenhall, who played nose guard. He was short at about 6-foot-1, 260 pounds and extremely quick. John was lined up on me all day long. I remember someone said something to me after the game that he had an outstanding number of tackles on Larry. Well, in the films it showed me blocking him and he had to turn around and chase Larry down. No tackles at the line of scrimmage, but he got some farther downfield. Larry gained 191 yards in that game. It was an outstanding day for him, one of his better days and therefore one of my better days.

The game had some challenging moments. Sonny ruptured his Achilles and had to leave the game. Billy came in, but this wasn't anything new because Billy and Sonny had been substituting all season long. When someone gets hurt like that you have to remain focused on the game. That may sound callous now, but at the time of an injury to anybody, when you're in the middle of a game, you don't have much time to think, "Golly, Sonny's out and Billy's in. How do we feel? Let's take a vote." You just go ahead and do the best you can.

I divided my career by playing seven years before George Allen and seven with him as coach. I can tell you that without a doubt that it's a heck of a lot more fun to win than it is to lose. We didn't have a winning season except for that one season with Lombardi. But under George we never had a losing season. We were in the playoffs five out of seven years. And to have five out of seven in the playoffs and seven out of seven being winning seasons, it was great.

GONE FISHIN'

Since retiring after the 1977 season, Hauss returned to Georgia to live year-round and went into the financial industry. He and his wife, Janis, college sweethearts at Georgia, have a daughter, who has two daughters of her own. When Hauss isn't working, there's a good chance he's fishing on the Altamaha River, where there are flathead catfish, largemouth bass, redbreast sunfish, and more. You name it—Hauss has caught it.

He's still close to many of his teammates, especially Billy Kilmer, who he sees a couple times a year when the Kilmers pass through Georgia traveling north from Florida.

On the topic of today's NFL, Hauss could spend hours telling you how much the game has changed in the past 30 years, but the biggest thing that sticks in his craw is the showmanship. That's why he really enjoyed watching the Colts and his favorite center, Jeff Saturday, win the Super Bowl last year.

"For me, it's important to see professionals act professional. And those guys act like what pros ought to act like," he says. "You see a guy score a touchdown and act like he knows what he's doing. Same with a guy making a tackle. He doesn't jump up and point and all that. To me it takes away from the game when you start pointing, shouting, and showboating."

Hauss laughs when he thinks about guys from his era carrying on like some of the players do now. "I'm pretty sure Larry Brown never did a cartwheel or grabbed some pom-ponms."

For all of Hauss' downplaying, one thing is for sure; he ought to be considered for the Hall of Fame. In 14 years he played in five Pro Bowls and started 192 consecutive games. When *Sports Illustrated* actually did a feature on centers for their 1975 NFL annual, the two players they focused on were Hall of Fame center Jim Otto and Hauss.

Of course, Hauss will be the first to tell you that he spends more time thinking about fishing and giving sound financial advice than anything remotely connected to the Hall of Fame. "I really don't give much thought to the Hall of Fame," he says. "I don't think there's ever going to be a way to recognize offensive linemen. I mean, there are some offensive linemen in the Hall of Fame who had teammates who were better. But they got in for some reason.

"And really when you think of the Hall of Fame, who cares? What does it do? I'm trying to think if I would be making more money if I was in the Hall of Fame. I don't think so. I don't think there's any effect on my life one way or the other. I think it means more to me that I was chosen one of the 70 Greatest Redskins. That means someone who knew something about me thought enough of my performance to recognize me. But one thing's for sure. You don't need to dwell on it. As far as I can tell, when we open the doors of this bank, the people I'm going to be dealing with don't really care if I'm in the Hall of Fame or not. They just want to know if I'm going to lend them some money."

And let's face it, centers don't get much recognition and, according to Hauss with his tongue firmly in cheek, they don't do much to deserve it.

"Someone once asked me what centers do and I told them, 'Well, we keep the quarterbacks from having to pick the ball up off the ground. We hand the ball to the quarterback. If we're doing a decent job we may find somebody to block. Otherwise, I guess our main job is to give the ball to the quarterback.'"

For the humble and dry-witted Hauss, that's the way he prefers to think about it.

Chapter 19

BILL DUDLEY

"Versatility" is a loosely defined word when it comes to describing NFL running backs. It's a term whose meaning seems to get narrower as time goes by. As Rams great Marshall Faulk retired as the ninth leading rusher in NFL history this past year, media experts hailed his versatility. Not only could he run the ball, they said, but he could also catch. But Faulk never returned a single punt or kickoff during his career. The same can be said of the Buffalo Bills' recent Hall of Famer Thurman Thomas. A generation older than Faulk, Thomas also never returned a punt or kick, and he attempted just one pass, which went incomplete.

In fact, you have to go back as far as the 1970s, to Broncos legend Floyd Little, to find someone who epitomized versatility. Little retired as the seventh leading rusher in NFL history, averaged over 11 yards a catch with 2,415 receiving yards, plus totaled more than 3,400 yards as a punt and kick returner. And he threw the half-back option as well.

The truth is, as versatile as Little was, only one NFL player can really be considred "Most Versatile Ever." He's former Redskins running back Bill Dudley. A member of the Pro Football Hall of Fame since 1966, "Bullet" Bill literally did it all.

During his extraordinary career, which spanned 1942, 1945-51 and 53, Dudley, known mostly for his tough running, was equally adept at catching the ball, throwing the ball, returning punts and kickoffs, playing defense, and kicking field goals and extra points. He even handled punting duties and did his share of blocking.

"My forte was playing the game with my head and my body," says Dudley, who turned a spry 85 in December 2006. "You need your whole body to play. Not just your legs or your arms, but your mind, too."

Dudley never thought too much about his versatility or that he was one of the stars of the NFL.

"I was a complete football player. I liked to play the game. I loved the competition and I knew something about it," he says. "But I would prefer to have been on a championship team than to be in the Hall of Fame. Don't get me wrong. Being elected to the Pro Football Hall of Fame is an outstanding achievement. But it took an awful lot of work from everyone to get me there."

When discussing his career, Dudley is more than humble. He frankly doesn't understand what all the fuss was about him. He's almost embarrassed by the individual accolades and prefers to downplay his accomplishments.

Dudley's outstanding pro career can be divided into four parts: three years with the Pittsburgh Steelers; an interruption after his first season to serve in World War II; three years with the Detroit Lions; and three final seasons with the Washington Redskins.

Born December 24, 1921, in Bluefield, Virginia, William McGarvey Dudley, was extremely athletic, dominating his high school football team even though he looked like a skinny boy scout. It took the 5-foot-9, 110-pound young man a couple of tries to make the team, but once he impressed the coach enough to earn a spot, he quickly became the team's star.

If you guessed his speed was the secret to The Bullet's running ability, you're wrong. "I was probably one of the slowest players around,"

Redskins Hall of Famer **Bill Dudley** was the NFL's most versatile running back ever. The humble star led the league in rushing twice, plus punt and kickoff returns. He once led the NFL with 10 interceptions. Dudley also handled punting and kicking duties, and he passed for close to 1,000 yards.

Nate Fine/WireImage.com

he says. "I was timed at an all-star game once and came in 12th place out of 14." Then why the nickname?

"They were looking for a moniker to get publicity and they attached 'Bullet,'" says Dudley. "It stuck even though I wasn't fast and never have been. But I had a good take off. I had good balance. I guess I faked people well, and could follow my interference. I wasn't big enough to run over people, but I wasn't going to stand tall and let someone get me. I tried to get down under. I never tried any fancy pirouettes. Lynn Swann could do that, not me."

By the time he was a high school senior at Graham High, Dudley's versatility showed through. In a tight game against Princeton High, Dudley kicked the winning field goal with seconds left.

He enrolled at the University of Virginia and hoped to play football. Again, his size gave coaches a false impression of his abilities. He made the team, but only as a punter.

After proving he was a capable back in practice, Dudley got his chance when injuries befell members in the starting backfield. After a few games filling in as halfback, he not only became a starter, but the star. One player he looked up to was the quarterback for the local professional team, Sammy Baugh of the Washington Redskins.

"He was the guy I watched as far back as when I was at the University of Virginia," says Dudley. "I used to marvel at the way he played even then. They ran the single wing and Sam handled the ball on every play. He was the best all-around football player I ever saw."

At that point Dudley was only about 150 pounds and not quite 5-foot-10. "Eventually, I became an All-American, but we never won a lot of games at Virginia, which was the only thing I cared about."

What Dudley avoids mentioning is that he was considered by many to be the finest football player in the country. As a senior in 1941, he placed fifth in the Heisman voting. And he won the Maxwell award for outstanding player. More impressive, though, is that when the 1942 NFL Draft was held, Dudley's was the first name called by the Pittsburgh Steelers.

NFL CALLS, NOT COUNTRY

Most people fortunate enough to be the first player selected in the NFL draft would be beside themselves with joy. Not Bill Dudley.

That's because when World War II broke out, it was Dudley's dream to serve his country, not play in the NFL. But to his dismay, he wasn't 21 and couldn't get his parents' consent to enlist.

So instead, the now fully grown, 5-foot-10, 182-pound rookie settled for the NFL. He led the entire league in rushing with 696 yards. He also led the NFL in punt returns and had the league's highest kick return average. He also passed for 438 yards and two touchdowns and had three interceptions.

"To be honest, I never thought about leading the league in rushing as a rookie or any of that other stuff," says Dudley. "It never occurred to me. These individual achievements—I never thought a whole lot about them. They were just things that happened."

The average person can't relate to leading the NFL in rushing and thinking nothing of it. But that's the case with Dudley; he's just being Bill, honest and unassuming.

Finally, after becoming all the rage as the NFL's star rookie, Dudley finally got his wish. The U.S. armed services were now drafting all eligible men for the war effort and Dudley happily enlisted.

"I wanted to become a hot pilot and fly missions," says Dudley. "Instead, I became a B-25 instructor. I spent most of my time during the war as an instructor at Randolph Base in Texas. I was upset. I had an older brother who had been shot up and a kid brother who was flying off aircraft carriers ready to fly into Japan. And I was in Texas as an instructor."

To the chagrin of Dudley, his orders during the war were to join the armed services football team and entertain troops during the war. Again, it didn't occur to Dudley that he was considered a celebrity and one of the bright stars of the NFL. He just wanted to serve his country.

"A friend of mine flew the first B-17 bomber, called Jack the Ripper, that bombed Berlin. I contacted him and wanted so badly to fly with him, but my C.O. had given me orders to remain at Randolph field and play football and be an instructor. What else could I do? I was a good instructor and did a good job. During a war, you do what you're told."

Near the end of his tour of duty, Dudley finally got to fulfill his dream of flying a mission. "I got to co-pilot a B-29 that flew into Japan once," he said. "We didn't see any action, so I guess I was fortunate. But I just wanted to serve my country."

Dudley was named the armed services team's best player and led his squad to a perfect 12-0 record. As you can imagine, that meant very little to him—except the winning part.

STEEL CITY

Once his military obligation had been fulfilled, Dudley was honorably discharged and congratulated for his morale-boosting efforts. He returned to the Pittsburgh Steelers, a team he hadn't played for in more than two-and-a-half years, and rejoined his squad with just a few games left in the 1945 season.

He promptly started where he'd left off his rookie year in '42 and scored three touchdowns. Again, he didn't think much about his accomplishments. His focus was on helping his team win next season.

As the '46 season got underway, Dudley quickly established himself as the league's best runner. His 604 yards led the league again, topping the likes of future Hall of Famers, Steve Van Buren of the Eagles and Tony Canadeo of Green Bay. Dudley also led the NFL in punt returns a second time. Plus, he notched a league-high 10 interceptions. One of them he returned for a touchdown off his idol, Sammy Baugh.

The rest of the league was quickly finding out that Dudley was just as dominating on the defensive side of the ball. How did he become so accomplished on both sides of the line of scrimmage?

"When it came to defense, I just studied the scouting report and went out and did my job," says Dudley. Later he was informed that Eagles coach Greasy Neale once told his quarterback, "I don't want you throwing the ball in Bill Dudley's area." Giants coach Steve Owen used to tell his quarterback the same thing. "He told people that I was actually a better defensive back than an offensive back."

The all-world, all-versatile Dudley easily won the NFL MVP award. Of course, winning games is what mattered most to Dudley, and his Steelers went 5-5-1. Adding to the sting of a .500 record, Dudley found himself unwanted in Pittsburgh despite being the best running back in the league.

"I hurt my knee with Pittsburgh and they traded me to Detroit," says Dudley, simply. "I thought about retiring, but the Lions gave me a three-year, no-cut contract at $20,000 a year. Guaranteed."

THE LION'S SHARE

Getting a guaranteed contract worth $60,000 was a big payday at the time, similar to today's multimillion-dollar unrestricted free agent signings. But for Dudley, the substantial increase meant continuing to play at a high level. As usual, he delivered again in every way possible. He threw for two scores, rushed for 302 yards, caught 27 passes for 375 yards and seven touchdowns, averaged an incredible 16.5 yards on punt returns including one returned for a touchdown, and then added 359 yards on kick returns and another touchdown. Dudley also intercepted five passes and averaged over 43 yards a punt. All in all, he scored 13 touchdowns for his team in almost every possible way.

In 1948, Dudley missed a good part of the season due to injuries, but he still scored six touchdowns. The next season, back healthy, he rushed for over 400 yards, added another 200 in receptions, and another 500 yards in punt and kick returns, not to mention intercepting a key pass that led to a rare Lions victory.

According to Dudley, the Lions had the right to sign him as an assistant coach at the end of his contract. His salary would be less than the $20,000 he was making as a player, but still solid at $12,500. "But I was told that my coach, Bo McMillan, didn't want to pay me that kind of money to coach, if I didn't play," Dudley says. "So they worked out a trade with me to go to Washington. I don't know if that's true, but that's what I found out."

Chances are, with Dudley's experience and vast football knowledge, McMillan was probably more afraid that the future Hall of Famer would succeed him as an excellent coach.

COMING HOME

Even though he had been in the NFL since 1942, it wasn't until Dudley headed to Washington that he truly felt like he was coming home.

"When I was a youngster at Virginia, the Redskins were the team I followed," says Dudley. "Now I was not only going to get to play for them, but play with the great Sammy Baugh."

For most people, the chance to meet your idol is a memorable yet fleeting moment. But by then, Dudley had become one of the all-time greats, just like his idol.

"It was fantastic playing with Sam," says Dudley. "We roomed together and became very good friends as well as great competitors. We already competed against one another for years. Now we were on the same team."

Dudley had already intercepted a number of Baugh's passes as a Steeler and a Lion. He had even done his best Baugh impression as a passer. But when asked who was the better player, Dudley made it clear that there was no comparison.

"Hell yes, Sam was better than me," says Dudley abruptly. "I couldn't carry Sam's shoes."

Of course, Dudley has his share of humorous stories about Baugh.

"Sam was a great fellow and loved to chew tobacco," says Dudley, "He always had a cup that he'd spit into. It didn't matter if we were out somewhere or sitting around watching TV. The first thing Sam would do is get a big wad in his mouth and grab a second cup to spit in. He was always two fisted. It was funny to see him enjoying himself."

The thing that may have impressed Dudley the most about Baugh was his unpretentious personality. "He was a regular guy that went out there and played the game with a lot of enthusiasm. Sam always played with all his heart and knowledge. He was a fine, fine gentleman."

Dudley didn't disappoint his first season in the nation's capitol. He rushed for 339 yards and a blistering 5.1 average. In one game against the Eagles, Dudley ran for 101 yards on just 11 carries. He grabbed 22 passes for 303 yards, averaged 15.4 yards a punt return, and scored on an exciting touchdown scamper. Kicking-wise, he hit five field goals and 31 extra points. On the defensive side, he picked off two passes and averaged 41.8 yards on 14 punts.

"I had no idea I was carrying such a high average that season," says Dudley, when asked about five-plus rushing average. "I probably wasn't carrying the ball as much then. In '47, '48, and '49, teams started having more players choose [between] offense and defense. I was fortunate to continue playing both."

Playing for an owner like George Preston Marshall was also an experience for Dudley. "He didn't know much about football," Dudley says. "He was like a lot of owners today. Very interested in the game, but only seeing the score. They know very little about the internal functions of the game. They sometimes try to get too involved with the game and personnel and they shouldn't. But it's the owner's team and they're going to do what they want."

Dudley was the perfect gentleman off the field. But on the field, he was first and foremost a competitor. During his first year with the Redskins, Dudley got the chance for a little revenge when he faced the team that unceremoniously got rid of him when he was injured: the Pittsburgh Steelers.

GAME OF MY LIFE
BY BILL DUDLEY

The game against Pittsburgh my first year with the Redskins stands out to me. Playing against the Steelers gave me an extra incentive because they were my old team.

It was near the end of the season and we had lost to them in Pittsburgh earlier by a lopsided score of 26-7. This time, the game was at home in front of the great Washington fans. It was December and there was a nice chill in the air.

The Steelers had a good team and some great players, like Hall of Famer Ernie Stautner. Another guy on the team was defensive end Bill McPeak. He later became the Redskins coach!

I remember Sam was really into the game, because he knew how much the game meant to me. We connected on some key passes. Tackling was tough. I got a nose that's been smashed in a few times but somehow never been broken. I would duck my head and try to get my blows on my head and not my face.

Near the end of the game, I returned a punt for a touchdown that helped win the game. You always want to play well every time you step out onto the field. I played for my teammates and the most important thing was to win. I was proud that we won that day.

ONE OF THE GREATEST

Dudley would play another year with Baugh as the team's quarterback. Then in 1952, Baugh's final year, Dudley took a year off to contemplate life after football. But he missed it too much and returned for a final season in 1953.

By then the Redskins had a new quarterback. Replacing the 6-foot-2, 182-pound Slingin' Sammy Baugh was Eddie LeBaron, a 5-foot-9, 168-pound scrambler.

"Eddie was a fine football player," says Dudley. "He was a magician with the football. That was his forte. Eddie was probably the best ball-handler in the league. He could take the ball and fake it, hide it, and throw it. He was excellent. One time we were playing the Giants and he faked it so well that there wasn't anyone 10 yards from him when he crossed the goal line. They didn't know he had the ball."

Another player that Dudley admired was Packer great Don Hutson. "I played against him a few times. Don put the fear of God in the defense.

Most of the time we had a couple people on him. Let's put it this way—
I was never covering him by himself."

As someone who kicked his share of field goals, Dudley can tell you
who was the best kicker of his generation. "As far as I'm concerned, Lou
Groza was the greatest kicker that ever came down the line. I was at an
all-star game and Paul Brown was the coach. It was the end of practice
and Brown said, "Bill, you and Groza go down and practice your kicks."
I looked at him and said, "Coach, are you kidding?" I could kick the ball,
but I wasn't anywhere near as good as Lou. He was in a class by himself.
Paul never cracked a smile. He just looked back at me and said, "Get your
ass down there."

After retiring, Dudley coached and scouted for a couple years. But
as he was nearing the end of his career, he went into the life insurance and
estate planning business in 1951, because his older brother had done so
and had been very successful.

"I thought about coaching full-time, but in order to do that you
have to be away from your family a lot, and I didn't want to do that," he
says. "So I tried selling insurance and it wasn't easy. But I dedicated myself
to learning it and I stayed in it for 54 years. I was a million-dollar
producer for 30 years. It's a great business, but they still don't call you to
buy."

In 1966, Dudley was inducted into the Pro Football Hall of Fame—
becoming the first overall draft pick to be inducted. His accomplishments
read like the careers of six players combined. He threw 222 times for 985
yards and six touchdowns; rushed for 3,057 yards and 18 touchdowns,
caught 123 passes for 1,383 yards and another 18 scores. Returned 124
punts for 1,515 yards and three touchdowns, and 78 kickoffs for 1,743
yards and a score. While playing defense, he intercepted 23 passes for 459
yards and returned two for touchdowns. He punted 193 times for 7,304
yards for a 37.8 average. As a field goal kicker, he made 33 kicks and 121
extra points. All in all, Dudley accounted for 484 points and countless
incredible moments.

"If I had my druthers I would have preferred to be on a championship team," says Dudley. "Being in the Hall of Fame is a great feeling. But there's something about the camaraderie of any player playing any sport when they win. When it comes to a team sport like football, you owe so much of your success to coaches, teammates, and even [to people] as far back as my high school coaches. Any success you have must go back to all the people who have influenced your life. It's hard to put an emphasis on one person and say he deserves it over someone else."

Dudley marvels at his friendships with legendary players. He still calls Sammy Baugh, who is up in years and living with his son in Texas. "I've had the privilege to meet Jim Thorpe, Red Grange, and Bronko Nagurski. Not a whole lot of ball players can say it; I've met some of the modern guys, too. And to be named one of the 70 Greatest Redskins was a real honor."

But, above all, Dudley is a family man. Last year Dudley and his wife, Libba, celebrated their 60th wedding anniversary. He and his wife had four children, losing one child to leukemia in 1956. Dudley also has four grandchildren and hopes to someday have great-grandchildren. He makes his home in Lynchburg, Virginia, and still watches the Redskins and the University of Virginia whenever he can. His hobbies include golf and bridge.

So do his grandchildren make a big deal about having such a famous Hall of Famer for a grandfather? "Nah," he says with his pleasant Southern drawl. "We're all just family here."

Dudley wouldn't have it any other way.

Chapter 20

DOUG WILLIAMS

Before Super Bowl XXII, the only quarterback people were talking about was the reigning NFL MVP, Denver's John Elway. After the Redskins' 42-10 pasting of the Broncos, the only quarterback people were talking about was the new Super Bowl MVP, Washington's Doug Williams.

Although he played nine NFL seasons, Williams will forever be linked to this one game. Anyone who watched Super Bowl XXII saw a fireworks display of offense in one quarter that has yet to be duplicated. Down 10-0 in the second quarter, the Redskins exploded for 35 points. Williams led the charge with his rocket arm and cool leadership.

Days leading up to the game, no one much cared or asked if he could throw the ball. They just wanted to know, as one reporter allegedly asked, "How long have you been a black quarterback?"

After the game, Williams had not only broken the color barrier as the first African-American to start a Super Bowl, but he had also put up the best performance to date: 18-for-29, 340 yards and four touchdowns—the scores all coming in one quarter.

"Everyone talks about the Super Bowl," says Williams, "but to get there we had some big obstacles in our way. You've got to get to the playoffs and win the championship game before you're given the chance to compete in the Super Bowl." For Williams, though, the road to the Super Bowl was filled with seemingly impenetrable obstacles far from gridiron.

Douglas Lee Williams was born in Zachary, Louisiana, on August 8, 1955. He grew up in a region and during a time where he would come face to face with racial injustice on a daily basis.

"My hometown was just 30 minutes from where David Duke lived," says Williams.

The third youngest of four brothers and three sisters, Williams was always surrounded by sports. His parents, Laura and Robert, two athletes in their own right, believed that sports were a great way to keep out of trouble. So the Williams kids competed in practically everything.

"Football wasn't something I was interested in initially," he says. "I wanted to play basketball and baseball instead. But I wasn't tall enough to be a power forward, and I didn't have a 100-mile-an-hour fastball."

But at 6-foot-4 and 220 pounds, Williams was plenty big to play football. The problem was, he wanted to play quarterback. "I threw a pretty good football," Williams says. "I felt like I would be a good quarterback, but I was black."

DOUG WILLIAMS: QUARTERBACK

Every young, talented kid has a role model: someone who understands him, who encourages him, and helps him believe in himself. For young Doug, that man was his older brother, Robert.

"He was 15 years older than me. He was my hero," says Williams. "Robert not only coached me up, but he also became one of my first football coaches. He was my man."

Williams continued to play basketball and baseball through grade school and high school, although football became his new passion since

---

Doug Williams made history when he quarterbacked the 1987 Redskins to a stunning lopsided victory over the Denver Broncos in Super Bowl XXII. The rifle-armed leader not only outdueled the reigning MVP, John Elway, but also silenced critics once and for all. *Stephen Dunn/Getty Images*

he knew it was his ticket to college. By the time he graduated from Chaneyville High School, he was all-district in football and baseball, and all-state in basketball.

"I had a chance to play baseball at Louisiana State University," says Williams, "but I was already set to play football at Grambling State University. My brother went there and he was my hero, so deciding to go there was a no-brainer. Plus, it was my chance to play for a legend, Eddie Robinson."

At Grambling, Williams operated out of the Wing T, one of the most complicated offenses around. In the Wing T, the quarterback must be a deft ball handler and a master of the option. It took Williams a season to learn the system. But it took the coaching staff just one practice to see that Williams was special. He had a gifted arm that fired the football like a missile. He had to learn to lay off some passes because they would dislodge the fingers of the receivers.

Playing in the Wing T, however, taught Williams the importance of preparation and hard work. "It was a tough system to learn because there were so many variables," says Williams. "Footwork, ball handling, making quick decisions. It definitely prepared me for the next level."

Once Williams learned the offense, the rest of the league was in trouble. In four seasons, Williams led Grambling to three Southwest Athletic Conference (SWAC) championships, and three National Black College Championships. In his senior year, Williams led the Tigers to 10-1 record and another NBCC championship. He became the first black quarterback to be chosen to the first-team of the Associated Press All-America team. Additionally, Williams earned SWAC Player of the Year honors and finished fourth in the Heisman Trophy, won that year by Texas running back Earl Campbell.

His fourth-place finish was unprecedented by a black quarterback. Williams also finished highest among quarterbacks in the voting. Stanford quarterback Guy Benjamin finished sixth, Pittsburgh's Matt Cavanaugh seventh, and Michigan's Rick Leach, eighth.

BREAKING MORE BARRIERS

When the NFL draft came along, Williams broke another color barrier; he became the first African-American quarterback to be drafted in the first round and start at quarterback. The NFL's first African-American quarterback to start more than a couple games, Marlin Briscoe, was a 14th-round pick of the Denver Broncos in 1968. James Harris, who'd starred at Grambling back in the 1960s, had been selected in the eighth round in 1969 by the Buffalo Bills. And Joe Gilliam, who'd played at Tennessee State, had been picked in the 11th round by the Pittsburgh Steelers in the '72 draft.

The Tampa Bay Buccaneers changed history when they used the 17th overall pick in the first round of the 1978 NFL draft to get Williams. Even though the Buccaneers had only won two games in their two-year history, Williams was ecstatic.

"When I was a kid I only wanted to play college football for two guys: John McKay at USC and Eddie Robinson. By getting drafted by the Bucs, I finally got that opportunity to play for Coach McKay. I was so happy I got to play for both coaches. It was the best of both worlds."

Williams quickly became the starter. It took a while for his receivers to get used to the pure speed and velocity of his passes. *Sports Illustrated* even did a cartoon of Williams, transforming his arm to look like a rifle and his receivers to look like they were fragile china dolls. The caption read: "Easy, Doug, hands are hurtin' in Tampa Bay."

Despite playing behind an inexperienced line and a troupe of receivers—Morris Owens, Larry Mucker, and J.K. McKay, the coach's son—Williams led Tampa Bay to a 5-11 record his first season. A few of his wins turned heads, such as 16-10 win at Minnesota, where he outdueled Fran Tarkenton, and the win against the Atlanta Falcons with Steve Bartkowski. Both were playoff teams that year.

But then, in just his second season in Tampa in '79, Williams led the former laughingstock franchise to the precipice of the Super Bowl. Going 10-6 in the regular season, the Bucs hosted the Philadelphia Eagles in the first round in Tampa. Behind the great running of the late Ricky Bell, the former legendary USC tailback, Williams finally had some offensive support. Bell rushed for 1,263 yards that season, while new receiver Isaac Hagins and tight end Jimmie Giles combined for 1,271 yards and 10 touchdowns.

The Bucs beat Philly 16-10 as Bell graced the cover of *Sports Illustrated*. A week later, they lost to the Los Angeles Rams 9-0, who would go on to lose Super Bowl XIV to the Pittsburgh Steelers 31-19. Williams tied Ron Jaworski with 18 touchdown passes and became one of the top young signal-callers in the game.

"We had some good players," says Williams. "Ricky, Leroy Selman, David Lewis, Jimmie Giles, I thought I'd play for Tampa the rest of my career." Williams also liked playing for McKay. "He had his own way of handling himself. He was a dry-witted, one-liner kind of guy who always said what was on his mind."

But when Williams' contract was up in 1982, the love affair somehow dissolved. "I never would have dreamed of leaving the Buccaneers," says Williams. "But you quickly realize that it's a business. The '82 season was the last year of my contract. They wanted to renew it, but we disagreed on what I should be paid. I ended up sitting out the whole 1983 football season."

DESTINY TAKES A DETOUR

When the 1984 season rolled around, there was a new league starting up that lured numerous NFL players away for big money. Doug Williams was one of them.

Williams joined the USFL's Oklahoma Outlaws in 1984 and played most of the season before a knee injury sidelined him for the remaining eight games. The next season, the Outlaws merged with the Arizona Wranglers and became the Arizona Outlaws. His new coach was Frank Kush, the former Baltimore Colts and Arizona State coach. Kush had a reputation for abusing players, both verbally and physically. He would scream at players beyond normal discipline and grab their facemasks, twisting them during practice. In fact, the biggest reason John Elway did not want to play for Baltimore when they drafted him in 1983 was not because he disliked the city of Baltimore, which was what many reported. It was his distaste for Kush, who tried to recruit Elway to Arizona State back when he was a senior at Grenada High School in Los Angeles and the most sought after quarterback in the country.

But Williams, typical of his relaxed, cool demeanor, understood Kush and didn't hesitate to play for him. "Coach Kush was a tough, disciplined coach," says Williams. "He just wanted you to do your job. I had no problem with that."

Despite name players like Williams, Herschel Walker, Brian Sipe, Reggie White, Steve Young, and Doug Flutie, the USFL could not compete with the NFL and folded after the 1985 season. Williams had been searching for his next employer when the Redskins called.

Joe Theismann had retired following that horrendous broken leg, and Jay Schroeder took over as the new starting quarterback. Coach Joe Gibbs wanted a veteran guy to backup Schroeder and got Williams' rights by sending a fifth-round pick to the Bucs.

Williams didn't know what to expect going to the Redskins. It had been three years since he took a snap in an NFL game, and now he was resigned to carrying a clipboard. Schroeder was only in his second year after coming out of UCLA and had the second most visible job in the country—Redskins starting quarterback. Schroeder played admirably, compiling 4,109 yards passing and 22 touchdowns. He also threw 22 picks. Still, the Redskins got to the NFC Championship game where the Giants blanked them 17-0.

As the '87 season got under way, Williams found himself playing in the season opener against the Eagles after Schroeder suffered a sprained shoulder. Showing no rust, Williams threw for 272 yards and two touchdowns and the Redskins won 34-24. The next week Williams started, but Washington lost 20-21 to Atlanta. Intent on redeeming himself, he had to sit for the next 24 days as another players strike, the second in six years, ensued. Lucky for the Redskins, they fielded a great strike team that won all three games. By the time the regular players returned, Schroeder was healthy and regained the starting role. But the team struggled in a loss to the Eagles, and Williams, once again, was elevated to starter.

Then, as the topsy-turvy quarterback battle went on, it was Williams who got hurt against the Lions. He strained his back, and Schroeder took over for the next five games until Gibbs switched back to Williams during the final game against the Vikings. It was the third time Gibbs had inserted Williams during the season.

It was a must-win for the Redskins, and Williams, as usual, made it exciting. With 6:51 left in the third quarter and the game tied at 7, Williams tossed a touchdown to Ricky Sanders to make it 14-7. Then, suddenly looking like a guy who hadn't played in five games, Williams threw two picks and Minnesota scored 21 unanswered points, making it 24-14. Undaunted, Williams collected himself and courageously led the team to tie the game with 10 points late in the fourth quarter, including a bomb to Sanders of 51 yards.

The game went into overtime and Williams found Sanders twice again, once for 22 yards another for 10 yards and a first down at the Vikings 20. After an 11-yard run by running back George Rogers, Redskins kicker Ali Haji-Sheikh booted a 26-yarder for the victory. In relief, Williams had gone 11-of-22 for 217 yards, two touchdowns and two picks. But Gibbs couldn't ignore the biggest stat. It was a "W."

Now in the playoffs, Gibbs had a quandary at quarterback. Williams was 3-0 coming off the bench in relief, but 0-2 as a starter. Still, the team played with a spark whenever Williams was in the game. Gibbs went with a gut feeling and started the former USFL star. It was one of his greatest decisions ever.

GOING TO THE SUPER BOWL

The San Francisco 49ers were considered hands down the best team in 1987. They went 13-2 in the strike-shortened, 15-game regular season and won their last three games by a combined score of 124-7. So when the 8-7 Vikings went to Candlestick Park and upset San Francisco, 36-

24, they had knocked off a team for the ages. The shocking loss turned the race to the Super Bowl upside down.

Washington, meanwhile, had its own playoff challenges. Tied for the third best record in the NFC, they narrowly defeated the Chicago Bears, 21-17, at subzero Solider Field. Chicago looked unstoppable, taking a 14-0 lead. Then Williams found his man, Sanders, for a 32-yard gain, and Rogers scored from the three to cut it to 14-7. Williams tied the game with a touchdown pass to tight end Clint Didier. What happened next is one of the most memorable plays in Redskins history. Darrell Green gathered in the frozen pigskin, launched his 5-foot-8 frame over a few grasping defenders, and sliced through the hearts of Chicago on his way to a scintillating 52-yard touchdown. The Redskins rejoiced, 21-17.

The NFC Championship would now go through Washington. The Redskins' foe this time was, once again, the Minnesota Vikings; it had been only three weeks since they'd played and gone into overtime. Plus, after upsetting the 49ers and annihilating the Saints, 44-10, the Vikings were suddenly the team to beat.

In an ugly game in which Williams completed just nine of 26 passes for 119 yards, the Redskins defense carried the day, sacking Vikings quarterback Wade Wilson eight times. Still, when it mattered most, Williams led the Redskins on a pivotal drive. Known for getting quick leads, the Vikings held the ball first for over eight minutes but failed to score. Williams and the Redskins took over and went 98 yards, highlighted by a 42-yard touchdown pass to running back Kelvin Bryant. That first touchdown proved huge on a day when the defenses dominated.

The Vikings tied the game at the half and then traded field goals to make it 10-10 going into the fourth quarter. With five minutes left in the game, Williams fired a 43-yard pass to receiver Gary Clark down inside the 10-yard line. The Vikings defense tightened, and Williams faced a third-and-6 at the 7-yard line.

The play called for Clark to run a corner route, but he saw that the Vikings were in a zone. Williams and Clark both read the same thing and

Clark changed it to find an open spot in the middle of the end zone. Williams threw the ball hard and low, and Clark made the catch for a 17-10 lead.

With less than five minutes left, Minnesota drove the ball to the Redskins 12 yard line with 1:12 on the clock. They got to the 6, then Wilson went 0-3 on passes. Now, on fourth down, Vikings running back Darrin Nelson caught a pass at the goal line, but it was knocked away by Green. The Redskins were going back to the Super Bowl. This time, Doug Williams was their quarterback.

GAME OF MY LIFE
BY DOUG WILLIAMS

A good friend of mine once told me, "It's not how you drive, it's how you arrive." Being given the opportunity to help lead a team to the Super Bowl is all I ever wanted.

I thought it was going to happen in Tampa, but it didn't. I ended up sitting out and playing in the USFL for a couple years. Looking back, it didn't matter. I still ended up with the Redskins and we went to the Super Bowl. I look at it this way: there are some guys who drove the same car their whole career. But if I got to change from the Volkswagen to a Cadillac, well, that was fine with me.

The great thing about the Super Bowl was that we had two weeks to mentally, physically, and emotionally prepare. We did that. For me it was a dream come true. I remember flying to San Diego and not knowing what to expect. But I was fortunate that I was on a veteran team with a bunch of guys who had been there. A friend of mine, Robert Piper, who hired me at Grambling, used to always tell me, "If you don't belong somewhere, just act like you do." Even though I had never been to a Super Bowl, you couldn't tell I hadn't been. I carried myself like I did. Yes, it was the Super Bowl, but the truth is at the end of the day, it was a game. I think that's how I looked at it. The Super Bowl was actually for corporate America and the media. The football game was for the players.

There was no doubt that once we qualified for the Super Bowl, it was no match. The Broncos were something like nine-point favorites. But the matchmakers didn't look at it realistically. They saw Doug Williams versus John Elway.

John was young, and he could have probably beaten me in a footrace back then. But it wasn't that kind of party. I didn't look at it as going head to head with John Elway. I looked at it as head to head with Broncos defensive players like Rick Hunley, Steve Wilson, and Karl Mecklenburg. I didn't care about John. He had to worry about the Dexter Manley, Monte Coleman, Barry Wilburn, and Darrell Green handling him. Now you hear all that media about Peyton Manning playing his brother, Eli, but they never played each other: their *teams* played each other. How come the media never made a bigger deal about Tiki Barber going against his brother, Ronde? They actually went at it.

In a game like the Super Bowl, nobody really knows what is going to happen. But you practice to execute. Fortunately for us that was the greatest execution of a game plan ever. We scored 35 points in that one quarter, but the way we did it, it was more than that. Usually scoring a touchdown takes a 10- to 12-play drive. But we scored 35 points in 18 plays. Think about that: 35 points in 18 plays. It was unbelievable.

Even when we were down 10-0 and I left the game with a hyper-extended knee, I knew we were going to win. When I came back in after two plays and tossed that touchdown pass to Ricky Sanders, I knew we were on our way. We never panicked because—quite simply—we'd had the best week of practice we ever had in my whole life. There was little doubt we were going to win the football game. I mean, we were down 14-0 to the Bears in the playoffs and it was 13 below. Here in San Diego, it was 88 degrees. No worries.

We basically did whatever we wanted, through the air and on the ground. It was Timmy Smith's first start. George Rogers had been banged up, so Timmy came in and gave our team that extra burst. He came off like gangbusters. 204 yards!

When the game was over and we had won, 42-10, I felt like a lot of weight had been taken off my shoulders for many reasons. There were a lot of people that I would have liked to tell where to get off. But I just raised my hand, raised my helmet, and was just proud at what had just happened. There were no more questions.

SUPER BOWL MVP

Williams played for the Redskins for two more seasons before retiring. His final regular-season stats read: 16, 998 career yards passing, 100 touchdowns, 93 interceptions; plus 884 yards rushing and 15 touchdowns. But the real stats were in the playoffs when it counted most. As a Buccaneer, Williams had had fewer weapons and went 1-3 in the post season, his win over the Eagles in '79 his lone victory. But as a Redskin, Williams went 3-0 with tough victories over the Bears, the Vikings, and the Super Bowl victory against the Broncos.

When the Super Bowl XXII MVP tried to come back from back surgery in '89, the Redskins released him.

"When the Redskins released me, I just felt it was time to go," says Williams. He coached high school football for a couple of years, worked as a scout, broadcast football games for BET network and, in 1997, he returned to his alma mater and became head football coach at Grambling. Over the next six seasons, Williams' teams went from 3-8 in '97 to 5-6 his first season. His second season, the Tigers went 7-4, then his third the team went 10-2 and won the first of three-straight NCAA Division I-AA National Black College and SWAC Championships. Along with it came three-straight coach of the year honors.

Having righted his college program, Williams left Grambling in 2004 to return to his first NFL team, the Buccaneers, as a personnel executive. When not pouring his heart and soul into making Tampa Bay a better club, he dotes on his family—including his four children: Ashley, Adrian, Doug, Jr., and Jasmine.

He recalls his playing days fondly and his role as a trailblazer proudly. "It's part of what you did," he says. "It could have been worse. I could have been one of the great quarterbacks who was never thought of, that's the way I look at it."

To make sure that many of those trailblazer quarterbacks are remembered, Williams, Marlin Briscoe, James Harris, Warren Moon, collaborated with *New York Times* sportswriter William Rhoden on a new book entitled *Third and a Mile: From Fritz Pollard to Michael Vick - An Oral History of the Trials, Tears and Triumphs of the Black Quarterback.*

"We felt it was important that our story was told," says Williams simply.

But Williams already wrote the biggest chapter with his performance in Super Bowl XXII.

Chapter 21

SANTANA MOSS

It was hailed as one of the richest wide receiver drafts in NFL history. A draft filled with supposed eye-popping future stars. The 2001 NFL Draft featured blue-chip receivers like Michigan All-America David Terrell and North Carolina State's Koren Robinson, both tall, talented top-10 picks. Terrell was drafted 8th by the Chicago Bears and Robinson 9th by the Seattle Seahawks.

The Washington Redskins had the 15th pick in the draft and needed a receiver. Redskins owner Daniel Snyder was smitten with University of Miami receiver Santana Moss, a 5-10, 189-pound burner. But new coach Marty Schottenheimer preferred the size of Clemson's 6-2, 219-pound Rod Gardner. So when the Redskins were on the clock, Schottenheimer denied Snyder by choosing Gardner as the third receiver in the draft. The New York Jets wasted no time to move up grab the next pick—selecting Moss at 16.

A record six receivers were taken in that first round. A few became busts, such as Terrell, Robinson, and UCLA's Freddie Mitchell, taken 25th by the Philadelphia Eagles. But several shined like Moss. The Colts drafting Reggie Wayne at 30, Moss's teammate at Miami was one. Oregon State's Chad (Ochocinco) Johnson and Utah's Steve Smith were drafted in the second and third-rounds, respectively, by the Cincinnati Bengals and Carolina Panthers.

The drafting of Gardner over Moss drew instant criticism from many Redskins fans. The U, as Miami had become known as, was a national powerhouse with NFL-ready stars. Along with receivers Moss and Wayne, the team featured Andre Johnson, running back Clinton Portis, tight end Jeremy Shockey, and two safeties by the names of Ed Reed and Sean Taylor.

Early on in their careers it was Gardner, not Moss, who seemed to be the better pro. Moss suffered a meniscus tear in his knee his rookie season and even though the Jets wanted him to hurry back, his agent advised him to sit out until it was completely healed. It was a wise move, but Moss did not catch a pass until Week 12. He finished the season with just two catches for 40 yards. Gardner had 46 catches for 641 yards and four scores. The next season Gardner seemed to be a budding star with 71 catches for 1006 yards and eight TDs. Moss stepped up his second season with 30 catches for 433 yards and four TDs despite starting only one game. But where he really blossomed was as a punt return-er—leading the league with two TD returns and a whopping 16.5-yard average. Still many media questioned whether being primarily a punt returner was worthy of first-round status?

THIRD SEASON A CHARM

The NFL is all about making the most of one's opportunity. For Moss that opportunity came in his third season. A concussion limited the playing time of Jets star receiver Wayne Chrebet, and Moss found himself starting Week 2 against the Dolphins. He delivered with five catches for 142 yards and a 32-yard TD catch from QB Vinny Testaverde. But the next week though he had one catch for 17 yards vs. the Patriots. Then he had five catches for 65 yards against the Cowboys, and a TD vs. the Bills.

In his first season with the Redskins, Santana Moss quickly displayed his dramatic deep-threat capabilities in Week 2 against the rival Dallas Cowboys. He caught 5 passes for 159 yards and 2 long TDs in the final minutes of the game including a thrilling 70-yarder to win it 14-13.

AP Images/Evan Tucci

But it wasn't until Week 7 when Moss took off for good. The Jets were playing the Texans, the same week that Moss likes to say "The article" arrived. Moss remembers: "It usually takes three years for a receiver to click in the NFL. I was hurt most of my first season and showed promise my second. Then my third season I had a 100-yard game against the Dolphins. We were set to play the Texans and I heard about this negative article about me on game day. I'm not the type to read the newspapers because there's so much negativity. But this reporter wrote a negative article about me, I think, out of spite because I couldn't do an interview with him due to a prior commitment I had made. Wayne Chrebet told me, 'I have the article about you. I am going to put it in your bag but don't want you to read it until after the game.' This gave me even more desire to have a good game. I was confident and you need confidence in order to make it life. I kept a level head. That game I had 111 yards and a TD and we won 19-14. After that I had arrived."

Indeed. After that big win over the Texans, Moss scored on a 60 yarder the following week against the Eagles. Then against the rival New York Giants, Moss lit up the Big Apple with 10 catches for 121 yards and 3 TDs. He proved unstoppable again the next week playing the Raiders with 146 yards and a 65-yard TD. Then a 48-yard TD against the Colts. And against the Jaguars, Moss caught the game-winning TD from QB Chad Pennington with just 26 ticks left. Moss had not only arrived, he was scoring at will and made the reporter look vindictive and foolish. He finished the season as a Pro Bowler and team MVP with 74 catches for 1,105 yards and 10 TDs.

So after a rough NFL beginning how was Moss able to turn it around? To gain a full appreciation, one has to heed his words, "You have to understand where I came from."

THE BEGINNING

Santana Terrell Moss was born June 1, 1979, to Lloyd and Natalie Moss in Miami, Florida. His parents were hard-working people. Lloyd was a corrections officer and Natalie was a food-service manager. He grew up in Liberty City, perhaps the toughest section of Miami, with his younger brother Sinorice, who would follow his brother to the University of Miami and play four seasons with the NY Giants. Both realized early on that athletics was the way to rise above these streets.

"You grow up in an environment like that and you learn what it takes to survive; how you have to be focused and motivated to make something of yourself," said Moss. "People wonder why a lot of the guys from Miami are so good at athletics. Guys like Clinton Portis and Reggie Wayne, we've known each other a long time. We knew the dedication it took to get us where we wanted to go."

Still it wasn't always easy and for Moss, facing the threat of street violence every day. The turning point came one day sitting on the porch at his grandmother's house in downtown Miami. "Down the road was this Holiday Inn, and one day this huge bus passed by," recalled Moss. "My uncle looked at me and said, 'Hey do you know who's on that bus—the Miami Dolphins. They're headed to the Orange Bowl to play today.' So I looked up and waved at the bus and saw Dan Marino. Right then I knew I wanted to be an NFL player on one of those buses."

Moss found the route to the NFL through Carol City High School, where he was asked to block more than catch, then to the University of Miami where he never lost focus to live out that dream. In typical Moss fashion, he started as a walk-on at the U and by the third game of the season he was awarded a scholarship. By the time he left Miami he was a first-team All-America and broke Michael Irvin's record with 2,546 receiving yards and became the school's all-time leader in all-purpose yards with 4,394. Not surprisingly, Moss was also a track star, competing in the 55-, 60-, and 100-meter dash and the long jump and triple jump.

With Moss's athletic prowess, it's no wonder Snyder was salivating when the Miami star was still available at the 15th pick in the 2003 draft. And even though Schottenheimer would choose Gardner, Moss finally found a way to get to DC.

THE TRADE

After a breakout 2003 season, Moss experienced frustration in 2004. Although the team made the playoffs Moss was doing more blocking than receiving. He caught just 45 passes for 838 yards and 5 TDs in a conservative offense. It reminded him of high school where his team rarely threw the ball.

Moss told his agent he wanted a trade and knew that the Redskins wanted a deep-play threat. He also had heard that Redskins receiver Laveranues Coles wanted to return to the Jets. It was the perfect scenario and Moss finally got his wish. After four years with the Jets, he would finally join the Washington Redskins for the 2005 season, the year after legendary Coach Joe Gibbs had decided to come out of retirement to return the Burgundy & Gold to prominence. But the big question was with a new team and new playbook, how would Moss fare?

GAME OF MY LIFE
BY SANTANA MOSS

In Week Two of my first season with the Redskins in 2005, we played the Dallas Cowboys at Texas Stadium on *Monday Night Football*. That game stands out the most because of the significance of that game. I've probably played better in other games but this Cowboys game my first season with the Redskins was my most memorable. It was on Monday night. Coach Joe Gibbs against Bill Parcells. I heard we hadn't beaten the Cowboys in two years and hadn't won at Texas stadium in 10 years. All that just motivated me.

I had a good game in Week 1 against the Bears with four catches for 96 yards, but we didn't score a TD and won 9-6 on three field goals. When you come from where I came from and a team like the Redskins trades for you to be The Guy—the deep threat who scores the big TDs, you want to show everyone that you were worth it. That week we all pushed each other to get ready. We knew coach Gibbs really wanted to beat the Cowboys.

I was familiar with Dallas. I had played them a few times with the Jets and had good games. But I never realized just how big the rivalry was until that game. So I was intent on playing well and helping my new teammates win. Now I have a lot of confidence in my abilities but when the first half ended, I didn't have a single catch in the game and I felt a little frustrated. I had been open a couple times but Mark Brunell and I didn't connect. I knew that was not up to my standards. I took full responsibility. So when the second half started I had this determined look on my face. I caught a few passes in the third quarter but only for a handful of yards. [Clinton] Portis saw me and asked what was going on. I told him I was frustrated because I knew I could get open deep but the plays we were running weren't designed for that. We had worked on this post-corner post play in practice and I knew it would work. He said, "Tell the coach!" Well, I'm not the kind of player that would ever tell a coach what to do. That's just not the way I was brought up. So Portis went and told Gibbs that I could beat their corner Aaron Glenn on that play and Gibbs told him, "Ok, let's run it!"

Aaron Glenn was a former teammate on the Jets and now he was on the Cowboys. I remember Reggie Wayne, one of my best friends, would beat Aaron on certain longer routes like this. Aaron was our best corner when I was on the Jets but he had a tendency to jump the routes. Every time we played the Colts, Reggie would beat Aaron on a post-corner post. It's a copycat league, so we had practiced that route the week of the Cowboys game.

But we hadn't run it in the game and now we were down 13-0 with less than four minutes left. We were inside the 40-yard line and it was a 4th and 15—now or never. The play finally came in. I was lined up on the right side and there was Glenn. So I ran my route and sure enough, he jumped the corner route and I turned toward the post. Just as I stepped into the end zone Mark laid the ball right there. Safety Roy Williams was a hair too late and I snagged it falling down for a 39-yard TD.

Now it was 13-7 and it was a ball game. I remember coming to the sidelines and seeing the determination on my teammates. Portis slapped me on the back and I heard the coach say when we get the ball back we're going to run it again.

We hadn't done much offensively the whole game, now we all believed. You could see it in everyone's faces. The defense really came through and we got the ball back with less than three minutes left. The ball was on the 30 with no time outs. The play came in again. I was sure that Glenn would know the play and I could see Williams inching toward me. But I knew I could beat them again. I got a jump on Glenn and both of them bit on the corner route again, which let me get separation. Mark did a great job at avoiding linebacker De-Marcus Ware. He stepped up in the pocket and put everything he had into the pass. It was on a rope and I grabbed it at the 20 and sped un-touched for a 70-yard TD. I heard later that Mr. Snyder was jumping up and down crazy in the owner's suite. I was excited but knew there was plenty of time left.

The Cowboys got the ball back and started moving downfield. QB Drew Bledsoe threw this out pattern to Joey Galloway and Sean Taylor really brought the wood. He broke up the pass and that helped seal the 14-13 victory. We all exploded on the sideline. It was such an emotional roller-coaster ride. A great victory for our team and the organization and to know that I had delivered when it counted most meant the world to me. Even though it was early in the season it felt like a championship game. Coach Gibbs even got a Gatorade bath. Looking back, I didn't have a great total game. But those two TDs at the end really put me over the top and showed Redskins fans that I could be the deep threat they were waiting for.

A NEW BEGINNING

As Redskins fans know that dramatic Week 2 game in 2005 was the first of many spectacular performances by Moss for the Burgundy & Gold. He earned his first Pro Bowl that season with 84 catches for 1,483 yards and 9 scores. Since then Moss has followed that season with two more 1,000-plus seasons and has scored 45 TDs as a Redskin. He's remained the Redskins big-play threat going into 9 seasons now.

But time catches up to even the speediest of receivers. In 2012 at the age of 33, Moss found himself relegated to spot duty as a slot receiver and third-down specialist. Still, even with limited play, Moss continued to draw raves. He caught 41 passes for 573 yards yet scored a team-high 8 TD receptions, most from rookie phenom QB Robert Griffin III.

Moss found the young QB to be very mature. "RGIII is a team guy, a hard worker and he takes great pride in preparation," said Moss. "That's what makes Coach Mike Shanahan a great coach. His preparation. I told RG III last season that even though you're a rookie we have a veteran team and you need to dig deep because most NFL games are close."

Echoing Moss's sentiments, RG III said last season, "I don't try to give myself excuses because I'm a rookie . . . the team doesn't look at me as a rookie. I'm a leader."

"RG III has been brought up the right way. He comes from a military background and he really can be as good as he wants to be," said Moss. "He came in being known as a running quarterback but he proved that he's a great passer. Even with his injury, I know he will get better and I expect some great things this season."

Moss is so hyped for his 13th NFL season that he took a pay cut to stay with the Redskins. When asked why, he answered candidly, "I was no longer a starter and my salary was based on being a starter. My ego isn't that big. I know when I walk out on that field I still play like I'm a starter, but I'm a team-player first."

AFTER THE FINAL TD

Now going into the 2013 season, Moss is 34 and knows that his illustrious NFL career is winding down. He's lived his NFL dream but it's obvious the reason he's still playing at a high level is the ultimate dream of winning a championship. It eluded Dan Marino, the Hall of Fame QB who made such an impression on Moss as a youngster.

Although the media always tried to compare Gardner's career with Moss's, he did not. "I never followed Rod Gardner's career," said Moss. "I think the media looked at that and took it out of proportion. I didn't care. My dream was to play in the NFL and to show people who I am. I've never worried about what other people thought. That's not the way I was brought up and that's not who I am."

Moss's parents raised him right. Lloyd and Natalie Moss are still married and Moss followed suit, marrying his high school sweetheart LaTosha. They have three children and when Moss's playing days are over he wants to give back by building homes for low-income families near the tough Miami area where he grew up.

"I've never forgotten where I came from, how I grew up, and who I am," said Moss. "I want to build homes for good, hardworking people who deserve a nice place to call home. That's so important for kids and young families."

After all, that's where dreams begin.

ACKNOWLEDGMENTS

This is my first book with Skyhorse Publishing, so I would like to thank Niels Aaboe for working with me to make this book a reality.

The next 21 people I'd like to thank are the Redskins greats who appear in this book. In no particular order: Mike Bass, Len Hauss, Billy Kilmer, Ken Harvey, Joe Theismann, Diron Talbert, Pat Fischer, Ron McDole, Sam Huff, Don Bosseler, "Bullet" Bill Dudley, Joe Washington, Dexter Manley, Roy "Sweet Pea" Jefferson, Jeff Bostic, Joe Jacoby, Mike Nelms, Rick "Doc" Walker, Larry Brown, Doug Williams, and Santana Moss. I can't begin to tell you how much I enjoyed talking with each of them. One in particular, Hall of Famer Bill Dudley, who was sharp as ever when I interviewed him in 2007, passed in 2010 at the age of 88. He reminded me what a humbling privilege it is to play in the NFL. All of them gave me the one precious thing that no one ever has enough of—their time.

While collecting contact information, I found a number of players went out of their way to help. Don Talbert, an NFL star in his own right, got me in touch with his brother, Diron. Rick Walker and Ron McDole got me in touch with numerous other Redskins greats. Sandy Sedlak was another great help; as Joe Theismann's longtime assistant, Sandy and I traded phone calls for weeks before she somehow found a nice block of time for Joe and me to converse. Thanks, Sandy.

Lastly, I'd like to thank my family and a few friends. My mom and dad, Nellie Ray Mackie and James W. Mackie, raised me to love sports—especially football. Even though my father has since passed, his influence is very much deep inside me. Much of what I write is from him nudging my arm. My dad's legacy continues to live in my son Luke who has many of my dad's qualities including his impish sense of humor. My siblings, Maryde Mackie Hand, Jeff Mackie, and Blythe Anne Mackie Lundstrom, have long supported all of my writing endeavors— even the really bad ones.

I'd also like to pay tribute to my two best friends growing up, Dave Apostolico, the author of a million terrific poker books, and Gregg Marvel, who loves to remind me how much I sucked at football. Together we've spent a trillion hours discussing the great games in exhausting, humorous detail—among other things. Another person is Hall of Famer Floyd Little. After writing two books together, Floyd Little's Tales from the Broncos Sideline and Promises to Keep, this magnanimous person has become a big brother to me and, at times, a father figure as well. His refreshing approach to life is an inspiration to me every day. I'm grateful to call him a friend. Also, I'd like to thank some old Redskins colleagues: Casey Husband, Gary Fitzgerald, and Steve Butchock. We had some fun, didn't we! Also, a special thanks to Suk Kim, the greatest Redskin fan I know. Suk and his wife, Jen, now have three boys, which only increases the chance that one of them may play for the Redskins!

I'd like to thank the two men to whom I dedicated the first edition of this book to, my brother Jeff's boys: Staff Sargent Jeffrey Brendan Mackie, 29 who did two tours of duty in Iraq and Afghanistan, and Kevin Patrick Mackie, 25, who did a tour of duty in Iraq and is now a police officer in Delaware. With my nephews safe return, I have dedicated this book to an old soldier and model American—Ray Ciesinski. Ray fought in World War II, survived being a prisoner of war and was awarded a Purple Heart among other medals. After the war, Ray went on to play football at the University of Delaware. He eschewed a tryout with the Chicago Bears to coach high school football, basketball, and track for 32 years at Newark High School in Delaware. He was elected to the Delaware Sports Hall of Fame in 2002. He was also my mom's inseparable companion for 13 wonderful years and one of the greatest men I've known. Ray passed at the age of 89 on June 10, 2011, but his love for football and sportsmanship touched hundreds of lives.